Leading Schools to Learn, Grow, and Thrive

Leading Schools to Learn, Grow, and Thrive provides a unique approach to preparing prospective education leaders by combining theory, research, and practice. Grounded in organizational and leadership theory, this book helps leaders understand their schools and districts from multiple perspectives and develop their own leadership aspirations, approaches, and missions. Well-known authors Brazer, Bauer, and Johnson present authentic practical problems, illuminate them with appropriate theory and research, and give readers opportunities to solve common puzzles as a means to grow wisdom about how to lead, especially when confronted with complex challenges. This book is an invaluable resource for aspiring leaders, one that readers will reference as they proceed through their leadership coursework and keep close at hand throughout their leadership career.

Special Features:

- Vignettes—introduce the reader to real-life dilemmas that impact teaching and learning and provide a central reference point for discussions of theory, research, and practice.
- Theory and Research—frameworks and examples inform common leadership challenges, helping readers expand their knowledge and experience base to explore situations similar to their own contexts.
- Puzzles—real-world situations test knowledge and provide opportunities to practice ideas for effective leadership.
- *Thought Partner Conversations (TPCs)* and *Extended Web Activities (EWAs)*—additional thought activities, opportunities for reflection, and suggestions for discussion provoke puzzle solving.
- eResources—complementary resources for instructors and students, including a set of authentic role-playing scenarios.

S. David Brazer is Associate Professor of Educational Leadership at Stanford University, USA.

Scott C. Bauer is Professor of Education and Associate Dean of Advanced Education and Doctoral Programs at the University of Colorado, Denver, USA.

Bob L. Johnson, Jr. is Professor of Educational Leadership and Policy at the University of Alabama, USA.

Leading Schools to Learn, Grow, and Thrive

Using Theory to Strengthen Practice

S. David Brazer, Scott C. Bauer,
and Bob L. Johnson, Jr.

Routledge
Taylor & Francis Group

NEW YORK AND LONDON

First published 2019
by Routledge
52 Vanderbilt Avenue, New York, NY 10017

and by Routledge
2 Park Square, Milton Park, Abingdon, Oxon, OX14 4RN

Routledge is an imprint of the Taylor & Francis Group, an informa business

Library of Congress Cataloging-in-Publication Data
Names: Brazer, S. David, author. | Bauer, Scott C. (Scott Charles), author. | Johnson, Bob L., 1956- author.
Title: Leading schools to learn, grow, and thrive : using theory to strengthen practice / By S. David Brazer, Scott C. Bauer, and Bob L. Johnson, Jr.
Description: New York : Routledge, 2019. | Includes bibliographical references.
Identifiers: LCCN 2018034610| ISBN 9781138039094 (hbk) | ISBN 9781138039100 (pbk) | ISBN 9781315176123 (ebk) | ISBN 9781351708814 (Web PDF) | ISBN 9781351708807 (ePUB) | ISBN 9781351708791 (mobi/kindle)
Subjects: LCSH: Educational leadership. | School management and organization. | Education–Research.
Classification: LCC LB2806 .B72 2019 | DDC 371.2–dc23
LC record available at https://lccn.loc.gov/2018034610

ISBN: 978-1-138-03909-4 (hbk)
ISBN: 978-1-138-03910-0 (pbk)
ISBN: 978-1-315-17612-3 (ebk)

Typeset in Sabon and Helvetica
by Wearset Ltd, Boldon, Tyne and Wear

Visit the eResources: www.routledge.com/9781138039100

For my children—Leah, Henry, Sam, and Noah—who have motivated me to think about schools every day of their lives—SDB.

For Peggy, (still) the love of my life—SCB.

To those exceptional educators in the Oak Ridge City School System who were an important part of my journey through school. I cherish your memory and remain forever indebted to your investment in the lives of the sons and daughters of the Manhattan Project, of which I am one—BLJJ.

Contents

Figures

Tables

Preface

Can leadership be taught? Some might argue that it can't, that leaders are born and not made, or that leadership can only be learned on the job. Although we would agree that some individuals are endowed with leadership dispositions, we do not believe that anyone comes ready-made to lead schools and districts. Furthermore leadership traits, styles, or dispositions contain assumptions that may privilege specific characteristics that "fit" only in specific contexts. Consequently, our approach is to develop leadership knowledge for those who aspire to greater influence in schools and districts. Our intent is to provide a course text that helps prepare adept leaders through insightful application of theory and research to practical problems leaders face in their day-to-day work. Apart from a course, the book stands as the leader's companion for understanding schools and districts as organizations and how to lead them. We wish to develop in you, the reader, a broader perspective on how to think about leading schools and districts and to have you apply new thinking to intriguing challenges that suffuse educational settings every day. Each chapter of this book presents authentic practical problems, illuminates them with appropriate theory and research, and gives you opportunities to solve common puzzles as a means to growing your wisdom about how to lead.

We assume that you aspire to lead schools and school districts in some form or fashion. Although we focus primarily on schools, we have our eye on district leadership at times because schools interact with their districts and because many school leaders aspire to move into district-level leadership at some point in their careers. We write to a broad educator audience because answers to the questions "Who is a leader?" and "What do leaders do?" have evolved in the past 30 years. Education leaders have traditionally included assistant principals (APs), principals, and various positions in the central office with some variation of "superintendent" in their titles. But mandates to educate all children to a standard minimum level have spawned interest in having teachers and teacher leaders making decisions to address persistent teaching and learning challenges (Gronn, 2008; Harris, 2005; Leithwood, Harris, & Hopkins, 2008; Ogawa & White, 1994). High school graduates' college readiness as an emerging standard for school and district performance lends greater urgency to improving teaching and learning for all students. At the same time, the voices of policy makers, entrepreneurs, and philanthropists—all people who believe they can improve education from outside the traditional bureaucracy—are growing louder and carrying more weight. The mission of preparing all high school graduates to succeed in college is much more difficult to achieve than a high school diploma for all, which stood as the standard for decades. Thus, with higher stakes and greater competition over ideas, there are many different positions from which to lead—as a teacher, department head, grade-level team leader, teacher coach, AP, principal, curriculum specialist, assistant/associate superintendent, superintendent, board member, or parent—and those leaders will be tested to meet varied and sometimes conflicting demands from inside and outside their systems.

We propose to help you meet the exciting challenges of education leadership from a constructivist perspective, providing analytical tools that will help you understand schools, districts, and the contexts in which they operate more deeply and broadly. We begin with knowing how organizations function because those insights provide a solid foundation from which to lead (Brazer & Bauer, 2013). Consistent with constructivism, we do not tell you how to analyze the organizations in which you will work. Rather, we explain organization theories and describe how they can be used as tools. You will figure out which tools fit well in your hands and are appropriate to a given puzzle or task. The same is true for leadership theories that follow chapters on schools and districts as organizations. Our mechanisms for helping you learn how to apply various theories and research to leadership practice include vignettes, exercises, discussions, and puzzles you will investigate via open-ended sets of questions. This is an interactive book that brings you as close as we can to making practical leadership decisions to help you grow your own education leadership skills, knowledge, and dispositions.

Our knowledge of a given phenomenon increases the probability that we will become skilled at doing it. As we complicate our thinking about leadership (Weick, 1979), we place ourselves in a position to become better leaders. This distinction underscores the difference between knowing *about* and knowing *how* (Johnson, forthcoming; Johnson & Kruse, 2009). Although knowing *about* leadership does not guarantee one will *become* an effective leader, one cannot become an effective leader without knowing about leadership.

Knowledge about education leadership begins with your own experiences in schools and districts. It continues as you examine and consider the leadership literature, become familiar with its dominant theories, and compare these with your lived experiences. This thought process is generally known as *praxis*. It progresses further as you enter into conversations with others about this literature, seek to identify and refine emergent themes, articulate working assumptions, and reconcile competing theories with your experience.

EDUCATION LEADERSHIP

What do we mean by *leading* schools and districts? Cuban (1988) distinguishes between management and leadership by claiming that managing well makes schools and districts function competently, focusing on stability. Leading, on the other hand, involves changing and improving how these organizations run, motivating others to implement initiatives they would not otherwise be inclined to take on. Cuban claims not to privilege management over leadership or vice versa. Both are necessary and one may predominate depending on contemporary circumstances. Cuban's thesis that the bureaucratic and political nature of schools and districts compels education leaders toward a focus on management motivates, in part, our desire to write this book. An over-emphasis on management may lead to complacency and stagnation. Leadership focused on teaching and learning provides hope for improvement in an era when school performance is a source of constant criticism. We offer this book to help you learn how to lead the kinds of improvements many schools need. Yet we, like Cuban, dwell a great deal on managing well because it may be impossible to lead a school or district experiencing managerial dysfunction.

We read a great deal about leadership and end up asking ourselves, "Leadership for what?" In other words, we wonder what people aspire to lead *toward*. Our answer is that the primary purpose of leadership in schools and districts is to improve teaching and learning. Robinson (2011) calls what we have in mind student-centered leadership while others might refer to it as instructional leadership (IL) (Hallinger, 2003; Marks & Printy, 2003; Robinson, Lloyd, & Rowe, 2008). Despite our focus on teaching and learning, and the fact that Chapter 7 is titled "Leading Instruction," we do not wish to narrow the reader's perspective into one set of ideas. Rather, we take a more eclectic approach that we hope will help readers to see the big picture of leadership challenges and opportunities in schools and districts while bearing in mind that all educators' core mission is teaching and learning.

PRACTICAL PUZZLES

The word "problem" has negative connotations for many, but not for us. We see "problem" as synonymous with words such as puzzle, challenge, test, or gap. For some the meaning is closer to failure while for others it is more like an opportunity to try one's skills. It is this latter meaning that most informs our use of the word problem for this book. We want to provide means for you to try and then refine your skills, applying your professional experience and new knowledge derived from this book and the course it accompanies. We also wish to preserve a sense of open-endedness, which is why we emphasize puzzles—mysteries, if you like—throughout the book.

We draw from our own experiences, stories from students and colleagues, and field-based research involving teachers and administrators to put puzzles in front of you that you are likely to encounter in an effort to manage well and lead student and school performance improvement. For example, how would you work with a colleague who is both hampered by weak teaching practice and reluctant to participate in a collaborative team that could help him? Or, how do you meet a concerned parent's needs without doing a special favor that every other parent will come to expect? Perhaps most puzzling, how do you listen well to the superintendent's new idea about school reform without giving up all the hard work your school has engaged in over the past 3 years? These are the challenges that present dilemmas to school leaders every day. By encountering them here and in your course work, you have an opportunity to try out ideas under conditions of low risk and reduced stress.

Problems embedded in this book take different forms. Each chapter begins with a *vignette*—a short description of an ambiguous circumstance that requires some kind of decision making. The primary purpose of these vignettes is to provide vivid, real-world material to which you can apply the various theories and research we explain. We pose questions intended to put you into the shoes of leaders represented in vignettes. The vignettes contain unanswered questions and some difficult choices. We elaborate the vignettes as you move through each chapter and build from exercises and discussions to present *puzzles*, choosing this descriptor carefully because you will need to see the big picture in order to put the pieces together and arrive at some sort of resolution. Trouble is, some pieces might be difficult to see, don't quite fit, or are missing entirely. A major theme for us through all of these different kinds of problems is ambiguity, meaning they are open to more than one interpretation (*The Random House Dictionary of the English Language: College Edition*, 1968). Ambiguity suffuses the world of leading schools and districts. We recommend you get used to it now.

An important feature of the problems and puzzles we pose, and those you will encounter as a leader, is that solutions often differ based on what's going on and who you happen to be dealing with at the moment. Ready-made solutions are few and far between; "best practices" applied without consideration of the nuances of the situation seldom prove to be as powerful as advertised. We hope that as you examine these problems and puzzles you relate them to a unique context within which you work or may have experienced in the past. How puzzles are approached, what big ideas you apply to them, who you might bring into the discussion about how to address them, and so on, will likely differ based on features of the people, place, and time. A major part of your leadership learning is becoming well versed in reading the situation.

Stepping into Leadership

A special feature of this volume are the eResources that provide a set of authentic role-playing scenarios in which you and your classmates can test your leadership learning. Consistent with the open-ended nature of the puzzles presented in the text, the scenarios put you into situations in which you need to think on your feet to lead a group of colleagues to remedy a problem. The challenge will be clear, but the path forward is entirely up to you. The greatest value of role-playing comes from trying out your ideas, then debriefing with your instructor and peers to learn how the decisions you made and actions you took were received by others.

WHY THEORY?

Theory intimidates people. Not just those who see themselves as practitioners, but social scientists, natural scientists, artists and other academics (Weick, 1995). We suspect that some of the grand theories—Darwin's theory of evolution, Einstein's theory of relativity, or Keynes's *The General Theory of Employment, Interest, and*

Money—are sources of this intimidation. How could my own theorizing possibly compare to such complex, multi-faceted, comprehensive systems? Yet we theorize and work with theories all the time. Weick cuts theory down to size by claiming, "Theory belongs to the family of words that includes *guess, speculation, supposition, conjecture, proposition, hypothesis, conception, explanation, model*" (1995, p. 386, emphasis in the original). He goes on to point out that even when we don't have in mind "Grand Theory," we are theorizing all the time. When as a teacher you enter your classroom on a Monday morning, you carry a theory in your head about what sort of approach your students will need based on whether this Monday follows a weekend or an extended vacation. Likewise you have a theory about how teaching ought to be different before lunch as compared to after lunch. And, you test and revise these theories constantly based on how your students react to your teaching and what you understand about them as people. You know this, but you probably thought about it as guessing, supposing, or hypothesizing about what would happen in response to your teaching effort.

We propose (theorize?) that there is a set of theories that will help you make sense of the confusing daily life of education leaders that is fraught with the ambiguity that naturally comes from working with mysterious, moody, funny, happy, unpredictable children and adults who inhabit schools and districts every day. Weick (2001) helps us to explain why theory is valuable. When people encounter changes in their immediate environment, they act upon those changes based on perceptions and past experiences. Noticing the results, they make sense of them and act again. This kind of sensemaking in Weick's terms is theorizing based on lived experiences. We bring theories in our heads—our *theories of action*—to bear on experiences as we have them, which guides our behavior. Novel situations require theorizing—sensemaking—about what is going on so that we can understand and by so doing revise a theory or two in our heads. Our "theory testing" is a primary source of learning. If through this book and your course work we can make insightful theory accessible in your mental toolkit, your interpretations of your experiences as a school leader might help make you wiser.

This perspective suggests that theory is vital to performance, including leadership, as opposed to being some sort of academic esoterica. Our challenge as authors is to put the "right" theories in front of you in a manner you will find useful. We distill what we have learned from different theoretical traditions as we apply them to educational settings so that you can see their utility. Some will speak to you and seem intuitively helpful; others may be harder to access or use. We also provide extensive citations and references you can pursue if you encounter theoretical propositions you would like to explore further.

THEORY INFORMS RESEARCH

We define research simply as the collection and analysis of data—both quantitative and qualitative. Similar to theory, educators often believe that research is for someone else, someone who isn't busy planning for and being with students every day. One of the positive effects of the No Child Left Behind Act may have been to emphasize the importance of research-based practice. What this means to us is that there is practical knowledge to be gained from learning researchers' conclusions regarding problems and contexts similar to those in which we are working. For example, when considering whether to support bilingual education in my school district, it would be helpful to know the history of and research into various kinds of bilingual programs that have existed in US education (Goldenberg & Wagner, 2015). That knowledge would help me in two ways: (1) I would understand which theories of second language acquisition have been validated and to what extent, and (2) I would learn if my school district context seems promising for bilingual education in light of systematically organized findings from other school districts published in this and other articles.

The research we present in this volume is focused on leadership results rather than curriculum and instruction, but the idea is the same. One example is to explain what IL looks like in practice. On its face it seems like a good idea to lead instruction, thus it is a theory that holds promise. But does it work and if so what does it do? These questions are not fully answered, but Robinson, Lloyd, and Rowe (2008) provide intriguing insights we spotlight in Chapter 7. Sound empirical research is based on good theory so that authors are presenting more than just interesting facts. Theory allows them to explain a system or process, to describe how their facts fit into a larger picture. Sometimes the fit is not good, however, leading to empirical findings invalidating a theory partially or completely. Thus, theorizing happens as a result of research based on other theory. The two are inseparable.

What has this to do with you, a prospective education leader? Just as we believe you are theorizing all the time already, we also think that action research—research conducted in your school or district for practical purposes—is helpful to you (Bauer & Brazer, 2012). A promising way to improve teaching and learning is to collect data to answer questions such as: How are our students performing in second grade

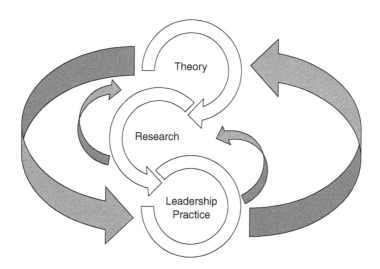

FIGURE P.1 Interactions among Theory, Research, and Leadership Practice

English/language arts (ELA)? Why do students who are eligible for free and reduced price meals receive higher proportions of Ds and Fs in algebra I? What is the 3-year trend line for middle school science performance among students who speak a language other than English at home? We present research that we hope will inform your leadership practice, and we advocate that you access published research and conduct your own action research as you try to improve your school or district performance (Bauer & Brazer, 2012). Just as with theory, our aim is to show you how to translate research into practice, and why you should do so. The interactions among theory, research, and practice that we emphasize are depicted in Figure P.1.

ORGANIZATION OF THE TEXT

Translating theory and research into practice is a major theme of this book. Each chapter is organized to do that based on engaging problems of practice. Our devices for applying theory and research to practice are featured in the following content descriptions that appear generally in this order:

- A vignette: a scene typical of some type of situation in a school or district that involves multiple actors with different perspectives and presents one or more problems of practice. These vignettes should look familiar to educators with just a few years of experience, though they may be unfamiliar by level. Those who work in elementary schools may not recognize the specifics of a vignette set at the middle school level, but they will likely be able to generalize from their own experience to the situation presented. The purpose of the vignette is to introduce the reader to real-life situations that impact teaching and learning in some way to provide a central reference point for discussions of theory, research, and practice that follow.
- Theory: ideas about how the world works. Organizational theory is both a guide for leadership practice and an analytical tool that helps the leader make sense of familiar and exotic circumstances that exist in the intense jobs we collectively call education leadership (Brazer & Bauer, 2013; Brazer, Kruse, & Conley, 2014; Johnson & Kruse, 2009). Our ambition is that this text will help you to appreciate the value of theory as a means to understanding leadership practice and guiding your leadership development.
- Research: reports of what others have found about situations similar to yours, and your own investigations into your school or district outcomes. We use research to expand your experience base. When we discuss research, it will be with an eye toward informing a specific leadership challenge common to particular circumstances.
- Puzzles: real-world situations that test what you are learning as you proceed through this book and the class(es) in which it is assigned. The puzzles that appear at the end of each chapter provide opportunities for you to use what you have gained from your reading to road test your ideas for effective leadership. For example, if you are convinced by theory and research that effective teams have

clear goals, complementary expertise, and a number of other characteristics (Katzenbach & Smith, 2006), whom would you pick from a hypothetical school to be on your leadership team? What would be your rationale behind these choices? The puzzles put you into the position of thinking like an education leader.

Spread within each chapter are additional thought activities, opportunities for reflection, and suggestions for discussion that we hope will provoke some smaller-scale puzzle solving and thus enrich your understanding. We have labeled one type *thought partner conversations (TPCs)* and another *extended web activities (EWAs)*. The TPCs may serve as short conversation starters in a face-to-face or online class that you can share with a shoulder buddy or critical friend, or they may be used as instigators for discussion board conversations in an online environment. We envision the EWAs as opportunities for you to extend your learning by conducting brief web searches to locate additional material and probe alternative meanings of the theory or research you are learning.

The book has two parts. Part I focuses on organizational theories that help prospective leaders to understand the contexts in which they will work. Part II addresses leadership more directly with an emphasis on leadership theories that can be put to use in different situations and at the discretion of the user. We explain the chapter contents and flow in the introductions to each part.

We hope that you will enjoy reading this book as it reminds you of situations you have encountered in schools and, possibly, alters your interpretations of or perspectives on them. Our vision when writing the book is that it will be an invaluable resource to you, that you will look back through it as you proceed through your leadership coursework and that you will keep it close at hand for reference as you build your leadership career.

REFERENCES

Bauer, S.C., & Brazer, S.D. (2012). *Using research to lead school improvement: Turning evidence into action.* Thousand Oaks, CA: Sage Publications.

Brazer, S.D., & Bauer, S.C. (2013). Preparing instructional leaders: A model. *Educational Administration Quarterly, 49*(4), 645–684.

Brazer, S.D., Kruse, S.D., & Conley, S. (2014). Organizational theory and leadership navigation. *Journal of Research on Leadership Education,* 1–19. DOI: 10.1177/1942775114532640.

Cuban, L. (1988). *The managerial imperative and the practice of leadership in schools.* Albany, NY: State University of New York Press.

Goldenberg, C., & Wagner, K. (2015). Bilingual education: Reviving an American tradition. *American Educator, 39*(3), 28–32.

Gronn, P. (2008). The future of distributed leadership. *Journal of Educational Administration, 46*(2), 141–158.

Hallinger, P. (2003). Leading educational change: Reflections on the practice of instructional and transformational leadership. *Cambridge Journal of Education, 33*(3), 329–352.

Harris, A. (2005). Leading or misleading? Distributed leadership and school improvement. *Journal of Curriculum Studies, 37*(3), 255–265.

Johnson, B.L., Jr. (forthcoming). Leadership as "disciplined imagination": Developing the Cognitive Agile Leader. In Bob L. Johnson, Jr. and Sharon H. Kruse (Eds.). *Exploring the ideas of Karl Weick in educational organizations: Extended perspectives on leading, organizing, and organizational learning*. New York: Routledge.

Johnson, B.L., Jr., & Kruse, S.D. (2009). *Decision making for educational leaders: Underexamined dimensions and issues*. Albany, NY: State University of New York Press.

Katzenbach, J., & Smith, D. (2006). *The wisdom of teams: Creating the high-performance organization*. New York: HarperCollins.

Leithwood, K., Harris, A., & Hopkins, D. (2008). Seven strong claims about successful school leadership. *School Leadership & Management, 28*(1), 27–42. DOI: 10.1080/1363243070 1800060.

Marks, H., & Printy, S. (2003). Principal leadership and school performance: An integration of transformational and instructional leadership. *Educational Administration Quarterly, 39*(3), 370–397.

Ogawa, R., & White, P. (1994). School-based management: An overview. In S. P. Mohrman, *The Random House dictionary of the English language* (1968). New York: Random House.

Robinson, V. (2011). *Student-centered leadership*. San Francisco: Jossey-Bass.

Robinson, V., Lloyd, C., & Rowe, K. (2008). The impact of leadership on student outcomes: An analysis of the differential effects of leadership types. *Educational Administration Quarterly, 44*(5), 635–674.

Weick, K.E. (1979). *The social psychology of organizing* (2nd ed.). Reading, MA: Addison-Wesley Publishing Company.

Weick, K.E. (1995). What theory is not, theorizing is. *Administrative Science Quarterly, 40*(3), 385–390.

Weick, K.E. (2001). *Making sense of the organization*. Malden, MA: Blackwell Publishing.

Wohlstetter, and associates (Eds.) (1994). *Designing high performance schools: Strategies for school based management*. San Francisco: Jossey-Bass.

Acknowledgments

We would like to express our sincere gratitude to the following people who read early drafts of chapters of this book:

Stanford University Graduate School of Education Policy, Organization, and Leadership Studies students: Ben Bowman, Rei Nakamura, Maggie Sharp, Casey Ulrich, and Ally Voss.

Emi Kuboyama, Associate Director, Leadership Degree Programs, Stanford University.

William Rich, Professor Emeritus, California State University, Chico.

We also wish to thank our editor, Heather Jarrow, for her endless patience and good cheer.

1

Understanding Organizations

Can you imagine anyone leading an activity without some sort of minimal organization? Neither can we. The reason is that leading means working with other people. When people come together for a common purpose, they naturally form into some sort of organization. It could be formal or informal, but groups of people tend to organize their work. In that process, leaders are often selected or emerge. If you think back to the days when your age was a single digit, you may recall how your friends in the neighborhood or birthday party guests would get organized for play. Often it worked well and everyone had fun, but sometimes it didn't and it wasn't. Reasons might include one kid dominating to make a game fun for him but no one else. Another child might have cheated. Or maybe no one led, creating a situation in which no one knew what to do and everyone got bored. Your world as an adult educator has different problems to solve, but just as when you were young, the work will get done inside some sort of organization.

Thought Partner Conversation

Take a few minutes with a critical friend and discuss: What can we learn about organizing from watching a group of children on the playground? What are some of the values of organizing, and what are some of the predictable hurdles that groups generally need to overcome to make things work?

The ubiquity and necessity of organizations causes us to begin this book intended to help you develop as a leader with *organization theory*. It is vital that you expand and enrich your perspective on how organizations emerge, develop, and function if you aspire to lead one. That organization could be as small as a four-person teacher collaborative team, as large as a school district of 50,000 students, or as temporary as a task force. You will be a more effective leader with frameworks you can use to unlock the mysteries of organizational behavior.

BUILDING AN ORGANIZATIONAL PERSPECTIVE

The first four chapters of this book draw heavily from organization theory to explain how individuals in schools and districts interact with each other and with the systems within which they work. Chapter 1 emphasizes the structural characteristics of schools and districts and weaves that together with how people interrelate under these organizational circumstances. We explain how structures both assist competent management and how they might get in the way. Human factors such as interpersonal relationships, motivation, and leadership choices further illuminate the ways in which schools and districts operate in sometimes unexpected ways.

Chapter 2 changes perspective substantially by considering how schools and districts interact with people and organizations outside their walls—i.e., it takes an *open systems* view of the educational enterprise (Scott, 2003). Resources and threats exist in the organizational environment of schooling, and leaders need to understand which is which in order to maximize opportunities and minimize threats. Doing so is made particularly challenging by the uncertainty and ambiguity involved in trying to understand how schools and districts are affected by policy, politics, beliefs, and myths.

Chapter 3 goes many steps further in making the familiar strange by explaining schools and districts as organized anarchies (Cohen, March, & Olsen, 1972; March & Simon, 1993). When knowledge is limited about any given event, goal, or challenge facing educators, decision making is more difficult. Political overlays can push decision making even further from what might be perceived as rational, systematic, or in the best interest of students. Since decision making is a critical part of leading, exploring how it works and challenging common assumptions are essential building blocks in developing an understanding of leading schools and districts.

Chapter 4 addresses organizational learning from a social–psychological perspective on why and how organizations make changes they anticipate will improve performance. Neither all organizationally based nor specifically about leadership, organizational learning is an interpersonal explanation for why the status quo exists, why it is so difficult to change, and what meaningful change looks like. This brings us to our basic position with respect to improving student and school performance: schools and districts must continually learn where aspirations and outcomes diverge and search for means to bring outcomes in line with aspirations (Argyris & Schon, 1974, 1978).

Chapter 5 is a transition into Part II's focus on ways of leading schools because it explores specific leadership theories that have evolved over time. We want you to see a broad range of how leadership has been defined and how it intersects with organizations and the people in them to inform how you might use the leadership tools presented in Part II.

Every chapter in Part I contains problems of practice that we ask you to analyze using an organizational lens. This helps to sharpen your ability to see past your singular perspective or a view of schools and districts as sets of random relationships. The vignettes, exercises, and puzzles help you to clarify at least some of the ambiguity endemic to organization theory.

Extended Web Activities

Before you proceed to Chapter 1, explore your school system's website (or, if you are not currently working in one, a website of a district you know) and see if you can locate symbols of organizing—for instance, the organization chart depicting the system's administrative structure. From this search, what might you be able to tell about how leaders have gone about creating the organization's structure? Anything jump out at you as interesting or maybe a little puzzling?

REFERENCES

Argyris, C, & Schon, D. (1974). *Theory in practice: Increasing professional effectiveness.* San Francisco: Jossey-Bass.

Argyris, C., & Schon, D. (1978). *Organizational learning: A theory of action perspective.* Reading, MA: Addison-Wesley.

Cohen, M.D., March, J.G., & Olsen, J.P. (1972). A garbage can model of organizational choice. *Administrative Sciences Quarterly, 17*(1), 1–25.

March, J.D., & Simon, H.A. (1993). *Organizations* (2nd ed.). Oxford, UK: Blackwell.

Scott, W.R. (2003). *Organizations: Rational, natural and open systems* (5th ed.). Upper Saddle River, NJ: Prentice Hall.

CHAPTER 1

Understanding Schools and Districts as Organizations

Not long after the start of the school year, the high school principal assigns two important tasks to a newly credentialed AP who has just joined the administrative team and is new to the school. First, he tells the new AP that she will be evaluating the calculus teacher this year as one of 20 teachers on her evaluation docket. The calculus teacher, Ms. Alakhi, has been teaching math since the AP was in second grade, has a somewhat fearsome reputation among faculty and students, and is revered by parents and other teachers for her ability to help students earn 5s on both levels of the Advanced Placement calculus examinations. The second, more urgent task is to mediate and resolve a dispute between two special education teachers who are quarreling over how a particular student was handled. Ms. Moore is the student's resource specialist (responsible for his individual education plan (IEP)) and his math teacher. Mr. Allen is the student's special education English teacher. Mr. Allen convinced the student's mother to de-certify him from special education because he "doesn't really need it" without consulting Ms. Moore. Ms. Moore is furious and this latest incident has fueled a long-standing feud between Ms. Moore and Mr. Allen. The first task seems intimidating, the second just weird. The principal wishes her the best of luck as he rushes off to a meeting at the central office.

Thought Partner Conversation

If you were the AP in the opening vignette, how would you react to your assignments? Where would you start, and why? Who might you consult for advice?

WHERE DO YOU START? THE TWIN FOUNDATIONS OF ORGANIZATIONAL THEORY

A major theme of this book is that teachers, students, parents, and administrators operate within schools and districts that share characteristics with many different types of organizations. Understanding the dynamics among individuals, groups, and the organizations in which they are embedded is critical to unlocking the puzzles of how schools and districts work and reveals opportunities for leadership. One powerful lever education leaders have is the design of their various spheres of influence. Too often, however, leaders accept the status quo for how work is organized, which can lead to organizational contradictions that stymie innovation and improvement. Understanding important features and nuances of organizational structure, design, and human interaction is a good place to begin thinking about how to lead complex organizations. This chapter begins our discussion of schools and districts as organizations by exploring structural and human resource theories that represent the twin foundations of organizational theory, each contributing important insights into organizational life.

Leadership preparation programs have a strong tendency to emphasize rational behavior because they are rooted in US culture that prizes efficiency and productivity. The larger field of organizational theory developed on this same foundation. Early theorists tended to focus on the rational pursuit of clear and agreed-upon outcomes as a defining characteristic of organizations, which were conceived to be purposive collectives of people joined by the glue of shared goals and objectives. More recently it has become cliché to observe that goals are in fact often ambiguous and may be numerous and inconsistent. Rationality—if at all possible given the human condition—is elusive at best. Further, people working in organizations probably have goals of their own, which might compete with the organization's, leading to something less than cooperation. Efficiency and productivity may be worthy goals in schools and districts, but evidence of those characteristics can be hard to pin down in the face of ambiguity and human characteristics. Nevertheless, when educators are faced with a complicated puzzle, they will tend to seek rationality as they propose specific and explicit means linked to stated goals. They might reflect on their school or district's mission or vision, review rules of behavior, consider their own job description, and investigate what their supervisor wants as they strive toward high performance.

In his insightful (and sometimes comic) essay on the origins of organizational theory, Perrow (1973) characterizes structural or mechanistic models as "the forces of darkness" primarily because they tend to ignore the human dimensions of organizational life. In contrast, human relations or human resource theories, which built on structural foundations and succeeded them as organizational studies matured, were the "forces of light" because they added a concern for individuals' needs and such things as employee involvement and job satisfaction. Just the same, Perrow observes, managers were not so quick to dismiss structural thought.

> When asked, they acknowledged that they preferred clear lines of communication, clear specifications of authority and responsibility, and clear knowledge of whom they were responsible to. They were as wont to say "there ought to be a rule about this," as to say "there are too many rules around here," as wont to say "next week we've got to get organized" as to say "there is too much red tape."
>
> (1973, p. 6)

The thinking introduced in structural and human resource traditions is necessary background for students of school and district organization. The "big ideas" embedded in these works are as important to education leaders today as they were to organizational thought 100 years ago, at least as bases for understanding contemporary work in educational organizations.

Thought Partner Conversation

Structural theories are characterized as "forces of darkness" and human resource theories as "forces of light." The implication is that one is bad or evil, the other good or beneficial. In your opinion, are these perspectives opposites? In what ways are they the same or different? Do you think of one as positive, and the other negative? Why?

We strive to untangle the puzzling ways in which schools and districts work by introducing some key ideas from the structural tradition in organizational theory, and progress from there to the human side of school and district leadership. To foreshadow, both offer critical perspectives to understand what to do to solve problems associated with such things as performance assessment and resolving disputes among faculty. In microcosm, the two administrative tasks in the opening vignette illustrate common dilemmas faced by leaders all the time. It would be common to hear that the new AP should just do her job, applying what she learned about teacher evaluation to the task of evaluating the calculus teacher and common sense to the dispute about a special education student's status. It is easy to default to a hierarchical model of leadership that says the AP has authority to carry out evaluation and to be the final arbiter for IEPs and special education eligibility, therefore resolving both issues. The rules, roles, and relationships spelled out in structure offer guidance for action. It would be naïve, however, to think that these situations are not more complicated than they appear and therefore require some subtle approaches. Further, the age, gender, ethnicity, and other identity factors of the new AP and those with whom she is working, coupled with her lack of prior administrative experience apart from an internship, are likely to create both constraints and openings, though the latter may be hidden from view in the short term. Structural and human resources concepts that illuminate how educators and leaders interact and why can help to make sense of the challenges presented in the vignette.

Our fictional AP will likely think first about her rank and responsibilities at the high school. By virtue of her administrative credential, she is empowered by the state and the local school board that hired her to evaluate teacher performance. The principal has assigned her to the calculus teacher, making it her duty to provide the best feedback she can. At the same time, there are human relations considerations the new AP will likely ponder. The calculus teacher is intimidating to a new administrator who probably remembers little of the details of the calculus she took in college. As a new person at the high school, she is eager to build positive relationships among the faculty. Difficult as that may be with the calculus teacher, the prospects in special education seem more daunting. Again, her position as an administrator gives her certain positional authority, but the situation is less under her control than teacher evaluation. She cannot undo the student's de-certification from special education and she may not be sure what exactly she can mandate in terms of teacher behavior. Goals of providing the best possible education to all students and meeting the needs of students with disabilities do not appear to be particularly helpful for guiding her thinking and action. The AP may need to learn how to negotiate her way between what the school and district demand of her and what she can accomplish with the personalities she encounters.

Using theory to inform educational leadership practice can be confusing to the reader new to both. To help focus your thinking in this and subsequent chapters, we provide a set of questions to consider.

Essential Questions—Structural
- What role does structure play in defining the "rules of the game" for leaders?
- How do organizational and individual goals and objectives impact the leader's role?
- Why do people come to work in schools and districts?

SOLVING PUZZLES FROM A STRUCTURAL PERSPECTIVE

The term "structure" focuses attention on the *form* of the organization. Bush (2011) describes it this way: "Structure refers to the formal pattern of relationships between people in organizations. It expresses the ways in which individuals relate to each other in order to achieve organizational objectives" (p. 42). Rules, policies, and procedures that define how teachers, administrators, and staff work, who has authority to make decisions, how people are held accountable, and how individuals and groups are arranged hierarchically and in various departments or subunits are all parts of structure.

Structural models are often associated with a select few theorists whose work emerged in the early stages of the twentieth century (Bauer & Brazer, forthcoming). Notably, Max Weber's thoughts on bureaucracy and Frederick Taylor's principles of scientific management have become virtually synonymous with structural or "formal" models, as Bush (2011) calls them. Weber's work, in particular, was so important that Scott (1975) marks the English translations of his key publications in the late 1940s as the beginning of the study of organizations as a field. It is hard to argue with the fact that the bureaucratic form is often the default image we have of organizations, and its (presumed) faults are the impetus for much contemporary theory. Taylor's theory, focusing more on how individual jobs are defined and arranged within the organization (Weisbord, 2012), similarly introduced the importance of efficiency in the organization of work in ways that prize specialization of task and organizational coordination; values we often assume as fundamental to organizational life. Exploration of these two theorists' ideas, and the criticisms of them, provide valuable insights into education leadership thought and behavior.

WEBER'S BUREAUCRACY

First and foremost, Max Weber (1864–1920) was a social historian; in offering his theory of bureaucracy, Weber described what he saw happening as societies transitioned from agrarian economies and monarchic governmental systems into industrial economies that spawned larger and more complex organizations. Weber "endeavored to understand the changing bases of the social order as more traditional social structure rooted in shared culture, low mobility, and extended kinship ties gave way to a more mobile, differentiated, and impersonal order" (Scott, 2003, p. xvi). His "ideal type" bureaucracy was offered not as a hope or suggestion of preference, but as a theoretical statement of what a "pure" bureaucracy might look like.

The origin of Weber's conceptualization was rooted in his observations about the basis of authority within organizational life. He posited three types, of which rational–legal generated bureaucracy (Scott & Davis, 2007, p. 47):

- Traditional authority—resting on an established belief in the sanctity of immemorial traditions and the legitimacy of those exercising authority under them.
- Rational–legal authority—resting on a belief in the "legality" of patterns of normative rules and the right of those elevated to authority under such rules to issue commands.
- Charismatic authority—resting on devotion to the specific and exceptional sanctity, heroism, or exemplary character of an individual person, and of the normative patterns or order revealed or ordained by him or her.

Differences in authority were tied to people's beliefs about the legitimacy of authority relations (Scott & Davis, 2007). Each authority type tended to yield a distinctive type of organizational structure, with bureaucracies emerging from rational–legal authority structures. Weber observed, in his time, a shift from reliance on traditional authority to rational–legal authority and hence, the growth of bureaucracy. The primary elements of the organizational form, as summarized by Perrow (1986, p. 3), include:

1. Equal treatment for all employees.
2. Reliance on expertise, skills, and experience relevant to the position.
3. No extra-organizational prerogatives of the position; that is, the position is seen as belonging to the organization, not the person. The employee cannot use it for personal ends.
4. Specific standards of work and output.
5. Extensive record keeping dealing with the work and output.
6. Establishment and enforcement of rules and regulations that serve the interests of the organization.
7. Recognition that rules and regulations bind managers as well as employees, thus employees can hold management to the terms of the employment contract.

Scott and Davis (2007) add to these the notions of a fixed division of labor, hierarchy of offices, and employment viewed as a career. These characteristics became virtually synonymous with large-scale organization—including school districts—so much so that most, if not all, models of organizational structure include the concepts of depersonalized work relationships, rule- or norm-driven behavior, rationality, hierarchy, and specialization (Tosi, 2009).

> **Thought Partner Conversation**
>
> Bureaucracy remains a dominant organizational form, and schools are often described as bureaucratic in nature. When you look at the attributes of Weber's bureaucracy, to what degree do the administrative structures and processes you are familiar with epitomize the "ideal type?" In what ways do they differ? Why?

The emergence of bureaucracy bestowed substantial advantages on growing organizations. In bureaucracy, the emphasis on formal rules and procedures replaced favoritism and nepotism rampant in traditional organizations. Depersonalizing various organizational functions provided a degree of fairness that was rare previously. Specialization "leverages the power of the division of labor" (Godwyn & Gittell, 2012, p. 73). By limiting the scope of responsibility and span of control of individual actors, bureaucracy also addresses the limited rationality inherent in individuals as decision makers (March & Simon, 1993) by providing opportunities and expectations to pool disparate knowledge. Hierarchy provides a clear picture of reporting relationships and an unambiguous statement of jurisdiction based on competence. Professionalism defines mechanisms for individuals to know how to progress in their career pursuits and provides the possibility that individual learning and development will be rewarded.

Although schools and districts today are often criticized for their bureaucratic nature, it wasn't always so. As the common school movement picked up momentum in the 1830s and 1840s, first in Massachusetts, then later spreading throughout the Midwest and West, organization was loose and personalized. The nostalgic children's books of Laura Ingalls Wilder paint a picture of common school learning and teaching that is mostly consistent with more scholarly publications (Tyack & Hansot, 1982). Teachers, particularly in sparsely populated areas on the frontier, had little if any more education than what we would think of as eighth grade today. They were hired by local school boards after passing written and oral examinations administered in person by itinerant superintendents, and they often boarded with local families. They taught in unruly one-room school houses children who might range in age from 5 to 14 years old, depending on the season of the year because older boys were needed in the fields at planting and harvest times (Tyack & Hansot, 1982; Wilder, 1941/1971). Teaching was inconsistent at best and was often viewed as a temporary occupation prior to marriage for women and more promising business prospects for men.

Nineteenth-century urban centers had schools and systems that likely looked substantially better organized than the one-room schoolhouses on the prairie. But up through the middle of that century, public schools were mostly intended as a means to educating the children of poor and immigrant families in an effort to socialize them to the world of work. Many experiments focused on how to structure schooling efficiently, and they struggled in non-bureaucratic systems characterized by favoritism, political infighting, and graft (Cuban, 1988; Tyack, 1974).

By the turn of the twentieth century, bureaucracy was viewed as an important means of rationalizing and improving education and has been deeply entrenched in

US education for over 100 years. Ellwood P. Cubberley and fellow reformers known as the administrative progressives advocated for creation of professional bureaucracies in the name of efficiency and anti-corruption. Good government initiatives gradually removed personal relations and political spoils from education systems and inserted common professional education for teachers and administrators, impersonal criteria for hiring, job specialization (e.g., separating the roles of superintendents, principals, and teachers), and formal rules and roles governing professional behavior (state education codes, teacher and administrator credentialing, district policies and procedures) (Cuban, 1988; Tyack, 1974).

Weber's conceptualization of bureaucracy, Scott and Davis (2007) write, was a statement related to how organizational participants were dealing with various problems or defects apparent in existing organizational forms, focusing largely on power relations and the plight of subordinates within large organizational units. Cubberley was especially drawn to this function of bureaucracy based on his personal experience with rough-and-ready politics during his brief tenure as superintendent in San Diego in the opening years of the twentieth century (Tyack, 1974). The rational–legal bureaucracy provides protections against the particularism, favoritism, and nepotism rampant within school systems through the early twentieth century and other organizations reliant on traditional and even charismatic authority (Perrow, 1973). Further, "By supporting increased independence and discretion among lower administrative officials constrained by general administrative policies and specified procedures, bureaucratic systems are capable of handling more complex administrative tasks than traditional systems" (Scott & Davis, 2007, p. 50). Thus, in education, bureaucratization allowed for larger, more efficient school districts in growing urban centers that gradually shrugged off capricious hiring and firing, large and unwieldy school boards, and kickbacks to local officials for purchases of books and equipment.

Bureaucratic organizations are goal-seeking and goals defined by actors at the apex of the hierarchy are assumed to be both clear and supported by organizational members. The rules, procedures, and other elements of structure are intended to optimize pursuit of these agreed-upon organizational goals and objectives. When leaders create structures as solutions to problems the test of their effectiveness is in goal accomplishment. From the efforts of the early twentieth-century administrative progressives through today, the answers to efficiency and effectiveness questions in education have been elusive because of unclear and often conflicting goals and the difficulty of measuring meaningful education outputs. Education thus reveals major fissures in the ideal bureaucratic structure articulated by Weber. Fuzzy goals and ambiguous performance measures blur rules and roles and undermine pre-determined structure.

Thought Partner Conversation

In your experience, what are the most important goals of educational organizations? How have these changed over the last few decades? Do you find that schools tend to be optimally organized to meet these goals?

Another characteristic of structural models is the assumption of organizations as closed systems. That is, there is little consideration of varying organizational contexts and little attempt to acknowledge how differing demands from the external environment might impact the organization. The reality of education systems being more open than closed because of their political foundations be-deviled Cubberley and his fellow reformers striving to build efficient bureaucracies. As Thompson (1967/2003) predicted, in the face of externally imposed ambiguity they sought to close systems in their attempts to professionalize them and minimize the role of politicians. Administrative progressives were only partially successful in their efforts. Chapter 2 elaborates what we mean by schools and districts being "open" or having porous boundaries. The degree of control implied in a closed system was key to efforts to maximize bureaucratic efficiency in private enterprise, districts, and schools.

SCIENTIFIC MANAGEMENT

Frederick W. Taylor (1856–1915) worked most of his career as an engineer designing tools and factory set-ups in fabricating plants. His writing, like Weber's, must be understood in its historic context, the industrial Northeast United States in the latter 1800s and early part of the twentieth century, a time when low-income and ill-educated immigrants offered plentiful labor, but also a time when unions were emergent in many trades.

Judging from *The Principles of Scientific Management* (1911/1998), what bothered Taylor most was what he saw as twin problems of inefficient organization and low worker motivation (Weisbord, 2012). The latter characteristic, he claimed, was manifest in "soldiering"—the practice of working slowly to conserve energy and make a menial job palatable. Taylor's intent was to address inefficiency in the organization and worker motivation simultaneously. The key for Taylor was financial incentive. It was in industrialists' best interests to organize work more efficiently so that worker productivity would be increased and material waste would be minimized. By the same token, workers should share in the benefits of increased productivity through higher wages as a means of incentivizing them to work more efficiently in accordance with Taylor's very specific prescriptions.

> **Thought Partner Conversation**
>
> Taylor and his followers admired the scientific process and saw no problem with the idea of applying this logic to the design of work. In what ways do educators do this today? What are the benefits of such an approach, and what are the possible problems?

Taylor, his associates, and other contemporaries (e.g., Frank Gilbreth) used time-and-motion studies to figure out ways in which work could be completed in less time with less wasted energy and material. He immortalized the fate of the lowly pig iron loader in his speeches and in *The Principles of Scientific Management* (Weisbord, 2012). Reading his (some would claim fictionalized) account of the archetype of Schmidt the pig iron handler makes vivid the belief that men could be taught to get more work done with less fatigue and that they would be more satisfied workers, especially if their wages reflected their increased output.

Cubberley was early in the academic portion of his career when Taylor was delivering his lectures that were collected into *The Principles of Scientific Management* (1911/1998). Admiring Taylor and making specific references to the concept of scientific management, Cubberley devoted much of his energy to traveling around the country to assess school districts' efficiency. He did so through the use of standardized testing and curriculum audits that might look very familiar in the twenty-first century. Cubberley was not alone, of course, but his career, emphases, and influence help to explain why contemporary schools have grade levels with highly specified scope and sequencing, differentiated curricula in secondary schools, and bureaucracy that communicates rules, roles, and norms. Each of these features was originally intended to achieve greater efficiency through job specification, task specialization, and coordination—key principles in Taylor's work. Much of the change that Cubberley and other administrative progressives wrought deliberately mirrored the rationalization of work in heavy industry promoted by Taylor. Although we may use the image derisively today, Cubberley aspired to make schools more like factories because of his devotion to efficient use of educational resources (Cuban, 1988; Tyack, 1974).

How did bureaucratization of schooling improve efficiency? One important means was through undergraduate and graduate education. Education for teachers improved from the mid-nineteenth century forward as prospective teachers were expected to have the credential that accompanied completion of a 2-year normal school curriculum. Normal schools were the precursors in many instances to 4-year state colleges and universities in which teacher education expanded into a 4-year curriculum and/or a teacher education master's degree that followed a full baccalaureate major.

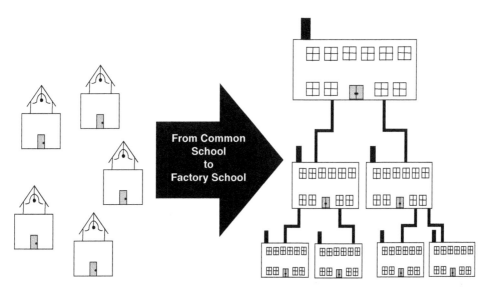

FIGURE 1.1 Schools Forming into Bureaucracies—Common Schools to Elementary Schools, Junior High Schools, and High Schools

> **Thought Partner Conversation**
>
> Suppose, for the moment, that you are the principal of your school, and you hired the renowned management consultant, Fred Taylor, to help you increase efficiency. If Fred spent a day in your school, what would he most likely recognize as consistent with his approach to organizing, and what would he most likely recommend?

Cubberley was instrumental in designing a master's-level curriculum for aspiring school administrators who had experience teaching. Thus, the professionalization of the principalship, superintendency, and other administrative roles followed on the greater professionalization of teaching. State requirements for these examples of professional credentialing legitimated the entire teacher and administrator education process. Roles became clearer as responsibilities of principals were differentiated from those of teachers (moving away from the concept of principal as "principal teacher" and toward school manager) (Cuban, 1988). A prominent example of this role definition is the codification of those holding administrative credentials being the sole personnel qualified to evaluate teachers. The administrative progressives argued that bureaucratic credentialing and role definition were akin to manufacturing's division of labor and organized supervision of work.

Imagine for a few minutes how the AP described in the vignette might respond to Weber, Taylor, and Cubberley. She would recognize herself as credentialed by the state to evaluate teachers and manage the school at the direction of the principal and superintendent. Her role is reasonably clear. She might note that differentiation of her role from that of Ms. Alakhi, the calculus teacher, helps to clarify their future interactions. Her place in the bureaucracy does not, however, ease her mind about having adequate expertise to evaluate Ms. Alakhi. The dispute between the special education teachers seems inexplicable through the lens of bureaucracy, possibly immobilizing the novice AP in her thinking. The virtues of and gaps in structural thinking might become clear to the AP as she engages in practice, as they were to those who criticized a purely structural approach to organizations.

> **Thought Partner Conversation**
>
> Before reading on about scholars' critiques of the structural models, how do you perceive them? In what ways do these models "ring true" and help you describe and explain organizational life in schools, and in what ways do they fall short?

Taylor believed that through scientific study, the "one best way" of doing a job could be discovered (Kanigel, 1997). Consistent organization, professional teacher and administrator preparation, and differentiated curricula were the "best practices" of their day, and many of the administrative progressives' reforms have been improved and are evident in contemporary school systems. Understanding the value of education bureaucracy and work arrangements within it doesn't mean that they are beyond criticism, however. Outcomes that appear less desirable today include treating teachers as interchangeable parts, not allowing for different rates of child development, and an inability to meet academic needs of large portions of the student population—all pathologies that may be at least partially attributable to a rigid, rule-driven system. These kinds of concerns are not new in education and are being addressed in many different ways across the US and around the world. Similarly, organization theorists have not been as enamored of the early structural theorists as was Cubberley.

CRITIQUE OF STRUCTURAL MODELS

Although it is hard to ignore the fundamental necessity of having rules and order in even the simplest organization, there are several problems with these models that have been recounted by theorists, researchers, and practitioners alike, prominent among them the notion that structural theorists tend to ignore the human dimensions of organizational life—dimensions that seem particularly important in the intensively interpersonal process of education. The AP in our vignette might be made somewhat comfortable by the clarity of her role, but she is also likely daunted by the interpersonal implications of evaluating a much more experienced educator and striving to help older adults get along in a professional manner. Bush (2011, pp. 63–66) summarizes major criticism of a purely structural approach, focusing on the concepts embedded in the notion of bureaucracy:

1. The assumption of organizations as goal oriented relies on additional assumptions that goals are clear and agreed-upon, criteria that do not work well in education. Schools have numerous and sometimes conflicting goals they address. Units within schools, such as departments, may have goals of their own that may sometimes seem out-of-sync with the school or district goals. The image of having a broad consensus on clear and well-articulated goals is at best problematic.
2. Unclear, ambiguous, or unknown goals common in education belie the notion that decision making within bureaucratic organizations is rational. Limits to rationality are well established by scholars such as March and Simon (1993), as is the notion that decision makers can and do make decisions based primarily on institutional norms rather than goals specific to a single organization (e.g., Meyer & Rowan, 1977; DiMaggio & Powell, 1983) (see Chapter 3).
3. Structural models tend to treat organizations as if they are independent of, rather than made up of people. There is little consideration of individual goals and the needs of people, or how these might differ from the needs of the organization.
4. Hierarchy and reliance on formal lines of authority and accountability may inhibit efficiency in schools by concentrating decision making among individuals who are distant from the classroom and who have less direct information needed to make decisions about teaching and learning processes.
5. Schools' organizational environments are varied and changing, contradicting the closed-system nature of the bureaucratic model that assumes environmental stability. Hierarchy, Perrow (1986) writes, promotes both rigidity and timidity in the face of change, resulting in "delays and sluggishness" (p. 29) and, in general indecision rather than efficiency.

In addition to early conceptions of organizations leaving out important features, many theorists have been concerned that Cubberley-type pursuit of efficiency through bureaucracy may be misguided. Merton was bothered by the notion that bureaucrats may be more loyal to the organization's rules and procedures than to the needs of clients, and Argyris (1999) worried that emphasis on formal structure and rationality in organizations would lead to learned incompetence. The combination of structure, supported by rules mechanically adhered to, could be seen as key to schools' inability to change as environmental factors such as demographics, politics, and technology shift over time. With bureaucrats in mind, Merton captures why teachers are particularly resistant to being changed by would-be reformers. "[B]ureaucratic officials affectively identify themselves with their way of life. They have a pride of craft which leads them to resist change in established routines; at least, those changes which are felt to be imposed by others" (quoted from Shafritz, Ott, & Jang, 2011, p. 111). Weber himself cautioned against the potential sins of bureaucracy, particularly the potential for the concentration of power in the hands of a few and the dehumanizing nature of reliance on rules and order to govern and constrain the degrees of freedom exercised by individuals and groups. He famously warned of bureaucracy as an "iron cage" (DiMaggio & Powell, 1983; Scott & Davis, 2007). Other theorists have questioned the assumption that bureaucracy and hierarchy are necessarily efficient.

Heckscher and Donnellon (1994) asserted that, by its very nature, bureaucracy wastes human intelligence as individuals need to adhere to rules that inhibit rather than facilitate their work. Follett (1949) believed that the bureaucratic form tends to limit cooperation by failing to foster horizontal relationships. Scholars looking at the impact of technology on structure (e.g., Burns & Stalker, 1961; Woodward, 1965) questioned whether the bureaucratic form might best fit only certain kinds of industries and be ill-suited to many, including schools, precisely because of the lack of goal clarity and widely varied and changeable demands made on workers as they enact their jobs.

In terms of the more micro-focused theories such as scientific management, Perrow (1986) and Weisbord (2012) note that a lasting effect of Taylorism is the separation of thinking and doing, that is, taking decision making about the conduct of work away from workers and placing it in the hands of engineers or technical experts. Deskilling labor serves to reduce costs and to make owners less dependent on any individual worker. There have been many attempts over the past 100 years to systematize schooling by providing teacher proof curricula and routinizing what are thought to be effective pedagogical practices (Eisner, 2002). In school districts, the result was the emergence of central office curriculum experts and other officials who took on the tasks associated with creating programs, pacing charts, and assessments—a managerial class that centralized "technical" aspects of educating and, in effect, reduced teachers' and school leaders' discretion over critical dimensions of the teaching and learning process. A current manifestation of attempts to constrain school-based decision making appears to be the tendency for charter management organizations and school districts to specify certain teaching practices down to the daily lesson level. A century after Taylor and Cubberley, there continues to be debate over the centralization of design and creativity in education and what role centrally-mandated programs and practices play in promoting educational outcomes.

There is evidence to suggest that Taylor would have abhorred what his principles became in practice, especially in the context of assembly line factories and other industries (Kanigel, 1997; Weisbord, 2012). Taylor's core principles included simplifying tasks, reducing conflict, and developing each individual to their highest capabilities, values that are hard to find fault with in his day or in the present. But Taylor seemed to ignore two properties of organizations that are vital to consider: First, Taylor neglected to notice that organizations exist in a wider environment; they are open systems. Taylor, perhaps more than any other theorist, treated the organization as a closed system, as if all relevant variables that could affect production could be accounted for, studied, and controlled. Second, Taylor seemed not to notice that all organizations are social as well as technical systems—they are populated by human beings. As we will see in the next section, organization theorists took up the issue of people inside organizations a decade or so after Taylor's death (and we will tackle the question of open systems in Chapter 2).

Thought Partner Conversation

Management theorists have observed that Taylor's separation of thinking and doing—planning from the execution of work—has had a far-reaching impact on how we organize work. How has this manifest itself in schools—what are the effects, both positive and negative?

HUMAN RELATIONS AND THE MOTIVATION TO WORK

Many students who enter education leadership programs start from a belief that they need to learn how to manage the systems in which they have typically worked as teachers or counselors. Understanding rules, roles, and relationships is of great importance to the prospective and novice administrator, but there is more to leadership than merely learning how to keep the school or district running from day to day. Schools consist of a variety of people who come to work in them—students, teachers, and administrators—and who have an interest in their outcomes—parents, the community, and policymakers. Thus, understanding how people actually function within schools and districts, separate from what we might expect in general terms, is essential for knowing how to build relationships and ultimately to lead these organizations. The opening vignette illustrates this point by bringing up two situations drawn from our own practice as school administrators in which the behavior and/or perceptions of the people involved are out-of-sync with organization charts and professional expectations.

We offer the following essential questions to help you refocus your attention on the human interactions that often defy bureaucratic explanations. Note the first question is repeated from our first set of essential questions because structural and human relations theorists both addressed this question but answered it differently.

Essential Questions—Human Relations
- Why do people come to work in schools and districts?
- What are effective means of motivating individuals and groups to work toward common goals?
- How are formal and informal relations and organization important in schools and school systems?

Interpersonal relationships are not unique to school sites, of course. The AP perspective presented in the vignette is drawn from a school embedded in a larger school district. Resources and relationships between schools and the central office present threats and opportunities. For example, if an AP seeks advice and assistance from the director of special education services at the central office, how will she be received? The director has choices of his own to make with respect to how he wants to lead his department and to work with site-level administrators throughout the system. Perceiving an expanding web of relationships bears careful analysis, but it is probably easiest to start from the perspective of individuals.

Engineers and psychologists have been interested in the motivation of those who work in organizations for at least the past 100 years. Engineers and psychologists may seem like odd bedfellows, but their interests converge on the question of why people work and how to get them to perform more effectively in their jobs. They share a common belief that "happy" workers produce more output of higher quality.

Thought Partner Conversation

We might have just as easily pointed out that principals and teachers assume that happy students are productive learners. Is the relationship between satisfaction and outcomes really so simple? Discuss what you believe about this, and challenge yourselves to come up with alternative explanations as well.

Until approximately the turn of the twentieth century, most factories were far more chaotic—and dangerous—than we would expect today. As more of the working population was moving from farm to factory work, and as younger children were being excluded from labor by means of compulsory education laws (Tyack & Hansot, 1982), upward pressure on workers' wages motivated factory managers to achieve greater efficiency. Part of that drive included reducing the frequency of industrial accidents and stabilizing the workforce to reap the benefits of on-the-job training—both of which improve worker productivity. We begin our examination of interpersonal relationships in schools and districts in the factories of America's industrial period because the theorists and practitioners who aspired to improve those conditions provide important insights for how prospective and practicing education leaders might think about their effectiveness today.

Motivation Revealed

Elton Mayo (1880–1949), a sociologist, psychologist, and psychotherapist, supervised investigations that inadvertently revealed at least one reason for improved worker performance. His graduate student, Fritz Roethlisberger, carried out time-and-motion studies and altered the work environment in the now-famous Hawthorne experiments. Attempting a controlled clinical trial approach to changes in work environment, Roethlisberger found that treatments intended to make telephone switch assemblers' working conditions better improved output. But so did treatments intended to make working conditions *worse*. And more to their surprise, whatever he tried in the experimental rooms, he got the same improved output in the control rooms. When Roethlisberger and his colleagues asked workers about these results, assembly workers told them that they were pleased by the extra attention they received and wanted to do a particularly good job for the researchers and the company. Thus, the Hawthorne Effect that generates positive outcomes just from additional attention (Scott, 2003; Smith, 1980).

WHAT IF WE APPLIED HAWTHORNE FINDINGS TO HIGH SCHOOLS?

Students in high schools often feel anonymous and sometimes seek out anonymity to avoid work or insulate themselves from potential failure. If we structured high schools to pay more attention to students as individuals, would that help them to perform better?

The answer is maybe. In the 1990s the idea of creating small schools by breaking up high schools into "houses" or other smaller configurations was a popular reform fueled by Gates Foundation money. Gates ultimately abandoned the idea in the belief that no substantial gains in student achievement were demonstrated (Kahneman, 2011), but houses live on at least in some schools (see, for example, William C. Overfelt High School in San Jose, CA and Hillsdale High School in San Mateo, CA).

Duncan-Andrade (2009) has identified teachers who are able to relate to their students on a personal level as being more effective in reaching students academically. His answer to the question about treating students more as individuals would appear to be, "yes" if children have greater opportunities to feel love and belonging. (See discussion of Maslow's Hierarchy below.)

Thought Partner Conversation

What motivates you to work hard(er), and what tends to deflate you a bit? Are these the same kinds of things that affect your co-workers and students? Here's a harder question: What do you mean by "motivation?"

It is possible that improved output observed by Taylor was also generated by the Hawthorne Effect, but he wouldn't have thought about that because the Hawthorne experiment results were not published until well after his death. Efforts to improve industrial processes teach us that how people are treated matters in terms of how they behave. Interestingly, the behavioral response cannot be entirely controlled by management, only influenced. What has all this to do with education leadership?

The calculus teacher and the special education teachers whom we met at the beginning of the chapter are similar to workers studied in that their behaviors are also driven by their personal and professional motivation. When principals and superintendents understand student, teacher, and administrator motivation, then they are better able to create the circumstances in which motivation to meet desired educational goals improves. Three psychologists whose mid-twentieth century work interests us the most for this discussion provide important insights into professionals' motivation for conducting what Fullan (2001) calls knowledge work that is much closer to what teachers and administrators do as compared to pig iron handlers or telephone switch assemblers.

Motivation Explained

In the 1940s, Abraham Maslow theorized his now well-known hierarchy of human needs, which adds nuance to an understanding of why people choose to work and how they behave while at work. Human needs of the most basic sort begin with food, clothing, and shelter—the physiological needs—and physical safety (Maslow, 1943). It is easy to see how these needs are reflected in schools through free and reduced priced meal programs that feed hungry children and administrators' concerns with keeping school campuses safe. Children who are hungry or in fear of their physical safety are not in a situation where they can maximize learning. Thus, schools and districts want to ensure physiological comfort and physical safety to improve prospects that all children are ready to learn. Likewise for adults. Although we are not likely to be concerned about whether they are hungry when they start the work day, it is important to job performance that teachers and administrators go to work with confidence that their physical safety is assured.

USING THE LENS OF HUMAN NEEDS

There are many factors embedded in the profile of the calculus teacher that might make her intimidating to the novice AP. Just the fact of her apparent success over a 30-year career places a burden of modesty on anyone presuming to evaluate her teaching performance. But thinking about her perspective by considering her human needs might make evaluation less anxiety producing for the AP.

The calculus teacher is comfortable in the school setting. She likely has her professional and personal friends, or she probably wouldn't have remained at the school for so long. Nevertheless, she like most of us probably has an unlimited need for esteem (i.e., recognition for a job well done) and self-actualization or being the kind of teacher she aspires to be.

The AP might encounter more success evaluating the calculus teacher if she focuses on the process of bolstering Ms. Alakhi's esteem and self-actualization so that she has a heightened sense of satisfaction as a result of the feedback she receives. If successful in this way, the AP is also far more likely to be able to offer constructive criticism that will further improve her performance, either by reinforcing effective techniques, making helpful suggestions for improvement, or a combination of the two.

Love and belonging are not far behind, at least with respect to how children are treated, particularly within elementary schools. Even in secondary schools there is growing interest in supporting students' affective needs so that they can focus on learning. We observe this interest through research on the effects of social and emotional learning generally and the tactic of intervening to mitigate stereotype threat and implicit bias (Steele, 2010; Walton & Cohen, 2011; Yeager & Walton, 2011). Intuitively, it is not a long leap from thinking about children's needs for love and belonging to considering similar needs for teachers and other adults. Teachers who have a sense that the school values their presence, takes good care of them, and has a clear place for them within the social network that inevitably develops when people work in an organization seem more likely to want to do a good job in their specific roles. Thus, moving from factory settings into schools and districts, emphasis shifts from economic gain and physical pain (most closely associated with physiological and safety needs) into the realm of the more emotional or affective needs. It is important to emphasize a change in perspective from understanding work as physical labor to looking at educators as focused on cognitive processes. Both kinds of work require motivation, but the motivations may be different.

Knowledge workers such as teachers and administrators are likely motivated by how they are perceived by peers, students, and parents—the esteem in which they are held—and whether or not they achieve professional fulfillment—self-actualization. We address these two highest levels of Maslow's Hierarchy in more detail in the next section as they are employed by another organizational theory.

Simplistic approaches to school leadership and management may not take into account Maslow's Hierarchy and may therefore be limited in their effect. If all school and district leaders do is focus on physiological and safety needs, perhaps with a little love and belonging thrown in, they are not likely to achieve improved performance for either teachers or students. The school will be merely a humane factory if it does not appeal to the higher motivations of students and teachers. Another mid-twentieth century theorist understood this problem and built a new theory of management based on the wisdom of Maslow's Hierarchy.

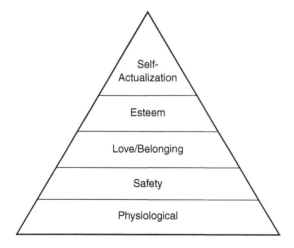

FIGURE 1.2 Graphic Representation of Maslow's Hierarchy of Human Needs

Thought Partner Conversation

Marion and Gonzales (2014) suggest a terrific thought exercise related to Maslow's theory. Suppose you were to rewrite the Hierarchy of Needs for the present day and with schools in mind. Would it differ? What would your hierarchy look like? Would it look different for a preschool as compared with an elementary, middle, or high school? Why or why not?

Differentiated Management Theories

The publication of "A Theory of Human Motivation," in which Maslow (1943) explains his hierarchy of human needs, had a profound influence on Douglas McGregor (1906–1964). Yet another engineer, this time with an additional advanced degree in psychology, McGregor made the argument mentioned in the previous section—once a lower stage in Maslow's Hierarchy has been satisfied—safety, for example—it no longer serves as a motivator for improved performance (Maslow, 1943; McGregor, 1960/2006). It is important to pause here to recognize that McGregor never claimed that this insight applies to all work settings. He was careful to differentiate labor and routine behavior from knowledge work or what we might think of as professional work. It may well be true that miners or factory workers are incentivized by higher pay and better working conditions (particularly those that enhance safety) because the nature of their jobs and compensation are such that those needs remain precarious. McGregor recognized that the nature of labor was such that few if any workers would achieve much esteem or self-actualization from engaging in repetitive tasks. But people within organizations who are well paid and make decisions that determine the direction of the organization and those who work within it—those engaged in knowledge work—are more likely to have the first three needs in the pyramid in Figure 1.2 met and will therefore be more motivated by opportunities for esteem and self-actualization.

McGregor took the assumptions of Taylor and others who focused on efficiency and called those approaches to management Theory X. Leaders who operate from a Theory X perspective assume that people do not want to work (which is certainly a rational thought if one's work consists of loading pig iron ingots onto a railroad car). Those whose work itself is unmotivating can only be motivated with money—either by providing more of it or threatening to take it away—and by minimizing chronic pain endemic to labor. It was McGregor's insight that if higher levels of motivation were not available in the workplace, they would be sought outside. Thus, doing a better job addressing physiological and safety needs will not create greater loyalty to the organization or a drive for improved performance, but it may free up workers' time and energy to address other interests or hobbies that gratify higher needs. Adhering to Theory X beliefs that people need to be coerced to engage in work they would not otherwise choose to do is neither good nor bad in McGregor's view. It is appropriate to certain work settings and managers should be forthright about the relationships among managers, workers, and the organization (McGregor, 1960/2006).

In developing his alternative, Theory Y, McGregor began by disagreeing with basic assumptions about why people work and what employees are capable of doing. His Theory Y perspective asserts that work is as natural to human beings as recreation or rest. Removing the compulsion to work assumption reveals other motivating factors apart from income and freedom from pain or discomfort. Psychic rewards that stem from esteem and self-actualization can drive employee commitment to achieving organizational objectives, which in turn generates a greater sense of responsibility toward the organization. Emphasizing the sentient nature of human beings in the work place rather than seeing them as extension of machines on the factory floor leads to the conclusion that wisdom is widespread in the workforce and there is much untapped potential when constrained by Theory X assumptions.

> [Theory Y] assumptions involve sharply different implications for managerial strategy than do those of Theory X. They are dynamic rather than static: They indicate the possibility of human growth and development; they stress the necessity for selective adaptation rather than for a single absolute form of control. They are not framed in terms of the least common denominator of the factory hand, but in terms of a resource which has substantial possibilities.
>
> (McGregor, 1960/2006, p. 66)

The concept of tapping into teachers' expertise to solve teaching and learning problems has driven much of the interest in teacher collaboration of the past 40 years (e.g., Grossman, Wineburg, & Woolworth, 2001; Malen, Ogawa, & Kranz, 1990; McLaughlin & Talbert, 2001; Ogawa & White, 1994; Van Lare, Brazer, Bauer, & Smith, 2013). Collaboration among teachers and others could be an avenue into generating esteem and self-actualization as teacher performance and student outcomes improve.

Schools are not actually factories and teaching is not labor in the classic sense, despite the administrative progressives' fascination with efficiency (Cuban, 1988; Tyack, 1974). Clear to anyone working within education, schools and districts involve a great deal of interpersonal interaction as teachers and students engage in the process of transmitting and generating knowledge. Thus potential for esteem and self-actualization abounds. This kind of setting, McGregor said, calls for a Theory Y approach to management in which organizational members have opportunities to earn the esteem of colleagues and others and can become the kinds of professionals they aspire to be (McGregor, 1960/2006). In education, we can imagine teachers and administrators creating innovative classrooms, schools, and districts they believe will generate the most powerful learning outcomes and achieve academic goals such as narrowed achievement gaps and higher rates of college admission and persistence.

A school leader who wishes to take a Theory Y approach must be realistic about the circumstances she faces in a particular school or district. No matter how well thought-out and how enlightened one's approach to school leadership may be, not everyone will be receptive to Theory Y approaches for a variety of reasons that likely include selfishness, burnout, and neglect. By the same token, school leaders should be adept at working with countless teachers and administrators who engage in their work because they want to make a difference for young people, they want to expand opportunities and try to help students achieve life goals. Reading the landscape is critical. Yet another organizational psychologist provides some important navigational aids, but first a slight detour.

Expansion of Maslow and Theory Y. While Maslow was developing his hierarchy of human needs in the early 1940s, a Jewish Austrian psychiatrist, Viktor Frankl (1905–1997), was languishing in Nazi concentration camps. To keep his mind occupied, he engaged in field-based research, asking why some concentration camp inmates survived for long periods of time and others did not. His conclusion was that survival had less to do with physical health than with maintaining an important goal larger than oneself, often enacted as helping others to survive (Frankl, 1959/2006).

JUSTICE RUTH BADER GINSBERG ON SELF-TRANSCENDENCE

When Justice Ginsburg delivered the Rathbun Lecture at Stanford University on February 6, 2017, she made the following comments on the topic of a "meaningful life":

I tell the law students I address now and then, if you're going to be a lawyer and just practice your profession, well, you have a skill, so you're very much like a plumber. ... If you want to be a true professional, you will do something outside yourself. ... Something to repair tears in your community. Something to make life a little better for people less fortunate than you. That's what I think a meaningful life is—living not for oneself, but for one's community (downloaded February 9, 2017 from http://news.stanford.edu).

The pursuit of a meaningful life, of self-transcendence, may be the most powerful motivator for any educator.

Extended Web Activities

Do a web search to learn more about the idea of self-transcendence. Do you find this concept a useful expansion of Maslow's ideas? Why or why not?

After his release at the end of World War II, Frankl developed a new approach to psychotherapy that emphasized the importance of life goals. In doing so, he claimed that Maslow had not gone far enough. The truly fulfilled adult would move beyond self-actualization into self-transcendence—the devotion to a goal beyond the self (Frankl, 1959/2006). Self-transcendence is a natural fit for education because of the dedication of many educators who have little hope of becoming wealthy or being particularly well treated professionally as they help children to succeed. The adept school leader employing Theory Y-type strategies would do well to find ways for fellow educators to achieve self-transcendence.

Opportunities and Barriers for Theory Y Leadership

Psychologist Frederick Herzberg and his colleagues conducted field studies among engineers and accountants associated with the steel industry around Pittsburgh in the 1950s to learn what motivated professionals in their work (Herzberg, Mausner, & Snyderman, 1959/1993). Through their analysis of survey data, they discovered specific, concrete elements of esteem and self-actualization. They collected these into the broader category of "job satisfiers," or work experiences that generated short- and long-term positive feelings among engineers and accountants. The linkages among the writings of Maslow, McGregor, and Herzberg et al. are significant. Conducting their research as McGregor was working out Theory Y, Herzberg and colleagues found that recognition for a job well done, goal achievement, and increased responsibility fed professionals' need for esteem—others' and their own belief that they were performing at a high level in their professional roles. Consistent experience of this kind of feedback combined with the individual's appreciation for the work itself constituted "a complex of factors leading to this sense of personal growth and self-actualization" (Herzberg et al., p. 70). Thus, Maslow theorizes a hierarchy of human needs that Herzberg, Mausner, and Snyderman are able to detect in the workplace, and McGregor further conceptualizes important leadership choices—Theory X and Theory Y—that allow leaders to tap into individuals' motivations in an effort to improve performance.

From the perspective of a novice AP, the path ahead may seem clear. Find ways to provide recognition, focus on goal achievement, and increase teachers' responsibility. Thinking about the work lives of teachers, however, it quickly becomes obvious that the process is not so simple. Although education has been professionalized over more than 100 years, teaching is unlike many other professions in that key satisfiers such as goal achievement or increased responsibility (i.e., promotion) are ambiguous, extremely rare, or non-existent. Thus, esteem might be achieved through private and public recognition of a job well done, but attempts to do so can be fraught with problems. Recognition of one teacher may cause jealousy from others and create perverse incentives through emphasizing outcomes measures such as standardized test scores. School and district leaders should be realistic about this situation and recognize that Herzberg and his team also learned the specifics of factors that tend to make professionals unhappy at work—the dissatisfiers or hygiene factors.

Herzberg et al. (1959/1993) were careful to point out that hygiene factors are distinct from, rather than the opposite of, satisfiers. Hygiene factors are heavily weighted toward management, rather than leadership because they stem from the *work environment*, as opposed to the satisfiers focused on the *work that people do* (Herzberg, 1966). School-based hygiene factors would include total compensation, number of preparations, class preparation time, out-of-class duties, and treatment by administration. Herzberg et al. (1959/1993) found that ineffective enactment of policies were the most frequent sources of dissatisfaction, but a close second were the ill-effects from poorly conceived but well-implemented policies. To bring this into an educational context, teachers are often frustrated by lax discipline that they blame on administration for being too soft or overwhelmed by student behavior. Likewise, principals and their assistants are frustrated when the central office ties their hands with teacher

HYGIENE FACTORS AND MOTIVATORS

One of the most intriguing aspects of Herzberg's work is that he and his colleagues found that what satisfies and motivates people at work is different from what dissatisfies them. The dissatisfiers, or *hygiene factors*, when absent, dissatisfy us. Hygiene factors include such things as:

- Organization policies
- Supervision
- Salary
- Relationship with peers at work
- Status

These are like Maslow's lower-level needs; when they are absent or insufficient, we are dissatisfied. When they meet expectations, well, fine. We are not motivated to excel by them.

What are the motivators—or using Maslow's terms, self-actualizers?

- Achievement
- Recognition
- The work itself
- Responsibility
- Advancement
- Growth

(Thought Partner Conversation—Do you agree with this scheme—and the attributes associated with hygiene factors and motivators? What would you add or delete?)

Source: Herzberg (1968)

evaluation procedures that may be alienating or ineffective. Further, teacher evaluation falls into the category of technical supervision, another major source of dissatisfaction. Teacher evaluation is an opportunity to build healthy professional relationships but often fails to do so either because of poor conceptualization (possibly using checklists), weak implementation (failure to observe long enough or frequently enough), or technical incompetence (not understanding calculus). Weak management generates dissatisfaction that creates demoralization within the school and district.

It might be tempting to conclude that if school leaders manage well, then the school and district will generate happy teachers who are motivated to help children learn at the peak of their capacity. Herzberg, were he still alive, would likely counter, "Not so fast." Adept management is a *necessary* condition for effective leadership (see, for example, Grissom & Loeb, 2011; Horng & Loeb, 2010), but not *sufficient*. The removal of dissatisfiers or the mitigation of those hygiene factors that get in the way of high-quality work is separate from satisfiers because they are limited to the work environment. Teachers, administrators, and very likely students require opportunities for esteem and self-actualization, not merely a good salary and clean classrooms, to perform at their peak. The satisfiers point the way to numerous leadership opportunities.

Worthy goals for the new AP would be to ensure that hygiene factors are taken care of to the extent possible, recognizing that teaching assignments, school safety, and adequate provision of supplies are within her grasp while larger issues such as total compensation are not. Minimizing dissatisfiers allows leadership to focus on generating as many satisfiers as possible—essentially implementing what is known about professional motivation at work. If Maslow, McGregor, and Herzberg are correct, improving teacher motivation will improve performance.

Extended Web Activities

Do a web search for the video, *Jumping for the Jelly Beans*, in which Herzberg himself explains his ideas. In it, Herzberg claims that motivation is a function of *ability and opportunity*—we need to feel able to do things AND we have to have the *opportunity* to do these things to be motivated to perform. Do you agree? How does this play out in schools?

CONCLUSION: LEADING KNOWLEDGE WORK

Understanding the power and limitations of structure and how people working within structures are motivated helps those in education administration to navigate their way through puzzling and sometimes threatening situations. Structure is necessary for organizations to function, but what should structure look like? Answering that question requires knowing what the structure is intended to achieve and how individuals respond to and shape structure based on their motivations and other factors. The interplay between structure and human relations is both fascinating and nuanced. We return to these twin foundations of organizational theory in subsequent chapters because they are fundamental to informing educational leadership.

By now we hope to have persuaded you that figuring out the purpose of structure and knowing how to work with individuals' motivations is central to on-the-job training of new leaders. As you strive to help others perform at their peak, you will need to consider opportunities and constraints present in the organizational structure in which you find yourself, the complex web of interpersonal relationships within that structure, and ways in which motivation is influenced by your behavior and the organizational climate you help to create.

A central theme of this book is that learning to lead involves considering how theory informs practice and using that knowledge to address practical problems that will help you to improve individual and system performance. It is equally important to bear in mind that education falls into the category of knowledge work—the use and generation of understanding of specific aspects of the world we live in. Your leadership must be well aligned with this type of work or you are likely to become very frustrated. We argue that the key to leading knowledge work is to lead learning—your own, students', and adults'. We address leading learning directly in Chapters 4 and 7, but we want you to know at this point that all of the other strategies and tactics we discuss in this book serve the purpose of leading learning.

Another important theme of this book is influence versus control. We emphasize organizational theory in Part I of this book because we believe leading well is predicated on understanding the organization—school or district—you purport to lead. Part of that understanding is knowing what you can control and what you can only influence. Thus, Chapter 2 removes the organization-as-closed-system assumption. Schools and districts do not stand alone, isolated from the outside world. On the contrary, educational leaders find themselves coping with and striving to influence many forces that come from beyond the walls of their buildings.

EXERCISE 1.1 BACK TO THE BEGINNING

We encourage you to use what you already know about how schools operate to search for opportunities and threats present in the new AP's world. It might be best to answer the questions in this exercise in a small group to benefit from the varied experiences of classmates. We suggest you record all of your answers and reconsider them when you have finished reading the chapter.

- In what ways does the AP's *position* in the high school give her potential influence with the calculus teacher?
- In what ways does this moment in the AP's career *limit* her influence with the calculus teacher?
- What seems structurally *appropriate* about the AP mediating a dispute between the two special educators?

  - In what way might interpersonal relations *limit* the appropriateness of the AP mediating a dispute between the two special educators?

- What steps could the AP take right away to *grow into* her role as an evaluator of experienced teachers and an effective mediator of disputes between adults?
- What are the leadership implications of the situations in which the AP finds herself?

EXERCISE 1.2 AN ANALYSIS OF YOUR OWN SCHOOL

Take some time to reflect on the current situation in your own school and complete the following table. As you do so, prepare to discuss:

- If you were on the administrative team, where would you focus your energy to have the greatest effect?
- How might the roles of principal and AP differ for addressing dissatisfiers and satisfiers?

WORKSHEET A

Satisfiers	Evidence of Their Existence	Influence on Individuals and/or the School	Ways to Maintain or Enhance Satisfiers
1.			
2.			

Dissatisfiers	Evidence of Their Existence	Influence on Individuals and/or the School	Ways to Mitigate or Eliminate Dissatisfiers
1.			
2.			

PUZZLE TO SOLVE

Although we use the metaphor of puzzles to help you think through common challenges in educational settings, we don't believe that the puzzles we put in front of you have one optimal solution. Having been exposed to and discussed the application of various concepts and theories, we provide these puzzles to help you think further about leading through common challenges characterized by ambiguity and complexity. They are intended to build from what you learned completing the chapter's exercises. We leave the puzzles open-ended so that you can discuss with your classmates and instructor how you would handle specific situations, allowing you to learn by puzzling through alone and with the insights of others. The puzzles in this and subsequent chapters differ from the exercises in that they require you to see more of the big picture and think about consequences over time. Doing so is an important process because sometimes short-term fixes create long-term unintended consequences.

PUZZLING THROUGH A DISPUTE

Mr. Allen has a history of reducing his caseload and class sizes as the year progresses. More insidious, the AP learns from the principal that Mr. Allen acts on a pattern of holding onto white students while de-certifying or transferring into Inclusion classes racial and language minority students. Ms. Moore is furious with him on three counts:

(1) the student was on her caseload so she should have been present for any discussion about de-certifying him from special education before the parent's mind was made up, (2) she strongly believes that this student requires special education support to have a reasonable chance to graduate with his class, and (3) the student is African American, thus fitting the questionable pattern of Mr. Allen's recommendations for student placement. Ms. Moore has a strong reputation as a special education teacher who is a full partner in Inclusion math classes with other teachers who respect her. Mr. Allen is the kind of teacher whom others avoid because of passive-aggressive and aggressive-aggressive behaviors that he employs to protect his comfortable position. Put yourself in the shoes of the AP with the understanding that Ms. Moore and Mr. Allen have had several similar conflicts in the past and are barely able to be in the same room together.

As you consider the task the new AP has been handed to settle this latest eruption in a long-standing conflict, answer the following questions:

1. What are likely to be the strongest motivations for each of these teachers?
2. Does this situation call for more of a Theory X or a Theory Y approach? What makes you think so?

   - In what ways might organizational hierarchy help or hurt this situation?
   - In what ways might human relations theory inform how to complement or mitigate the effects of hierarchy?
   - In what ways does your being new in the position present opportunities?
   - In what ways does your being new in the position require a cautious approach?

We have told you about as much as you are likely to know about Mr. Allen and Ms. Moore before you head into your first meeting with them after school tomorrow. Their interpersonal conflict may overshadow structural problems that are fueling it. What would you want to accomplish in this meeting and how would you go about it?

REFERENCES

Argyris, C. (1999). *On organizational learning* (2nd ed.). Oxford: Blackwell.

Bauer, S., & Brazer, S. (forthcoming). Structural theories of school organization. In M. Connolly, D. Eddy-Spicer, C. James, & S. Kruse (Eds.), *The Sage international handbook on school organization*.

Burns, T., & Stalker, G. (1961). *The management of innovation*. London: Tavistock.

Bush, T. (2011). *Theories of educational leadership & management* (4th ed.). Los Angeles: Sage.

Cuban, L. (1988). *The managerial imperative and the practice of leadership in schools*. Albany, NY: State University of New York Press.

DiMaggio, P., & Powell, W. (1983). The iron cage revisited: Institutional isomorphism and collective rationality in organizational fields. *American Sociological Review*, 48(2), 147–160.

Duncan-Andrade, J. (2009). Note to educators: Hope required when growing roses in concrete. *Harvard Education Review*, 79(2), 181–194.

Eisner, E. (2002). *The educational imagination: On the design and evaluation of school programs* (3rd ed.). Upper Saddle River, NJ: Pearson Education.

Follett, M. (1949). *Freedom and coordination: Lectures in business organization* (Reprint 1987). New York: Management Publications Trust.

Frankl, V. (1959/2006). *Man's search for meaning.* Boston: Beacon Press.

Fullan, M. (2001). *Leading in a culture of change.* San Francisco: Jossey-Bass.

Godwyn, M., & Gittell, J. (Eds.). (2012). *Sociology of organizations: Structures and relationships.* Los Angeles: Sage.

Grissom, J., & Loeb, S. (2011). Triangulating principal effectiveness: How perspectives of parents, teachers, and assistant principals identify the central importance of managerial skills. *American Educational Research Journal, 20*(10), 1–33.

Grossman, P., Wineburg, S., & Woolworth, S. (2001). Toward a theory of teacher community. *Teachers College Record, 103*(6), 942–1012.

Heckscher, C., & Donnellon, A. (1994). *The post-bureaucratic organization: New perspectives on organizational change.* Los Angeles: Sage Publications.

Herzberg, F. (1966). *Work and the nature of man.* New York: The World Publishing Company.

Herzberg, F. (1968). One more time: How do you motivate employees? *Harvard Business Review, 46*(1), 53–62.

Herzberg, F., Mausner, B., & Snyderman, B. (1959/1993). *The motivation to work.* New York: John Wiley & Sons.

Horng, E., & Loeb, S. (2010). New thinking about instructional leadership. *Phi Delta Kappan, 92*(3), 66–69.

Kanigel, R. (1997). *The one best way: Frederick Winslow Taylor and the enigma of efficiency.* New York: Viking.

Khaneman, D. (2011). *Thinking, fast and slow.* New York: Farrar, Straus, and Giroux.

Malen, B., Ogawa, R., & Kranz, J. (1990). What do we know about schoolbased management? A case study of the literature—a call for research. In W. Clune & J. Witte (Eds.), *Choice and control in American education: The practice of choice, decentralization and school restructuring* (Vol. 2, pp. 289–342). London: The Falmer Press.

March, J., & Simon, H. (1993). *Organizations* (2nd ed.). New York: John Wiley and Sons.

Marion, R., & Gonzales, L. (2014). *Leadership in education: Organizational theory for the practitioner* (2nd ed.). Long Grove, IL: Waveland Press.

Maslow, A.H. (1943). A theory of human motivation. *Psychological Review, 50*(4), 370–396.

McGregor, D. (1960/2006). *The human side of enterprise: Annotated edition* (J. Cutcher-Gershenfeld, ed.). New York: McGraw-Hill.

McLaughlin, M., & Talbrt, J. (2001). *Professional communities and the work of high school teaching.* Chicago: The University of Chicago Press.

Meyer, J., & Rowan, B. (1977). Institutional organizations: Formal structure as myth and ceremony. *American Journal of Sociology, 83*(2), 340–363.

Ogawa, R., & White, P. (1994). School-based management: an overview. In S. Mohrman, P. Wohlstetter, and associates (Eds.), *Designing high performance schools: Strategies for school-based management.* San Francisco: Jossey-Bass.

Perrow, C. (1973). The short and glorious history of organizational theory. *Organizational Dynamics, 2*(1), 2–15.

Perrow, C. (1986). *Complex organizations: A critical essay* (3rd ed.). New York: McGraw-Hill.

Scott, W.R. (1975). Organizational structure. *Annual Review of Sociology, 1*(1), 1–20.

Scott, W.R. (2003). *Organizations: Rational, natural, and open systems.* Upper Saddle River, NJ: Prentice Hall.

Scott, W.R., & Davis, G. (2007). *Organizations and organizing: Rational, natural and open systems perspectives.* Upper Saddle River, NJ: Pearson Prentice Hall.

Shafritz, J., Ott, J., & Jang, Y. (2011). *Classics of organization theory* (7th ed.). Boston: Wadsworth.

Smith, J.H. (1980). Three faces of Elton Mayo. BookBlast® Archive. https://bookblast.com/blog/bookblast-archive-the-three-faces-of-elton-mayo-j-h-smith-new-society-december-1980/.

Steele, C. (2010). *Whistling Vivaldi: How stereotypes affect us and what we can do.* New York: W.W. Norton.

Taylor, F.W. (1911/1998). *The principles of scientific management.* New York: Dover Publications.

Thompson, J. (1967/2003). *Organizations in action: Social science bases of administrative theory.* New Brunswick, NJ: Transaction Publishers.

Tosi, H. (2009). About theories of organization. In H. Tosi (Ed.), *Theories of Organization* (pp. 3–18). Los Angeles: Sage.

Tyack, D. (1974). *The one best system: A history of American urban education.* Cambridge, MA: Harvard University Press.

Tyack, D., & Hansot, E. (1982). *Managers of virtue: Public school leadership in America, 1820–1980.* New York: Basic Books.

Van Lare, M., Brazer, S., Bauer, S., & Smith, R. (2013). Professional learning communities using evidence: Examining teacher learning and organizational learning. In S. Conley & B. Cooper (Eds.), *Moving from teacher isolation to teacher collaboration: Enhancing professionalism and school quality* (pp. 157–182). Lanham, MD: Rowman and Littlefield.

Walton, G., & Cohen, G. (2011). A brief social-belonging intervention improves academic and health outcomes of minority students. *Science, 331*(1447). DOI: 10.1126/science.1198364.

Weisbord, M. (2012). *Productive workplaces revisited: Dignity, meaning, and community in the 21st century, 25th anniversary edition.* San Francisco: Jossey-Bass.

Wilder, L.I. (1941/1971). *Little town on the prairie.* New York: HarperCollins.

Woodward, J. (1965). *Industrial organization: Theory and practice.* London: Oxford University Press.

Yeager, D., & Walton, G. (2011). Social-psychological interventions in education: They're not magic. *Review of Educational Research, 81*(2), 267–301.

CHAPTER 2

Schools as Open Systems: There's a Whole World Out There

New AP Peter Tunin finds himself in a highly diverse inner-ring suburban middle school with an array of responsibilities, but discipline takes the lion's share of his time. Although he had hopes for spending more time learning to be an instructional leader, as the "new guy" he accepted the inevitable and determined to make the best of it. He took a deep dive into school discipline, setting out first to review historical data about patterns of infractions documented in past years, and next to examine the Positive Behavior Intervention and Supports strategies employed by the school.

In recent years, the Hispanic student population has increased dramatically in the school district, now accounting for fully one-quarter of the middle school's student population. Reviewing the data, a disturbing trend becomes apparent. Last year, Hispanic students accounted for 60 percent of the discipline cases recorded. Clearly, Peter thought, there's something going on here. So he decided to contact the parents of several of the students who show up in the data as repeat offenders. One parent in particular got his attention when he said, "Hey, I have no idea why the teachers are picking on my son. He's a big kid, and he says the teachers are scared of him, avoid him, and then jump down his throat at the slightest provocation. He says that they want him out of the room because they find him intimidating. Can you imagine? My kid, intimidating an adult teacher? He's 12 years old!" Another parent commented that she and her husband came to school to meet with a teacher, and the teacher seemed ill at ease and wouldn't make eye contact with them. "I was thinking," the mother said, "What, you think because I speak with an accent that I have some kind of disease or something?"

Peter mentioned his data and concerns at an administrative team meeting the week following his discussions with parents, and others expressed amazement. One person agreed that she feels that some of the teachers don't know how to deal with families from diverse backgrounds, even to the point of avoiding contact with them. The principal, listening attentively, said, "I'm not so sure this has anything to do with teachers' ability to relate to diverse populations. Let's let the teachers teach and not make too many assumptions about their motives. Take a hard look at the discipline system we have in place. I went to a principals' professional development session at the district last week. We learned about restorative justice (RJ), which the school system is advocating very strongly. Jefferson High School across town presented their RJ policy and some stats that show that this is making a big impact for them, and hey, they have roughly similar demographics as our school. I think this is the answer." Peter left the meeting, not sure what just happened or why.

STUDENTS ARE NOT PRODUCTS

An important reason why the machine metaphor doesn't work too well for schools and districts is that students are not output in the traditional sense of the factories upon which the rational systems theorists reflected. Schools and classrooms act upon students to be sure, but student reactions reach across a range and are unpredictable, unlike steel or chemicals.

Anyone who might doubt the permeable nature of school walls should consider students alone and all that they bring into schools and classrooms. Some carry with them rich experiences from preschool, their neighborhoods, or trips to Europe. Others carry trauma that may be personal or societally based. Students, and by extension schools, are influenced by the presence or absence of other forces in their lives such as faith-based organizations, government agencies, and their parents' employment circumstances. Personal and institutional influences present opportunities and threats; they ought to be responded to by schools, but they cannot be controlled.

INTRODUCTION

Classical theorists focused their attention on the operations of organizations and the specification of jobs and procedures within the four walls of these social enterprises. The complexities they worked to describe and explain lay within the organization. Understanding how work was organized—how workers were arranged, controlled, and motivated (to the extent they cared about the latter)—were daunting enough and demanded their full attention. Theorists like Weber puzzled through the explanation of how the social order morphed as a result of the transition from traditional to rational–legal bases of authority; Taylor strove to convince managers to apply science to the specification of jobs in order to maximize efficiencies and, he dreamed, promote cooperation on the otherwise contentious shop floor. Thus, structural theories are characterized as "closed systems models" in that they tend to focus on what happens within the organization (Marion & Gonzales, 2014), and barely (if at all) concern themselves with actors in other organizations or interactions among organizations in a larger environment.

Thinking about AP Peter Tunin grappling with ambiguity about the causes of student discipline, it seems evident that factors both inside and outside the school have influence on students' and teachers' experiences. What are external social forces that impinge on the administrative team's capacity to create and maintain a school environment that is welcoming, safe, and productive for all students? We learn little from classical theories about what goes on outside the firm (or school) or the impact of the environment on the nature and structure of work. Even the human relations theories, which take into account some of the complexities of inter- and intra-personal dynamics and motivation, tend to be closed systems views that focus on what goes on within the organization (Perrow, 1986; Tosi, 2009), largely ignoring influences from "outside."

As we noted in the previous chapter, another important dilemma embedded in classical theories is the assumption that organizational structures and processes emerge from rational decisions made by leaders (Kast & Rosenzweig, 1973; Scott & Davis, 2007). While we will deal with the assumption of rationality and its consequences more fully in later chapters, for the moment let us revisit a few of the central tenets of a core belief derived from the earliest structural theorists: form follows function. First, strict rationality assumes that the goals of the organization (function or organizational purpose) are clear and well known, at least to decision makers. Second, for decision makers to make rational decisions, they have access to and acquire the information necessary to do so. Third, the pace of change is modest at most, or the rationality of key decisions would be constantly challenged. It is no wonder, then, that Morgan (2006) characterizes the classical theories metaphorically as "machine models"— machines are stable, routine, their operations are ordered and predictable; they can be programmed or designed to meet highly specific production goals and objectives. Morgan notes that the classical theorists looked at organizing as a technical problem and sought specific, "right" ways to organize work.

Ask yourself: Is the organization that you work in and lead machine-like? Are classrooms, schools, and school systems mostly ordered and predictable? We would be loath to describe schools as "irrational" in their design and operation, yet some of what happens within them is difficult to describe as rational in terms of educational goals and objectives. Can we consider learning as strictly a technical problem? Is there one best way to teach? When we invoke the maxim that it takes a village to educate a child, what is this village of which we speak? Where is it located? Of what consequence is what goes on outside the classroom, school, and district in terms of how we organize, manage, and lead?

Thought Partner Conversation

Spend a moment or two with a critical friend answering the question posed above—when we say "it takes a village," who are we considering and why? Who might we be leaving out (and why)?

As you might have guessed, there is an alternative perspective to the closed systems view, namely considering organizations as open systems, "open" in the sense of existing within a broader context—an environment—filled with actors that influence decisions and processes that occur within schools and districts. Scott (1979) explains:

> When organizational structure is viewed as a limited set of factors which together may be arranged or modified to produce desired outcomes, then the logical model

employed is that of a closed system. When the structure itself is viewed as something to be explained at least in part by the operation of external forces and as not completely under the control of system participants, then the underlying image is that of an open system.

(p. 165)

Think about a school district and schools within it and the various educational, social, political, and economic influences that come from "outside" these systems:

- stakeholders who make demands—students, teachers, parents, administrators, and community members;
- entities whose policies and procedures impact educational practices—state education agency, federal government, policy analysis organizations; and
- governance structures of schools and districts—elected and/or appointed state officials (legislators, state superintendent of instruction, state board of education, etc.), elected school board members, and superintendents serving at the pleasure of their boards' majorities.

Suddenly, it seems easy to see numerous influences beyond the control of superintendents and school site administrators.

In this chapter, we move beyond the mechanistic and closed view of schools and districts as organizations and address the complexity of the open systems perspective. We begin by explaining what we mean by "system" in this context, and then provide a description of the open systems view. Along the way, we introduce a number of contemporary perspectives on school organization that rely on an open systems perspective. We conclude with a discussion of the role of the school's environment in solving the various puzzles leaders face as they seek to create effective schools. As you will see, a hallmark of moving to an open systems view is abandonment of the illusion of certainty in favor of acknowledging complexity and ambiguity in leaders' puzzle-solving work.

> Essential Questions
> 1. What is meant by a "system"?
> 2. What does it mean when a system is open as opposed to closed?
> 3. How might thinking of schools and districts as open systems change leaders' perspectives on opportunities and constraints confronting them?

SYSTEMS DEFINED

An Austrian biologist, Ludwig von Bertalanffy (1952, 1968), is credited with being the primary architect of what became known as general systems theory (GST) (Kast & Rosenzweig, 1973), a set of abstract ideas applied widely to the physical, biological, and social sciences. A system can be defined as "an organized, unitary whole composed of two or more interdependent parts, components, or subsystems and delineated by identifiable boundaries from its environmental suprasystem" (Kast & Rosenzweig, 1973, p. 10). Dissecting this simple definition highlights several of the most intriguing aspects of this perspective: the whole as made up of *inter*dependent parts; identifiable *boundaries* between these parts; and the fact of an *environment* beyond the boundary of the organization. Even in its simplest form, the systems perspective acknowledges complexity and the potential for variability, ambiguity, and change as any part of the system interacts with others. Considering schools and districts as organizations with permeable boundaries, located within complex systems might give the aspiring leader a headache. We provide a systematic (pun intended) pathway through the tangle.

Thought Partner Conversation

In what ways might you consider your school a system? What about each class you teach? Using the parts of the definition presented in the preceding paragraph, discuss with a critical friend whether the term "system" applies well to your school and a class you teach. Are there features that are easier to see and others that don't seem to apply?

The roots of the systems perspective in organizational studies date back to classical management theorists of the type discussed in Chapter 1. Although they tended to focus on a mechanistic view of how organizations work, many acknowledged (though did not incorporate) complexity and the existence of a world outside the four walls of the factory. As a key example, Barnard's (1938) definition of an organization as "a system of consciously coordinated activities of forces among two or more purposes" (p. 73) was influential in moving thought in this direction. Indeed, human relations theorists such as Barnard tended to add a focus on the informal, social organization and the interactions between and among people to the structural concern with the technical definition of tasks and roles (Scott & Davis, 2007). Although this was an important departure from classical theory, it too was limited. Viewing the organization only through a social lens is just as one-sided as viewing it only as a technical exercise, and the focus was squarely within the four walls of the firm. A conceptual bridge to open systems theorists, however, is that human relations theorists departed from structural theorists' tendencies to examine the material and visible to think about what was intangible and invisible, such as human needs, interactions, and motivations.

In the 1950s, scholars at the Tavistock Institute of Human Relations in England suggested that organizations are *socio-technical systems* (Morgan, 2006; Shafritz, Ott & Jang, 2005), that is, that organizing requires consideration of both the technical and social elements of work. In a sense, the characteristics of systems allowed scholars to merge some of the attributes and thought of the classical, mechanistic approach to understanding organization with those of the human relations theorists to begin to accommodate the notion that the technical and human dimensions interact or are integrated within the organization. As Kast and Rosenzweig (1973) note, "the technologies affect the types of inputs to and outputs from the organization. It is the social system, however, that determines the effectiveness and efficiency of the utilization of the technology" (p. 12).

Thought Partner Conversation

When theorists use the term technology, they are referring to how work is done. Discuss for a moment with a critical friend: What is the "core technology" of schools? Why might this be important to organizing?

Later scholars have been interested in describing the interrelationships between the technical core of education and social interactions that make it happen. Weick (1976) explained that educational organizations are loosely coupled in part because the technical core (i.e., how teaching and learning happen) is only dimly understood. Human beings impart meaning to what is happening in schools and generally trust what they and others are doing as correct. Cuban (1988) in his effort to demonstrate work and leadership similarities among teachers, principals, and superintendents claimed that historical images tended to combine technical and artistic as discerning characteristics of educators to generate a definition of education professional. Moving away from a strictly rational, closed-system approach to thinking about schools and districts demonstrates the importance of understanding systems operations that are both mechanistic and interpersonal; internally managed and externally influenced.

Thought Partner Conversation

With a critical friend, explore the metaphor of schools as loosely coupled systems. What elements of the organization are only loosely coupled? What might the effect be on leaders' ability to lead?

In its simplest form, we might think about the systems view of formal organization as involving the components depicted in Figure 2.1 (adapted from Connor, 1980). The components are organized into inputs (goals and constraints); throughputs (organizational design variables); and outputs or outcomes. As applied to schools, we would note that organizational purposes or goals are initiated by policy makers at various levels, primarily from the state and district. Other inputs include the quality and quantity of human resources available from which to staff the school; elements of the social and fiscal environment; and the universities, publishers, and vendors that help define the technologies available to achieve teaching and learning. The actual work of schooling is defined by various organizational design factors, such as the ways in which people, equipment, facilities, etc., are deployed; the way decisions are made; and the actual conduct of work. Outputs include a safe and orderly school climate, student learning, staff productivity, and so on. Changes to any parts of the system necessitate adaptation from other parts—and while in this simple conception we envision these interrelationships as unidirectional, we could easily argue that each part

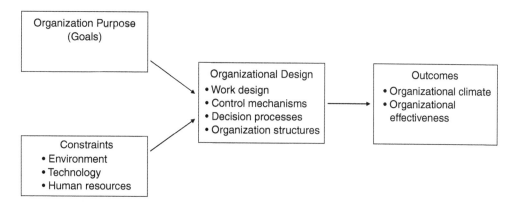

FIGURE 2.1 Simple Systems Diagram

influences the other, with feedback loops flowing back as the school impacts at a minimum its local environment, and learning outcomes impact decisions about the structure and process of the school's work. See Figure 2.2 as a school specific example of the general system depicted in Figure 2.1.

Peter Tunin, our somewhat beleaguered middle school AP from this chapter's opening vignette, could make good use of Figure 2.2 but he would need to fill in some blanks from the general example. With his school discipline hat on, good citizenship and social–emotional learning seem to be most in his purview, with educating for the next level left largely to others. His constraints remain unknown from the vignette and do not seem to be well informed by what we have listed in Figure 2.2. The student population is changing but it is not yet clear if that is more of an opportunity or a constraint. At the same time, something is happening in some teachers' classrooms that seems to be alienating the school's Hispanic students. Thinking about the interaction between demographic shifts and the middle school's status quo, the

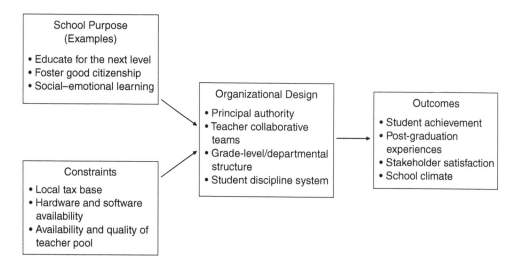

FIGURE 2.2 School as System Diagram

student discipline system is generating referrals, suspensions, and expulsions of Hispanic students well over twice their representation in the population. They bear the brunt of the school's negative messages about behavior. The principal has suggested a major shift to a RJ approach, an idea that comes from outside the school that could provide new ways to address student resistance to teacher authority and direction. Implementation of the new approach will also place constraints and open opportunities for Peter's work. Peter is left baffled because he cannot imagine how the administration could bring in a new system that would take a completely different approach to referrals and suspensions. Feeling overwhelmed by teachers' response to the changing population and the possibility of adopting a method used by a local high school, Peter is not certain at this point how to improve discipline outcomes.

Kast and Rosenzweig (1973) provide a more complex and realistic perspective on the systems model as applied to organizations. They conceive of the *internal organization* as being made up of several subsystems, each complex unto itself:

- Organizational goals and values make up one subsystem—these may be derived from outside the organization, but are also affected by internal actors.

  o In schools, particularly secondary schools, the instructional system is often perceived as separate from the disciplinary system, even though both should be focused on optimizing teaching and learning.

- The technical subsystem covers the knowledge required to perform the organization's work, and would include equipment, work processes, space, etc.

  o The technical subsystem in schools if often contested as exemplified by debates about how to achieve early literacy or the degree to which laboratory experiences should be emphasized in high school science courses.

- The psychosocial subsystem refers to individuals' behavior and motivation, status, group dynamics, and decision-making systems.

  o Teachers working at different grade levels or in different subject areas and students in different age cohorts are characterized by attributes such as collegiality, behavior, and achievement.

- The structural subsystem involves the organizational structure or form of work, including reporting relationships, departmentalization, formalization—the "org chart" and rule book.

  o As we established in Chapter 1, schools and districts tend to be highly structured into bureaucracies that have been familiar for at least 100 years.

- The managerial subsystem encompasses management of work—setting goals, planning, organizing, controlling, and evaluating.

  o Administrative teams are typically in charge of the managerial subsystem, but emphasis on teacher initiative through formal (coaches, grade-level leaders, department chairs, etc.) and informal roles has been growing over the past few decades.

Internal subsystems exist within and interact with the *environmental suprasystem* that affects every element of the internal organization—"the environment" includes all entities that interact with or even tangentially affect any element of the internal workings of the organization. Figure 2.3 presents a simplified graphic depiction of this model (adapted from Kast & Rosenzweig, 1973, p. 14 & 18). Note the overlaps between each internal subsystem plays as a unifying element that significantly impacts all other elements.

Organizations as Open Systems

In the preface of the second edition of their classic treatise on organization theory, March and Simon (1993) define organization as "systems of coordinated action among individuals and groups whose preferences, information, interests, or knowledge differ" (p. 2). How managers and leaders go about coordinating these actions is a significant puzzle, accomplished, they say, through control over information, roles, incentives, and organizational culture. The real-world difficulty, they observe further, is that the world we live in is more complex than these simple propositions allow:

> Effective control over organizational processes is limited, however, by the uncertainties and ambiguities of life, by the limited cognitive and affective capabilities of human actors, by the complexities of balancing trade-offs across time and space, and by threats of competition.
>
> (March & Simon, 1993, p. 2)

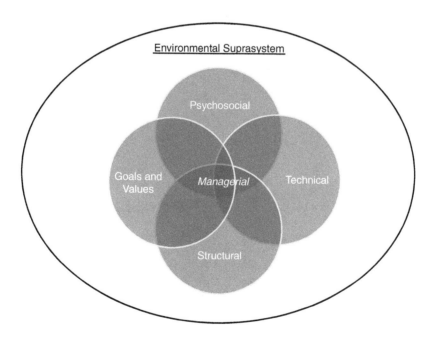

FIGURE 2.3 Organizational Systems

Thompson (1967, 2003) explains that complexity is a central conundrum in organizational theory. He concludes that "there are strong human tendencies to reduce various forms of knowledge to the closed-system variety, to rid them of all ultimate uncertainty," that is, "If we wish to predict accurately the state a system will be in presently, it helps immensely to be dealing with a *determinate system*" (p. 4). The rational model theories such as those described in the preceding chapter feature such assumptions. He goes on:

> If, instead of assuming closure, we assume that a system contains more variables than we can comprehend at one time, or that some of the variables are subject to influences we cannot control or predict, we must resort to a different sort of logic.
>
> (p. 6)

The alternative, he suggests, is a natural- or open systems approach in which "the complex organization is a set of interdependent parts which taken together make up a whole because each contributes something and receives something from the whole, which in turn is interdependent with some larger environment" (p. 6). Our discussion of Figure 2.4 that follows shortly describes how this works for schools

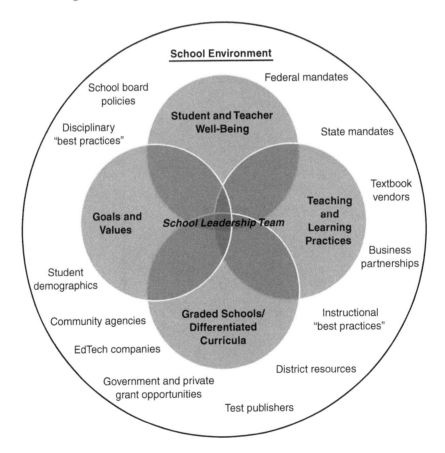

FIGURE 2.4 Schools as Open Systems

and districts. Schools are interdependent with one another and with strong influences in their environments such as the school board, the state education department, and the state legislature, which all give directives of one kind or another to the school.

To summarize, the open systems concept embraces and builds upon the notion of socio-technical systems, stressing the role of the environment, and raising questions about the very boundaries of formal organizations. When a parent comes to school for a conference with a teacher, or when we speak about parents as partners in a child's education, do the parents become a part of the organization or are they part of the environment? When we speak of "organization" in relation to schools, what are we speaking of—classes, the whole school, the school system? As Katz and Kahn (1966) ask, "How do we know that we are dealing with an organization? What are its boundaries? What behavior belongs to the organization and what behavior lies outside it?" (p. 14).

When introducing the concept of open systems in organizational studies, Morgan (2006) employed the metaphor of the organization as an organism: "We find ourselves thinking about them as living systems, existing in a wider environment on which they depend for the satisfaction of various needs" (p. 39). The organization belongs to a species; e.g., schools similar to one another in some respects but very different in others. In describing the nature of open systems, Katz and Kahn (1966) note that just like living systems, organizations draw energy from the environment and transform this energy to produce some outcomes. They have routines and processes through which they process their work and a complex series of work flows through which things are accomplished. Perhaps most important, they note, organizations as open systems are characterized by *equifinality*, meaning that the system can accomplish its work in a variety of different ways. Leaders in organizations adjust work processes and reorganize as needed to ensure the organization's survival as demands from the environment change. Leaders also act to buffer or reduce turbulence from the environment in order to maintain productivity.

Thought Partner Conversation

The concept of equifinality suggests that there is no one best way to conduct work, but that instead leaders and followers might organize work differently depending on their sense of goals and environmental demands. With a critical friend, discuss the implications of this in schools. In what ways is this principle in evidence, and in what ways are demands made on the school to limit it?

Viewing school organizations as complex open systems suggests, at a minimum, that teaching and learning practices are but one part of the enterprise, linked to and affected by myriad other parts that lie both within and outside of the organization. Figure 2.4 presents an application of the Kast and Rosenzweig model to the contemporary school environment. Note that the influences in the suprasystem are exemplary, not exhaustive.

> **Thought Partner Conversation**
>
> It is straightforward to see the environmental influencers on schools that embody legally defined stakeholders like the state. With a critical friend, examine Figure 2.4 and make a list of actors in your school's environment that we may have missed—to help think about this: What stakeholders in the school environment influence what we teach and how we teach?

What does all of this complexity mean for middle school AP Peter Tunin? Understanding the four circles in Figure 2.4 and how they interact with each other and with the school environment—i.e., assuming the school is an open system—helps him to see the nature of his work from multiple perspectives. Doing so may help him to manage student discipline in a manner more supportive to students individually and to classroom learning. Let's see how this works starting from the managerial function of the school leadership team in the middle of Figure 2.4.

Managerial—The School Leadership Team

A primary duty of Peter's is to manage the discipline system in his school. This typically involves working with the leadership team[1] to develop a vision for school discipline, establish and enforce an attendance policy, delineate procedures with teachers that would include articulating proper classroom decorum and appropriate responses to misbehavior, respond to referrals from the teacher to the AP in a timely fashion, suspend students for offenses stipulated in the state education code, and meet with parents to enlist their support in maintaining appropriate student behavior. As simple and concentrated in the school site as these responsibilities may seem, the school environment is, nevertheless, hard at work influencing Peter, the AP.

Administrative behavior and decision making are by their nature quite public and therefore have many reference points within and beyond school walls. The school board is likely to articulate a discipline policy that bounds AP behavior, and board policy is influenced by state policy and law. For example, most states prohibit corporal punishment. Another example at the time of this writing, the California Department of Education actively scrutinized school districts' suspension rates by ethnicity. San Francisco Unified School District (SFUSD) was admonished to address disproportionate suspension and expulsion rates of African American and Latino students. The district's response was typical: adopt a program (or in this case, two programs) to address the problem. By selecting RJ and Positive Behavior Interventions and Supports (PBIS), SFUSD drew upon resources outside itself—from the environment—and pushed them into the schools. In our scenario, Peter Tunin may be required to implement RJ as a response to the discipline challenges typical of middle schools and unique to the changing population at his school. He would need to graft the program onto the management imperatives already present in the school.

Suppose that Peter, in collaboration with the administrative team, wrote the discipline section of his school's faculty handbook to specify expectations for teachers for classroom management and school supervision. In his managerial role, he would explain all of the procedures required when students step outside the boundaries of acceptable behaviors, and he might even provide helpful advice and resources for teachers to support their classroom management and interactions with students. If Peter were in San Francisco, the state's concern about disproportionate suspensions and expulsions would ripple through the school district, into his school, and into the school's classrooms in the form of mandated RJ and PBIS practices. His handbook sections would need to be rewritten and a host of additional actions would follow. Resistance of varying force seems likely throughout this chain because school systems are made up of people with social–psychological needs, aspirations, and biases. No single stakeholder—student, teacher, administrator, school board, or state education agency—is entirely in control, nor is any without some measure of influence.

Goals and Values—What is the Purpose of Discipline?

The authors of this book have supervised literally hundreds of administrative interns—people such as yourselves who are preparing to lead schools. Although we don't encourage it, these interns frequently end up spending much of their time addressing student behaviors that are at cross-purposes with the educational intent of their schools, particularly high schools. What does this mean in practice? Oftentimes it means sitting in the high school cafeteria for an hour or more each morning greeting students who have arrived late to school and have been referred by their first period teachers to the intern to receive appropriate consequences and return to class as soon as possible. Imagining the line of students in a large high school waiting to be "processed," it seems evident that few students are likely to be in class anytime soon. Some are caught up in a one-time snare because of oversleeping or a flat tire on the way to school, but many students are repeat offenders, as any intern will tell you, who work their school's tardy policy and system to spend as little time in an early class as possible. Why do we perpetuate such systems?

Psychosocial—Student and Teacher Well-Being

In Chapter 1 we wrote about human motivation, based largely on Maslow's Hierarchy, and we did so mainly from an individual perspective. Considering individuals as part of a social system we call school and recognizing that psychosocial outcomes of students and teachers are both interrelated and differently motivated moves discipline beyond the mere management of programs and procedures.

What do kids want? To paraphrase the Cyndi Lauper hit from the 1980s: "Kids just want to have fun." Granted, that is probably overly simplistic, but we sometimes forget that our students are children who in middle school, for example, have a hard time delaying gratification and are not consistently future oriented. This presents a puzzle for teachers who are responsible for student learning such that they can succeed in high school and beyond. Adept teachers recognize the desire for fun and strive to build that into learning (see, for example, Cuban, 2018), while others have a hard time balancing fun and curriculum coverage. There are many ways in which classrooms can go awry when student and teacher motivations do not align, often

IMPLICIT BIAS AS A PSYCHOSOCIAL FACTOR

Working in a consultant role with a school district, one of us was told by parents and administrators alike that it was possible to walk down the hallways of a high school and know the academic level of the class inside a room just by peering through the window in the door. How? By the color of students' skin. It seems that, even though this school district adopted an open enrollment policy for advanced courses, few African American students were finding their way into honors and Advanced Placement classes. We should note that African Americans make up more than 40 percent of this school district's student population.

Whether the issue is discipline, as in Peter Tunin's case, or academics, students are well aware of messages sent by the patterns that occur in schools. These patterns may not be intentional and they may be generated by forces outside the school, but they are real and they send messages that students pick up and act upon.

leaving teachers isolated in the social systems that evolve in their classrooms. The psychosocial dynamics of a particular class might be discussed in the teachers' lounge with an opening statement such as, "My third period English class is hell on wheels."

What do teachers want? As the one person in the classroom responsible for the outcomes from 180 or more days of schooling, an important teacher motivation might best be summed up by a phrase from an old Frank Sinatra hit: "I did it my way." Teachers crave classroom control so that they can "cover" curriculum, teach in a manner they believe to be most effective given their content and the students they encounter, and go home at the end of the day feeling as though they made a difference in the lives of young people, often the main motivation for entering the profession. While in the act of teaching, teachers are usually socially isolated from peers. They may creatively try to generate a specific sense of community in their classrooms, but they are not in full control because students who are compelled to go to school may not feel motivated to participate in the classroom community in the manner the teacher expects. When teachers' and students' motivations are divergent or in conflict, they are most vulnerable to disciplinary incidents.

Classrooms are social systems that enact outcomes period by period, day by day, and so on. With roughly 900 hours per year of middle school teachers handling five different social systems each day or every other day (depending on the bell schedule), conflict is bound to occur. Teachers vary in their motivations and interpersonal skills and therefore vary in their disciplinary responses. Some never refer students to the AP, are in close touch with parents about aberrant student behavior, and continually strive to improve relations with their most troublesome students. Others send students to the office for a first offense of chewing gum or shooting spit wads. The classroom discipline challenge easily affects the whole school because of students' and teachers' collective psychosocial needs and the role of the AP as an important arbiter of discipline cases. But discipline has much larger social implications when students with specific identities—race, learning disability, or first language—run afoul of classroom and school systems with far greater frequency than their peers.

Peter Tunin should consider the psychosocial background of his students, which may include having witnessed the devastation of war in another country, physical abuse at home, the trauma of entering the US illegally, hunger, or any one of a number of social–psychological strains. All of these factors originate outside of the school and are brought through its doors every day. What students bring may be complicated by teachers' assumptions about them and the reactions that result. One teacher may be gentle and sympathetic to students whose life circumstances have placed them in a precarious position in the US economy while another may be irritated that she must teach teenagers who do not have command of English. Teacher reactions to students can range from benign to pernicious within a school environment replete with implicit bias. Peter and anyone in his shoes could easily feel overwhelmed by all of the influences that generate disciplinary incidents that impede learning. It is natural for the principal to seek help from off-the-shelf programs such as RJ, and doing so may help his students, teachers, and school. The principal's suggestion to see how Jefferson High School is handling discipline through RJ practices may link Peter to an important resource in his school's environment. The greatest certainty regarding students' and teachers' psychosocial dispositions is that Peter processing tardy students one at a time has little chance of improving the whole-school discipline system with all of its moving and unpredictable parts.

The Technical Core—Teaching and Learning Practices

Most of our discussion of principals' and others' leadership roles with respect to classroom teaching and learning is reserved for Chapter 7. In this chapter, we wish to point out administrators' management roles with respect to the technical core of teaching to continue our discussion of the managerial linkages to the various subsystems operating in schools.

Nearly all schools in the US today are strongly influenced by the testing regimes required by the states in which they are located. Standards-based standardized testing may be the single most obvious demonstration of the open nature of school and district systems. Typically, standards are adopted at the state level. As of this writing, 41 states, the District of Columbia, and four US territories and the Department of Defense Education Activity have adopted the Common Core State Standards (CCSS). Two state consortia have worked with test developers to create common assessments of CCSS, one is the Partnership for Assessment of Readiness for College and Careers (PARCC) and the other is the Smarter Balanced Assessment Consortium (SBAC) (www.corestandards.org/). The nine states that have not adopted CCSS have their own state-wide tests that may be a holdover from the No Child Left Behind (NCLB) era (see Virginia's Standards of Learning assessments, for example). Nevertheless, we would note that all states are influenced by the existence of and support for the CCSS—in an open system, this is inevitable.

School boards are required by state education codes to adopt curricula that address their states' standards and instruct their superintendents to run their systems in compliance with adopted standards and testing. Peter Tunin may therefore find himself assessing teacher performance in terms of teaching district curricula focused on state standards and running some portion of the annual testing apparatus that reveals how well students in his school are performing based on testing criteria.

If this sounds more bureaucratic than you might have imagined teaching and learning to be, that is not surprising. The accountability movement with its focus on student performance has wrought a large and complicated apparatus in an effort to understand how well students are served in their schools and districts this year and over time. The success or failure of the subtle work of improving teaching and learning—the technical core of schooling that open systems theorists might have recognized—is revealed to the larger public through test score reporting. As inaccurate or unjust as that may seem to many educators, it is a fact of school leader life and both instructional and testing processes must be managed in a way that allows the school to survive. We believe that with appropriate leadership of what Leithwood, Harris, and Hopkins (2008) refer to as the instructional program generates positive results on state-mandated and other forms of assessments. Thus, outside influences compel schools toward a specified set of standards and testing, but actions internal to the school generate results that influence outside perceptions. How that might be handled internal to the school, as we have said, we reserve for Chapter 7.

Structural—Graded Schools/Differentiated Curricula

Why do schools look the way they do? Why do primary schools have age-based grades and secondary schools have teachers and classrooms devoted to single subjects and feature multiple pathways for student progress? Long and involved answers to these questions can be found in many engaging historical texts (e.g., Cuban, 1988; Tyack, 1974; Tyack & Hansot, 1982). For now, a simplistic answer is: because that's what schools (for the most part) look like. A more sophisticated answer to these questions is presented later in this chapter when we discuss the effects of open systems concepts. Whatever the reasons, Peter and his colleagues find themselves managing segmented systems in which teachers specialize—either by grade level, by subject, or both—that present coordination challenges. The managerial responsibility that Peter and others take on by virtue of their administrative positions is ensuring vertical and lateral coordination such that students' progress toward the next level of schooling and, ultimately, graduating capable of further continuing their education and, one day, entering the world of work.

How the AP's coordination work looks probably varies considerably by school. Yet, there are common themes. Peter may have responsibility for helping fifth graders move from elementary school to become sixth graders in his middle school. Part of that process is learning from fifth grade teachers how well each rising sixth grader has progressed in core subject areas so that she or he can be placed in the appropriate specialized class. Peter may also have a mirror responsibility as eighth graders emerge into high school of informing their new school about their progress in middle school, again in an effort to place students in the classes that will serve them best, as determined by their teachers and, likely, their test scores. The transition of students from one school to the next clearly illustrates the webbed nature of schools as open systems.

Recall Chapter 1's discussion of structure. Grade levels, differentiated curricula, and different school levels are all intended to educate students "efficiently" in the sense that each student faces an appropriate academic challenge that moves him or her forward in the educational system and beyond. But the division of labor embedded in this segmented system also presents coordination or management challenges. It is difficult for Peter to know if all students have been informally and formally assessed accurately and whether they are progressing appropriately. In cases where progression seems slow or stalled, Peter and teachers should intervene, but how? That is a difficult question to answer without knowing *why* progress appears less than satisfactory. Numbers are overwhelming if Peter faces a middle school student population of 900 or more. Structural complication and segmentation are probably two of the greatest factors that contribute to Peter and others' focus on management, or what Cuban (1988) has called the managerial imperative.

Thought Partner Conversation

What if we considered your classroom (or a classroom) as an organization. With a critical friend, apply the systems framework we just used to analyze this smaller organization as an open system. To what degree does this framework help you understand the complex influences on individual teachers and students?

IMPLICATIONS OF OPEN SYSTEMS THINKING

Having briefly explored the world of schooling in terms of systems thinking, we return now to understanding where this newer, mid-twentieth century perspective on organizations led and how that further affects our thinking about schools and districts.

Thought Partner Conversation

Discuss all the ways a school might impact its environment—local, regional, and beyond. Then return to the notion of a teacher's classroom as an organization, and discuss the ways this organization might impact its environment. What mechanisms do we employ to coordinate these influences?

Katz and Kahn (1966), in their landmark book, *The social psychology of organizations,* noted that systems theory as applied to organizations is centrally concerned with relationships and the interdependence between elements within the organization and its external environment. One implication of this is that the organization is both impacted by its environment *and* affects this environment. The success of Peter Tunin's school as indicated by test scores (an external mandate) might influence how the environment (e.g., school district, community, politicians, etc.) treats his school. Subsystems rely on each other and a change in one may necessitate changes in others. In a school district, for example, this is easy to see when a delayed student pick-up at an elementary school affects the bus run for a neighboring middle school, or when students arrive at high school with an excellent foundation in math because of the work of elementary and middle school teachers. It is equally evident when a court case that started in Wyoming results in a precedent that necessitates that all schools nationwide begin to provide services for children with a particular characteristic, when a change in government results in alterations in funding allocations, or when opening a local factory results in the need to redistribute children across neighborhood schools.

In their work on systems *thinking*, Shaked and Schechter (2017) encourage leaders to see the system in its fullness, rather than merely as a sum of its parts, to see the parts "in the context of the whole" (p. 11).

> Systems thinking may be explained succinctly as an approach that puts the study of wholes before that of parts. This approach does not try to break systems down into parts in order to understand them; it concentrates its attention instead on how the parts act together in networks of interaction.
>
> (p. ix)

A systems-thinking approach that embraces organizations as complex systems stands in sharp contrast to the reductionist perspective endorsed by the notion that jobs can be most efficiently constructed through the division of labor and that parts of the whole might be connected through simple, linear cause-and-effect relationships—assertions very much consistent with models such as Taylor's scientific management. You may have noticed that in the sections above we struggled to describe how Peter's middle school fit into a larger web of systems because, for the sake of illustration, we were focused more on the parts than the whole.

> This systems-thinking approach upholds that the whole emerges from the interactions that transpire among its parts, and once it has emerged, it is that very whole that gives meaning to the parts. … Accordingly, the only way to fully understand a system is to understand its parts in relation to the whole.
>
> (Shaked & Schechter, 2017, p. 13)

Thought Partner Conversation

Do you agree with the notion that the only way to understand a system is to understand its parts in relation to the whole? Are there some parts that are easier to define than others? Are some more important to the success of "the whole?"

The Impact of Open Systems on Organizational Theories

Tosi (2009) suggests a taxonomy that divides organization theories along two axes: (1) organizations as rational, with fixed and certain goals and structures designed to optimally meet these goals, or organizations as natural systems that adapt and adjust

TABLE 2.1 A Typology of Organization Theories

	Closed Systems	Open Systems
Rational Models	Classical theories (bureaucracy, scientific management)	Contingency theories
Natural Models	Human relations theories	Institutional and ecological theories

Source: Adapted from Tosi, 2009, p. 12.

with some frequency; and (2) organizations as closed systems that are certain or determinate, with stable resources and little turbulence introduced from the environment, or organizations as open systems whose structures and processes are significantly impacted (if not determined) by the environment—such organizations are interdependent with or even co-constructed by entities beyond their boundary.

The theories introduced in Chapter 1 fit squarely in the "closed systems" category, with classical theories based on assumptions of rationality and human relations theories tending to assumptions more consistent with natural models. In the next sections, we explore the theories that emerged as most aligned with the *open systems* assumptions, models that we contend are increasingly helpful in understanding schools as organizations. To foreshadow, we close the chapter by wondering: Is the dichotomy, open and closed, best thought of as an either-or proposition? What would we learn if we thought of schools as both?

Contingency theories. The open systems perspective first gave rise to a variety of theories of organization that sought to embrace and account for increased sources of variability and ambiguity (or contingencies) that may impact organizing, while retaining some of the core assumptions of classical theories in terms of rationality. Kast and Rosenzweig (1973) summarize that contingency theories attempted to explain interactions among parts of organizations and their wholes simultaneously with organizations' interplay with their environments. The intent is to understand how organizations function under various conditions and circumstances in an effort to determine effective organizational responses to internal and external influences.

Scott (2003) asserts that the work of Lawrence and Lorsch (1967/1986) and Thompson (1967, 2003) "defined the contingency theory of organizations" and that "it remains, arguably, the most influential theory of organizations to this day" (p. xxi). It is easy to see why this might be the case. "Contingency theory states that there is no single organizational structure that is highly effective for all organizations," Donaldson (1996, p 57) wrote. "It sees the structure that is optimal as varying according to certain factors such as organizational strategy or size. Thus the optimal structure is contingent upon these factors which are termed the *contingency* factors." In this manner, contingency theorists embraced rather than ignored the myriad sources of variability that affect organizational design and work processes. They acknowledged that the organizational designs and managerial practices most appropriate for specific situations differ according to the nature and variability inherent in the work itself, the environment in which the enterprise exists, the technologies available to conduct the work, and so on.

Consistent with rational models, contingency theorists believed that an optimal structure could be found given knowledge of the contingencies most influencing the organization. Theorists working in this tradition focused their attention on different elements of the organizational system and characterized organizations along these dimensions (Kast & Rosenzweig, 1973). For example, Simon (1964) viewed closed systems as pursuing single goals whereas open systems are characterized by multiple goals and strategies that account for multiple constraints; Perrow (1967) emphasized simple technologies with few exceptions as characteristics of closed systems, whereas open systems are characterized by non-routine technologies with numerous exceptions and hence feature complex processes to deal with these may puzzles.

Thought Partner Conversation

With a critical friend, relate this notion of contingencies to differentiating instruction in a heterogeneously grouped classroom. What are some of the *contingencies* teachers typically need to take into account before deciding how to teach a lesson?

A thorough review of contingency theories is far beyond the scope of this chapter, though certain key elements of these models are important to understanding schools as open system organizations. First, as Donaldson (1996) summarized:

> The core assumption of structural contingency theory is that low uncertainty tasks are most effectively performed by centralized hierarchy since this is simple, quick and allows coordination cheaply. As task uncertainty increases, through innovation or the like, then the hierarchy needs to loosen control somewhat and be overlain by participatory, communicative structures.
>
> (p. 59)

This finding, which Donaldson characterizes as "the underlying theoretical unity of the ideas composing structural contingency" (p. 59), is profoundly important to understanding schools as work organizations. It suggests that routine, assembly line-like jobs with predictable and well-defined goals and technologies are best organized in tightly coupled hierarchical systems—managed in Theory X fashion as McGregor (1960/1996) theorized. Individuals conducting the work of such organizations seldom need to make consequential judgments or adjust to changing work objectives; experience few exceptions; find inputs to be within pre-ordained specifications and the work experience to be highly predictable. In contrast, consider organizations where goals are many, contested or sometimes conflicting; inputs are highly variable and unpredictable; and the work process itself is subject to many and varied changes requiring on-the-spot judgment. This kind of ambiguity and simultaneity of actions that require a constant stream of informed decisions are characteristic of schools and their component classrooms (Cuban 1988, 2018). Contingency theory would suggest that in these organizations, structures need to be more loosely coupled (Weick, 1976) and line workers (teachers and staff) need to be allowed to exercise judgment and have a great deal of control over the conduct of work.

Contingency theory provides a conceptual grounding for the critique of classical theories as applied to organizations such as schools, organizations in which goals and the very nature of work itself is highly variable and subject to many and myriad sources of turbulence. In schools, ambiguity is the rule and not the exception. Think of the vignette from Chapter 1 and Peter Tunin's situation described at the beginning of this chapter. Structures that are tight and reliant on high degrees of certainty, such as assigning a consequence for each instance of being tardy to class, generally prove ineffective and inefficient. Simultaneous and varied actions throughout the school mean that school leaders, especially principals, need to spend at least as much time seeking information as providing answers or giving directives or suggestions.

Thought Partner Conversation

Return to your exploration of the core technology of schooling, and the conclusion that in organizations like schools structures need to be loosely coupled and teachers need a degree of autonomy to make decisions in real time to accommodate variability. In what ways do you see teaching as being loosely coupled and requiring autonomy, and in what ways should teaching be more tightly coupled and consistent across classrooms? What are the essential tensions involved here?

KEEP YOUR HANDS OFF "MY" MONEY

The district office administrator in charge of providing Lesson Study as a means of improving teacher practice (see Chapter 7) runs this program from two major funding sources: (1) a special tax assessment the school district passed and renewed, and (2) a grant from a local university interested in studying the effects of Lesson Study on teachers' practice. As the person in charge of this teacher professional development, the administrator bridges from the school district environment to bring outside resources to bear on improving teaching and learning.

But budgets get tight and the Lesson Study program is small. At one point administrators higher up in the bureaucracy eyed the tax revenue Lesson Study was using and threatened to take it away. The administrator in charge of Lesson Study then had to engage in buffering his program against this threat, which he did by explaining how well it was helping to narrow achievement gaps and other student outcome challenges.

Kast and Rosenzweig (1973, pp. 315–318) present an exhaustive comparison of theorists' views of open and closed systems, which we adapted to construct Table 2.2. This table is especially helpful in contrasting the tendencies of closed systems theories similar to those reviewed in the previous chapter, and open systems approaches, including the structural contingency theories, which tend to characterize more contemporary views of schools as organizations. Taken as a whole, it is clear that the open systems view attempts to account for the reality of the contexts professional organizations such as schools experience. The theory accounts for the fact that the

TABLE 2.2 Attributes of Closed and Open Systems Perspectives on Organizations

Attribute	Tendency of Closed Systems	Tendency of Open Systems
Environment	Stable, certain, little impact on organizational structures and processes	Turbulent, changing, high impact on organizational structures and processes
Technologies	Stable	Dynamic
Boundaries	Closed	Permeable
Boundary relationships	Mostly closed, routine	Open; many participants; variable
Inputs	Mostly homogeneous	Mostly heterogeneous
Goal structure	Single goal maximizer; stressing efficiency, predictability, risk avoidance	Variable; goals change as the organization adjusts or adapts; stresses adaptability and problem solving
Goal setting	Hierarchical	Inclusive, participative
Predictability	Relatively determinate	Relatively uncertain

core technologies of such organizations are varied and require frequent adjustments and decisions by those doing the work; and that organizations such as schools are in a "fishbowl," metaphorically, open to the view and demands of multiple stakeholders, each of whom have overlapping but different demands. In such environments, leaders serve as "bridges" or boundary spanners with external agents, on the one hand, and spend a great deal of energy buffering teachers and students from external turbulence, on the other (Honig & Hatch, 2004).

In summary, then, by encompassing and defining what is legitimate, the institution represents a system of beliefs and constraints on individual or organizational action. It may affect what leaders can and cannot do—indeed, it can influence whether an organization is allowed to exist within a given field through our collective agreement on criteria of inclusion.

Institutional and Ecological Theories

Acknowledgment of the open nature of schools as organizations leads us to a more recent and intense view of schools as not merely residing within a demanding environment, but greatly affected by the environment in some fundamental ways. These perspectives draw on and expand earlier work on the nature of institutions in organizations' environments, where institutions are defined as regulative, normative, and cultural forces that provide stability or definition to aspects of social life (Scott & Davis, 2007). So, when we speak of the "institution of schooling" we are referring to a broad set of beliefs, rules, and values that define what makes a school a school based on societal assumptions. The institutional view, in its earlier iterations, focused on the organization as a whole which was viewed as organic and evolving with a natural history (Perrow, 1986). It stressed that organizations reside within an institutional environment that affects how the organization is structured, the choices leaders make in organizational life, and what is acceptable in the design and conduct of organiza-

INSTITUTIONS IN ORGANIZATIONAL THEORY

Scott and Davis (2007) provide a detailed definition of what organizational theorists generally mean when they use the term "institution." Scott (2001, p. 48) wrote: "*Institutions* are composed of cultural-cognitive, normative, and regulative elements that, together with associated activities and resources, provide stability and meaning to social life."

- As regulative systems, institutions provide rules, guidelines, or governance structures—they define "rules of the game" so to speak.
- As normative systems, they provide a moral framework for defining what is right.
- As cultural systems, institutions provide shared beliefs about "the way we do things" in a given circumstance, or a set of "social facts" that are taken-for-granted assumptions about what is proper or preferred.

tional processes. Institutional theory stressed how leaders' choices are shaped and mediated by the institutional (macro) environment. DiMaggio and Powell (1983) point out that the focus of institutional theory is on socially constructed meaning and how individual preferences are shaped by institutional thought. This perspective provides a sharp counterpoint to the rational actor view of organizational life. It came to the fore as scholars attempted to address a persistent and perplexing reality: Why is it that some policies or practices persist in the face of a seemingly widespread acceptance that they are outdated or out-of-sync with technical efficiency?

Within organizational studies, institutional theory has responded to empirical anomalies, to the fact that, as March and Olsen (1984, p. 747) put it, "what we observe in the world is inconsistent with the ways in which contemporary theories ask us to talk." As Powell and DiMaggio (1991) wrote:

> Studies of organizational and political change routinely point to findings that are hard to square with either rational-actor or functionalist accounts. ... Administrators and politicians champion programs that are established but not implemented; managers gather information assiduously, but fail to analyze it; experts are hired not for advice but to signal legitimacy.
>
> (p. 3)

In education, there are many and varied practices that are perpetuated even though they do not seem to be supported as the optimal or most efficient way to achieve the goal of each child reaching his or her potential as a learner. Considering the text box on p. 46, it seems impossible that the student participation outcome described is what educators in this system are seeking. How can we explain this? Theory based in a conventional assumption of rationality, i.e., that organizational practices are adopted and persist purely because they serve to meet clear and agreed-upon goals, are insufficient in helping to explain apparent anomalies in schools and how leaders respond to them.

Neo-institutional theory, which began to emerge in the late 1970s and 1980s, focused on the macro, institutional environment within which individual organizations operate, and the organizational structures and processes that exist industry-wide, that are national or international in scope. Institutional and ecological theorists focus on organizational fields, i.e., populations of like organizations that fulfill similar purposes and that operate in similar fashions; for instance, schools, labor unions, or hospitals. Theorists asked first why seemingly inefficient or ineffective structures and processes perpetuate in organizational life across a field, despite widespread acknowledgment that they do not work. As just one example, why is it that schools cling to an agrarian calendar decades after agriculture was replaced as a primary source of gainful employment and in locales in which it never was one, such as in urban centers?

In their influential paper, "Institutionalized organizations: Formal structure as myth and ceremony," Meyer and Rowan (1977) suggest that structures and technologies become institutionalized within a field as sources of *legitimacy*. Bureaucracy itself, they observe, has proliferated in part because of the widespread acceptance of the organizational form. What is critical to understand here is that the theory suggests that organizational forms and processes are adopted not for technical efficiency, but because they are widely accepted as the appropriate way of organizing. In highly institutional organizational fields such as education, where there are many external stakeholders making demands on the organizations and who serve as sources of the resources the organization needs to continue to survive, leaders are under constant pressure to conform to the *institutional rules* and adopt policies and practices that are seen as appropriate and effective.

Meyer and Rowan (1977) go on to observe that leaders in institutionalized organizations seek to protect the organization from evaluation on purely technical criteria, favoring instead inspection that focuses on conformance to institutionalized practices or evaluations that are ceremonial in nature. Hence, adoption of a well-established answer (such as RJ) is assessed in terms of whether the program was implemented, at least initially, rather than in terms of whether practice produced desired results, in this case reducing or eliminating inequities in discipline. By this logic, the school has responded to the problem by adopting an effective practice.

Thought Partner Conversation

With a critical friend, consider some changes that your school, school system or agency may have adopted in the past that you wondered about or thought "I don't understand why we are doing this." Can you understand the change from an institutional perspective? (Hint: Might the school have been under pressure to adopt the program or policy? By whom and why?)

To summarize, this perspective stressed that by adopting formal structures that adhere to the institutional environment, i.e., they are accepted as legitimate, an organization demonstrates that it is acting on collectively valued purposes. Failure to adopt institutionalized vocabulary, labels, structures, or processes would risk being seen as out-of-step with legitimized norms, and may be perceived as both negligent and irrational. Widespread adoption of such taken-for-granted structures and practices promotes legitimacy and survival for an individual organization and, across a field, supports stability.

Adoption of the legitimated policies and practices satisfies environmental actors as being efficient and effective, a proxy for close examination of actual outcomes.

A second and related question addressed by neo-institutional theorists is why there seems to be rather dramatic homogeneity of practices and arrangements within an organizational field. Why is it, for instance, that elementary schools in Seattle look much like those in Honolulu, New Jersey, and Portland, Maine? Pushed a little further, why do charter elementary schools in Cleveland operate in much the same fashion as independent schools in Phoenix? "Much of modern organizational theory posits a diverse and differentiated world of organizations and seeks to explain variation among organizations in structure and behavior…" DiMaggio and Powell (1991, p. 64) write. "We ask, instead, why there is such a startling homogeneity of organizational forms and practices, and we seek to explain homogeneity, not variation."

In their landmark paper, "The iron cage revisited: Institutional isomorphism and collective rationality in organizational fields," DiMaggio and Powell (1983) observe that in contemporary society the structuration of organizational fields—institutional forces—have become the primary impetus to homogenization. DiMaggio and Powell (1983, p. 66) define the term "isomorphism" as "a constraining process that forces one unit in a population to resemble other units that face the same environmental conditions." For example, we might observe the principal's motivation for his interest in RJ in the opening vignette as an instance of isomorphism—he perceived his school to be facing the same challenges as Jefferson High School, which is purported to be having great success with RJ. DiMaggio and Powell posit three primary mechanisms through which organizational isomorphism occurs:

1. coercive isomorphism that stems from political influence and the problem of legitimacy;
2. mimetic isomorphism resulting from standard responses to uncertainty, and
3. normative isomorphism, associated with professionalization (p. 67).

Coercive isomorphism includes, for example, sameness of practice that results from legal mandates, although mandated operating procedures might come from other sources such as a parent organization. A school being required to adopt a particular disciplinary system as a result of state sanction of the school district would be an example of coercive isomorphism. Mimetic isomorphism is thought to be a response to ambiguity or uncertainty that prompts leaders to seek sameness in approach as another organization that is perceived to be successful. As an example, a principal of a school with below average test scores adopting an after-school tutoring program because she is aware that highly successful schools in the district have such programs would be engaging in mimetic isomorphism. Finally, adoption of a nationally recognized online math instruction program because the profession has deemed this practice as a standard and efficient response to substandard math performance would be an example of normative isomorphism.

Isomorphism has some crucial advantages. Policies or practices that are seen as effective elsewhere are accepted as such when your organization adopts them. Successful implementation of the practice is assumed to be efficient or effective because it is known to be effective in schools like yours (sometimes in schools generally).

Adoption of externally legitimated processes reduces uncertainty that might be characteristic of trying something new (and unproven). And often, adoption of isomorphic answers to existing puzzles is rewarded with resources with which to adopt the practice (Meyer & Rowan, 1977). In our current institutional environment, these resources might come from the state, from school systems, and increasingly from foundations with deep pockets and an interest in specific legitimized answers. The connecting thread here is that technical rationality—adoption of a solution or practice because it is believed to be technically superior—may be replaced or at least augmented by legitimacy as a criterion for adoption.

To summarize, the neo-institutional perspective stresses that while leaders certainly make choices in organizational life, these choices are constrained to the extent that it is impossible to ignore the institutional environment, in particular the behavior of similar organizations in a field. Leaders experience pressures from stakeholders inside and outside the organization, and are under pressure to conform for the sake of legitimacy—which may be vital to the very ability of the organization itself to persist. Institutional norms—such as the agrarian calendar—assume a taken-for-granted nature; to not conform is to resist being seen as out-of-step with what is commonly known to be effective. These norms may even become codified in law, further restricting leaders' degrees of freedom. Leaders, it seems, seek answers based on more than their own knowledge or some sense of technical rationality; they observe like organizations, consult legal and professional organizations, and are constrained by concerns related to legitimacy alongside effectiveness and efficiency. In fact, forces in the environment determine, to a large extent, what is considered effective and efficient, and conformance to these institutional forces may be the only reasonable solution to many puzzles.

LEADERS FACING HIGH STAKES

Here is one of Thompson's (1967, 2003) many propositions about how leaders might react to a wide variety of organizational conditions and challenges that is well worth highlighting.

He speculated that in organizations with dynamic environments and uncertainty or variability regarding the core technology, under conditions of high-stakes accountability leaders will seek to treat the system as _closed_—in other words, to tighten reigns and stress predictability and sameness—and to "keep score" in relation to proxies for effectiveness rather than in terms of technical effectiveness. He also theorized that under such conditions, "score keepers" would stress comparisons with like organizations rather than technical outcomes (in other words, we may not be doing great, but we're doing as well as schools like ours).

These hypotheses would tend to suggest that the tighter the accountability demands on schools, the more likely leaders will feel pressured to seek legitimacy through adoption of institutionally defined solutions or best practices as accepted by important stakeholders.

Can you think of instances in your education career when legitimacy was sought under stress? Did someone proclaim that a new strategy was "best practice"? Was the strategy effective?

BEYOND OPEN VERSUS CLOSED

The mere fact of acknowledging that organizations are complex systems that exist within an external environment opens up a huge number of possibilities as we seek to describe, explain, and predict the work of schools as organizations. Viewing schools as systems with a variety of inputs, throughputs, and outputs helps us understand a level of complexity ignored by classical theories. Raising questions associated with environmental actors who supply various resources needed by schools and the sheer variety of stakeholders who exist in a school's environment who make demands and render judgments about legitimacy helps us understand further the context in which leaders make decisions and the powerful criteria that enter into this decision-making process that reach well beyond simple notions of technical efficiency.

Thompson (2003) stressed that from an open systems approach, organizations are viewed as problem-solving phenomena, thus the leaders' primary role is searching, learning, and deciding in a context in which choice alternatives are not always well known. "With this conception the central problem for complex organizations is one of coping with uncertainty" (p. 13). Technical rationality is possible only when one assumes that systems are *closed*, i.e., that all relevant variables are certain and accounted for; an open systems perspective assumes instead that uncertainty and variability are the rule, not the exception, hence alternative types of rationality are required. One consequence of a turbulent and unpredictable environment, Thompson hypothesized, is that leaders will attempt to seal or buffer the technical core of the organization—those doing the core work of the enterprise—from turbulence, and leaders will seek ways to smooth out or adapt to environmental changes that cannot be buffered.

Thompson (1967, 2003) embraced Parsons' (1960) notion that organizations are composed of three primary subsystems: production, managerial, and institutional. The production subsystem, i.e., where the actual work of the organization occurs, must be buffered most from environmental turbulence so that the work can go on more-or-less undisturbed. Managerial subsystems provide this buffering function, and must alternatively deal with turbulent environmental issues and "close off" the technical core as best as possible. The institutional subsystem is most open to the environment; it is "part of a wider social system which is the source of the 'meaning,' legitimation, or higher-level support which makes the implementation of the organization's goals possible" (Thompson, 2003, p. 11). The institutional subsystem needs to be most flexible and adaptable, and acts as a boundary spanner with environmental actors.

A consequence of Thompson's (1967, 2003) formulation is the astute notion that organizations are not best characterized as *either* open or closed, but rather that parts of the organization tend to be closed (those parts closest to the technical core) and others quite open (those closest to the institutional environment). "In Thompson's imaginative model, all organizations are simultaneously rational and natural systems; and all are both open and closed systems" (Scott, 2003, p. xx). This idea, it would seem, reminds us that understanding elements of both the closed and open systems perspectives are important to leading schools as organizations.

CONCLUSION

Returning for a moment to our opening vignette, recall that AP Peter Tunin is concerned about the disproportionate impact of school discipline on Hispanic students, particularly boys. His principal tosses out what seems to be a facile response to the situation that leaves Peter feeling unnerved. Peter's middle school and the disciplinary puzzle he faces are subject to forces that come from outside the school.

First, it is apparent that changes in the school's immediate environment contribute to the present circumstances. As the student population diversifies, so too does the need for teachers' skills and abilities. Theory that helps us recognize changes in the school context—in this case, changes in inputs from the environment—helps us gain an awareness of what is going on. Second, we might understand the principal's rush to action as an effort to provide a legitimate solution that serves, at a very basic level, as a symbolic indicator to various stakeholders that the school will do something to remedy a pattern of student treatment that could be perceived as unjust. Adopting a solution that a powerful environmental actor—the school district—endorses as preferred, and that another school that has been deemed "effective" uses, serves to signal that the response is appropriate, quite apart from the question of whether the actual source of the problem has anything to do with the school's existing discipline policy. Adopting RJ will likely be seen as appropriate, but there is no information available that it is effective and efficient. Thus a "logic of appropriateness" supplants a logic of efficiency (Meyer & Rowan, 1977), and important stakeholders (including parents, teachers, and administrators within the school and district) will observe that the problem is being addressed.

In closing, it seems important to note that nothing in this analysis should be construed as suggesting that the principal in this case is doing anything sinister or wrong; we make no such judgment. It is equally important, though, to observe that we would be hard-pressed to explain these occurrences from a purely rational, efficiency perspective. What an open systems perspective adds to our arsenal is a means of understanding how the open systems nature of schools as organizations impacts leaders' decisions and actions, and that ignoring the influence of pressures from various stakeholders in the environment would be unwise.

EXERCISE 2.1 FROM PROBLEMS TO SOLUTIONS

Imagine yourself in Mr. Tunin's position, as the new AP of a diverse, suburban middle school, and suppose that you decide to move forward to address the problem you've identified. Peter observed evidence that Hispanic students in his school were being disciplined at a much greater rate than other students—they accounted for 60 percent of the discipline cases recorded but make up only about 25 percent of the student population.

1. Explore all of the in-school and out-of-school factors that might cause this. Be sure to think 360 degrees around the problem—be as specific and inclusive as you

can be. Remember to include causes that relate to student, faculty, staff, other stakeholders from outside the school walls, as well as policy and procedures, norms, and informal aspects of school processes and culture.

2. Thinking about your own school or a school you know, and examining your list of potential causes, which of these would your staff have control over, and which would seem to be beyond your control? Why is knowing this important to your problem-solving efforts?

3. Again imagining your own school or a school you know, select the causes that you believe seem most likely to be relevant to reality—the most likely reasons such a discipline gap might exist. After selecting this short list of causes, explore ways you might address each of these causes—solutions that you would suggest that would help lessen or eliminate each cause.

    *   If you were in charge of attacking the problem, which solutions would you select first to implement, and why? What criteria did you use to make this decision?

    *   What more might you want to know about the problem, its causes, or the potential solutions in order to make this decision?

EXERCISE 2.2 OPEN TO WHOM?

When we speak about schools as open systems throughout this chapter, you might be wondering: Open to whom? Thinking about the issue Peter Tunin is facing at his school, make a list of all of the stakeholders who might potentially influence the problem and its solution. Then jot down your ideas about what it is each stakeholder might want—in what ways can you imagine them seeking to influence discipline policy and practice in the school? Finally, make a note of your thoughts about what sources of influence each stakeholder might bring to bear to "get their way."

WORKSHEET B

Stakeholder	What Do They Want?	What Are Their Sources of Influence?

EXERCISE 2.3 SCHOOL INPUTS AND OUTPUTS

In its most basic form, the systems view considers three categories of variables in relation to organizations: inputs, the social system or work processes, and outputs. Forgetting for the moment the work that goes on inside the school (the center column in the table that follows), answer the following questions:

1. What are a school's inputs? List as many of these are you can imagine, and try to be inclusive of all of the resources (human, technical, physical, etc.) that come from the school environment that help make the work of schools possible.

    *   What drives or influences which inputs a school seeks and/or what is made available?

2. What are a school's outputs?
3. In what ways does a school influence its environment?

WORKSHEET C

Inputs	Social System	Outputs
	School	
	(tasks, technologies, structures, humans)	

EXERCISE 2.4 TIGHT VERSUS LOOSE STRUCTURES

Contingency theory taught us that in organizations in which the goals are uncertain and the nature of work is highly variable and subject to frequent changes—for example, in schools—it is best to create structures and processes that are flexible and adaptable and to vest decision-making autonomy in those individuals who are on the "front line" delivering services.

1. Why is it so important to provide front-line actors—such as teachers—with the autonomy to make decisions?

    - For what kinds of decisions is it most important to provide teachers autonomy?
    - What are some of the consequences of this for leaders?
    - What sorts of limits exist on teacher autonomy? For what kinds of decisions do leaders need to retain tighter control? Why?

2. Returning to Peter Turin's situation, is it important to give teachers autonomy to make decisions regarding discipline? Of the several decision points involved in any discipline situation, for what decisions is teacher autonomy important, and for which decisions ought Peter be sure that administration made and enforced the decision?

    - What parts of the discipline process might best be variable or flexible, and what parts need to be certain or conforming to pre-established rules?
    - In what ways might you imagine that the current policy in Peter's school might have contributed to the apparent equity problem in the first place? Is it plausible that giving teachers autonomy led to this apparently unfair outcome?

BRIDGING AND BUFFERING PUZZLE

Adopt AP Peter Tunin's perspective. How can he take advantage of resources available in the environment of his middle school and protect the "technical core" of discipline at the same time so that he can play his part in improving enactment of student discipline that ensures a safe school environment conducive to learning? Accept reality as presented in the vignette and use the following prompts to craft a discipline strategy that will be fair and effective, reducing disproportionate impact on Hispanic students in the process.

1. What resources might be present both in the school and in the school's environment to which Peter should build bridges?

    - In what ways are families a resource?
    - Are there institutional resources Peter might find?
    - In what ways are teachers a resource?
    - Is the RJ program a resource or is it a threat? Why do you believe as you do?

2. What are the most substantial threats in the environment or in the school that Peter will need to buffer against to move a program forward to improve student discipline?

    •   Who probably has a stake in the discipline system as it exists? Why would they want to maintain the status quo?
    •   Who or what will threaten Peter and the school if the status quo does *not* change?
    •   How does student treatment in the current system threaten school discipline generally?

3. What are three to five steps that Peter Tunin should take to improve the fairness and effectiveness of student discipline at his school?

    •   Be as specific as possible about bridging and buffering actions you may recommend.

NOTE

1. We define the leadership team loosely. It could be a principal and APs, or it could include both administrators and non-administrative leaders, including coaches, department chairs, and other teacher leaders.

REFERENCES

Barnard, C. (1938). *The functions of the executive.* Cambridge, MA: Harvard University Press.

Common Core State Standards Initiative (n.d.). Preparing America's students for success. www.corestandards.org/.

Connor, Patrick E. (1980). *Organizations: Theory and design.* Chicago: Science Research Associates.

Cuban, L. (1988). *The managerial imperative and the practice of leadership in schools.* Buffalo, NY: SUNY Press.

Cuban, L. (2018). *The flight of a butterfly or the path of a bullet? Using technology to transform teaching and learning.* Cambridge, MA: Harvard Education Press.

DiMaggio, P., & Powell, W. (1983). The iron cage revisited: Institutional isomorphism and collective rationality in organizational fields. *American Sociological Review, 48*(2), 147–160.

DiMaggio, P., & Powell, W. (1991). Introduction. In W. Powell & P. DiMaggio (Eds.), *The new institutionalism in organizational analysis* (pp. 1–38). Chicago: University of Chicago Press.

Donaldson, L. (1996). The normal science of structural contingency theory. In S. Clegg, C. Hardy, & W. Nord (Eds.), *Handbook of organization studies* (pp. 55–66). London: Sage.

Honig, M., & Hatch, T. (2004). Crafting coherence: How schools strategically manage multiple, external demands. *Educational Researcher, 33*(8), 16–30.

Kast, F., & Rosenzweig, J. (1973). *Contingency views of organization and management.* Chicago: Science Research Associates.

Katz, D., & Kahn, R. (1966). *The social psychology of organizations.* New York: John Wiley & Sons.

Lawrence, P., & Lorsch, J. (1967/1986). *Organizations and environment.* Boston: Harvard Business School Press.

Leithwood, K., Harris, A., & Hopkins, D. (2008). Seven strong claims about successful school leadership. *School Leadership and Management, 28*(1), 27–42. DOI: 10.1080/13632430 701800060.

March, J., & Olsen, J. (1984). The new institutionalism: Organizational factors in political life. *American Political Science Review, 78*(3), 734–749.

March, J.G., & Simon, H.A. (1993). *Organizations.* Cambridge, MA: Blackwell.

Marion, R., & Gonzales, L. (2014). *Leadership in education: Organizational theory for the practitioner* (2nd ed.). Long Grove, IL: Waveland Press.

McGregor, D. (1960/2006). *The human side of enterprise: Annotated edition* (J. Cutcher-Gershenfeld, ed.). New York: McGraw-Hill.

Meyer, J., & Rowan, B. (1977). Institutionalized organizations: Formal structure as myth and ceremony. *The American Journal of Sociology, 83*(2), 340–363.

Morgan, G. (2006). *Images of organization.* Thousand Oaks, CA: Sage.

Parsons, T. (1960). *Structure and process in modern societies.* New York: The Free Press.

Perrow, C. (1967). A framework for the comparative analysis of organizations. *American Sociological Review, 32*(2), 194–208.

Perrow, C. (1986). *Complex organizations: A critical essay* (3rd ed.). New York: McGraw-Hill.

Scott, W. (1979). Organization structure. In M. Zey-Ferrel (Ed.), *Readings on dimensions of organizations: Environment, context, structure, process, and performance* (pp. 164–181). Santa Monica, CA: Goodyear Publishing Co.

Scott, W.R. (2003). Introduction to the Transaction edition. In J. Thompson, *Organizations in action: Social science bases of administrative theory* (2nd ed., pp. xv–xxiii). New Brunswick, NJ: Transaction Publishers.

Scott, W., & Davis, G. (2007). *Organizations and organizing: Rational, natural, and open systems perspectives.* Upper Saddle River, NJ: Pearson Prentice Hall.

Shafritz, J., Ott, J., & Jang, Y. (2005). *Classics of organization theory* (5th ed.). Belmont, CA: Wadsworth.

Shaked, H., & Schechter, C. (2017). *Systems thinking for school leaders: Holistic leadership for excellence in education.* Cham, Switzerland: Springer International Publishing.

Simon, H. (1964). On the concept of organizational goals. *Administrative Science Quarterly 9*(1), 1–22.

Thompson, J. (1967). *Organizations in action: Social science bases of administrative theory.* New York: McGraw-Hill.

Thompson, J. (2003). *Organizations in action: Social science bases of administrative theory* (2nd ed.). New Brunswick, NJ: Transaction Publishers.

Tosi, H. (2009). *Theories of organization.* Los Angeles: Sage.

Tyack, D. (1974). *The one best system: A history of American urban education.* Cambridge, MA: Harvard University Press.

Tyack, D., & Hansot, E. (1982). *Managers of virtue: Public school leadership in America, 1820–1980.* New York: Basic Books.

Von Bertalanffy, L. (1952). *Problems of life.* New York: Wiley.

Von Bertalanffy, L. (1968). *General systems theory.* New York: George Braziller.

Weick, K.E. (1976). Educational organizations as loosely coupled systems. *Administrative Sciences Quarterly, 21*(1), 1–19.

CHAPTER 3

School Leadership as Organized Anarchy: Taming the Untamable Beast

Stephanie Wright is the social studies department chair and the team lead for the Mustangs team at Harmony Mill Middle School (HMMS). She enjoys the variety in her work—teacher, formal and informal student advisor, manager for the social studies department, and team lead who ensures her team of six teachers improves the quality of teaching and learning that their 180 students experience. Stephanie thinks that verbs such as lead, run, or manage might seem like something of a stretch to anyone who observes her behavior day-to-day. In a diverse middle school of over 1,000 students in an urban setting, life is loud, crowded, full of emotion, and more than a little bit smelly. Stephanie has her classroom well under control and has a reputation for leading her department and team with competence. At the same time, she enjoys the sense of living on the edge that she gets from working in this high-functioning but somewhat wild middle school.

HMMS has come a long way since the current principal, Arnie Schmidt, took over 10 years ago. He came into the job big on shared decision making. He reorganized the school into teams that would be responsible for educating the whole child—i.e., monitoring and nurturing both academic and social–emotional development. When Stephanie was still relatively new to teaching, she jumped at the chance to serve in the two teacher leader roles she now holds. She is widely seen as an influential teacher in a school that has moved from one of the lowest performing middle schools in the district to one of the highest performing.

Although HMMS seems able to improve most students' academic performance, as indicated by rising test scores and relatively narrow achievement gaps, Stephanie is somewhat dismayed by her recent efforts to track student progress in high school. Three middle schools feed into Groveland High School, the other two whiter and higher income than HMMS. Early exploratory data analysis from Stephanie and district office administrators indicates that HMMS students are not well represented in honors, Advanced Placement, or other advanced courses. She is deeply concerned about what this may mean for her students' college opportunities. Thus far, Stephanie has had a hard time generating interest among Mustang teachers or HMMS administration in her action research. Everyone's academic focus seems to be on getting kids through eighth grade meeting state standards, no small achievement for the HMMS student population.

Stephanie often jokes with colleagues that it is "hard to maintain harmony in the mill." They feel pressed to ensure that all students are succeeding, but they are also expected to be adults of influence in the lives of all of the students on their team. With hormones running wild and students focused on anything and everything but building their academic futures, Stephanie often feels overwhelmed. When there are too many responsibilities and students seem determined to blow the place up, Stephanie walks in the door of her house and declares to her husband, "I'm drowning in chaos!" She often feels bewildered and exhausted by the contradictions and challenges built into teaching middle school students and helping her fellow teachers to improve student and school performance. Nevertheless, she gets up at 5:30 a.m. the next day, as usual, and starts all over again to be the best teacher leader she can be in a day she knows will be filled with unpredictability.

Thought Partner Conversation

Some of what Stephanie experiences is labeled in the literature *role conflict*—the feeling that there are required parts of one's role that are in conflict with each other. With a critical friend, identify these conflicts in the vignette, and perhaps also in your own experience. What are some of the possible consequences of role conflict for the school and for the individual?

WELCOME TO THE LAND OF CONFUSION

Jumbo shrimp, seriously funny, pretty ugly, awfully good, deafening silence, found missing, military intelligence, unbiased opinion, honest thief, dynamic equilibrium. Many of us incorporate such words into our day-to-day conversation. We do so consciously and unconsciously, with serious and humorous intent. What binds these pithy phrases together is the logic they share. What makes them humorous is the contradictory message each conveys. All are *oxymorons*.

An oxymoron is a rhetorical device that makes use of logical contradiction to: (1) emphasize a point, (2) highlight tensions or qualities not readily apparent, and/or (3) reveal a paradox. As a figure of speech, contradictory ideas are juxtaposed to create an effect. Shakespeare's famous line in *Romeo and Juliet*—"parting is such *sweet sorrow*"—captures the complex, paradoxical nature of love that is otherwise elusive (Shakespeare, 2015, p. 9). His skillful use of this oxymoron forces the audience to ponder the contradiction conveyed in it. Because of the physical separation that ensues, parting for lovers is *sorrowful*. Yet because of the hope generated by the anticipation of reuniting again, parting is likewise *sweet*.

The word *oxymoron* is itself an oxymoron. A single word derived from two Greek roots (*oxsý* + *mōron*), it conveys opposite ideas. Whereas the initial half of the compound (*oxús*) refers to that which is "sharp, keen or pointed," the second (*mōron*) speaks of that which is "dull, stupid or foolish." When combined, the roots convey contradictory ideas *simultaneously*: "sharp-dull, keen-stupid," and "pointed-foolish." It is in this sense that oxymoron is *autological*—the word itself is an example of an oxymoron as is *sophomore* (a single English word comprised of a Greek compound—*sophos*—'wise' + *moros*—'fool').

Rest assured that in reviewing this word and its etymology we are *not* implying that our readers are dumb, stupid, foolish, or sophomoric. To the contrary, the fact that you've reached this point in your career and are anticipating or serving in a leadership capacity implies the opposite. These ideas draw attention to how oxymorons underscore the contradictory elements, cross tendencies, and/or countervailing qualities of certain entities we encounter and experiences we have. As such, they caution against reductionist, hyper-simplistic, or binary thinking. Further, these ideas provide a context to explore the dynamics of educational leadership and school organizations.

Nor are we suggesting as the chapter title implies that schools are "beasts." The strategic choice of this noun represents the employment of a second literary device. A *hyperbole* is an intentional exaggeration, a rhetorical overstatement. And we open the chapter with a middle school vignette because everything can feel like an overstatement (and an oxymoron) in the early adolescent years. In this chapter, we state our case by overstating it a bit. As we will argue, there are certain school dynamics that lend themselves to leader control. There are others that do not. It is in this sense that schools are both tamable *and* untamable, domesticated yet wild—perhaps also like adolescents.

Previous chapters have provided a conceptual foundation for understanding the general nature of school organizations as we lay the groundwork for thinking about leadership within them. As argued in Chapter 1, understanding organizations begins with the twin pillars of structure and human working relationships. Leadership opportunities emerge when principals and other leaders understand how structure can help motivate people to engage in work and invest in the organization of which they are a part. Making spaces for Stephanie Wright to serve as a teacher leader is an example of such understanding. Whereas bureaucratic approaches typically hinder engagement, empowering structures and various forms of leadership are more conducive to it. Structures are used to facilitate meeting the organization's goals, in this case by empowering and involving a teacher as a leader.

An additional layer of complexity was added to our understanding in Chapter 2. Schools exist as *systems* "open" to the influences and uncertainties of the environments in which they exist. With this realization comes an abandonment of hyper-rational views of leadership and organizational life and a shift toward a more complex, ambiguous view of school leaders' roles. To add to this complexity, there is something of an oxymoron in our final observation in that chapter—that school organization may best be understood as both closed and open systems, that features of both perspectives coexist in order to make schools work.

Making use of a familiar and persistent oxymoron found in the literature, this chapter builds further on these ideas while adding an additional layer of complexity to them. Cohen, March, and Olsen (1972) have described educational organizations as *organized anarchies*. We thus begin the chapter with an exploration of this descriptor and the uncertainties it presents to principals as *decision makers*. We then move to identify those factors that contribute to decision uncertainty in schools: unknowns, ambiguities, and equivocalities. Each factor is defined and their cumulative effect on decision making described.

Extended Web Activities

The term *equivocality* is not often used in day-to-day speech or, for that matter, in much of the leadership literature (with some exceptions, which we will review in this chapter). Do a quick web search to come up with an acceptable working definition of the term and see if you can identify examples in your teaching and leadership practice.

Considered together these factors challenge prevailing myths about leading and organizing. We will argue that the assumptions on which these myths rest are of questionable validity. After exploring the meaning of *decision rationality*, we then provide examples of processes in schools that lend themselves to rational control *and* those which do not. Both types of processes define the context of many decisions principals make.

Thought Partner Conversation

Explore the following terms with a critical friend: ambiguity, uncertainty, and complexity. In what ways do these terms represent similar meanings, and how are they different? Why might it be important for a leader to know?

The chapter concludes by defining the *context* in which decisions are made and examining the elements found therein. *Decision context* refers to that collective array of factors that surround a given decision. Decisions arise from and are embedded in this context. After exploring this definition, we provide a framework intended to facilitate the identification and assessment of common elements found in most decision contexts. What are the contextual elements of a decision, and how do these inform the decisions leaders are called on to make? Our intent with this framework is to facilitate the development of skills needed to read, map, and effectively link elements found in the decision context with the decision-making process itself. In other words, we want to demonstrate to you, the reader, how to make sense of confusing and shifting situations, much as Stephanie does while working with contentious adults and students. Educational leaders must be ever vigilant in honing their decision-making skills, particularly in conditions of ambiguity and uncertainty.

Essential Questions

1. If schools are suffused with ambiguity and confusion, how can they possibly be understood, much less led?
2. How does understanding a school as an organized anarchy inform your thinking about how to lead it?
3. In what ways are teachers and principals able to mitigate the causes of ambiguity, uncertainty, and equivocality in their schools?

SCHOOLS AS "ORGANIZED ANARCHIES"

What does it mean to describe schools as *organized anarchies* and why is this somewhat obscure phrase something school leaders should know? Like other oxymorons, this designation by Cohen et al. (1972) presents cause for pause. It brings to the surface inherent tensions and uncertainties found in educational organizations.

Schools share vivid features of organized anarchies. Ever-present contradictions, and the paradoxes embedded in them, present ambiguities to which leaders must attend *if* the organization is to survive and/or achieve its goals. As organized anarchies, educational organizations share three defining features, two of which were surfaced in Chapters 1 and 2: (1) they have multiple, competing, and ill-defined organizational goals; (2) ambiguities surround the core task of teaching and learning which defines them; and (3) participation by organizational members and constituents is in a constant state of flux.

MULTIPLE, COMPETING, AND ILL-DEFINED GOALS

A defining feature of school organization is the existence of *multiple*, *competing*, and *ill-defined* goals. Each adjective in this sentence is significant. Every educator is keenly aware that there is not one, but many goals for public education. Each in turn informs the demands society makes on educators. For example, schools are expected to produce students who:

- read, write, and calculate at acceptable levels of proficiency;
- think and act independently;
- think and act morally and responsibly;
- possess the dispositions necessary to participate in and perpetuate a democratic way of life;
- possess marketable skills that contribute in positive ways to economic growth;
- reproduce cultural values while at the same time changing them;
- challenge and correct societal injustices.

Although each of these goals is commendable, they are not always compatible. Limited resources prevent the educational system from pursuing all with equal vigor. Furthermore, consensus regarding how these goals should be rank-ordered cannot be assumed.

Because partisan champions exist for each goal, the consensus that does exist at a given period of time is a result of political negotiation. In light of environmental changes and shifting demands—for example, the election of new members to a local school board or state legislature or the appointment of a new superintendent—this consensus is subject to change and renegotiation. The existence of *multiple* educational goals that are *contested* introduces uncertainty to many decisions principals are called on to make. A newly appointed superintendent selected for her strong emphasis on character education will introduce changes that shift focus away from that of her predecessor (e.g., college and career readiness) toward developing good citizens. Complicating matters further, a new superintendent is more likely to layer new initiatives on top of old, rather than replacing them (Tyack & Cuban, 1995). Principals and schools will be called on to adapt accordingly, keeping the old while adopting the new.

Uncertainty about the future is further complicated by the absence of measures that can assess the realization of goals in valid ways. Accountability demands are based on the assumption that institutions such as schools should "account for" how effectively and efficiently public funds are used to address public expectations (shifting though these expectations may be). Taxpayers want and deserve to know what schools have done with *their* tax dollars. A review of the educational goals or purposes listed above hints at the challenges associated with precise measurement of the extent to which these have been realized.

Impacts on students play out far into the future in adulthood. Although standardized achievement tests provide a potential snapshot of these effects, they fail to capture the long-term extent of goal realization. In spite of this, educational leaders must continually provide "evidence" of progress. Measures that produce quick, accessible and "quantifiable" results that often satiate accountability demands may not be tightly aligned with teaching and learning practices, rendering publicized results more symbolic than real (Meyer & Rowan, 1977). Principals therefore must make decisions that negotiate or compromise between the reality of teaching students and the symbolism of success sought by the public. This calls for the skillful management of expectations through a variety of ceremonial rituals, including strategic decisions regarding the publication of data that present a favorable profile of the school to the public (Bolman & Deal, 2013).

Thought Partner Conversation

With a critical friend, discuss the ways your school (or schools you know) make the public aware of how well they are performing—what evidence is shared, how is it shared, how often, and so on. How has this process changed in the past few years, and in what ways is this the "skillful management of expectations"?

TEACHING AND LEARNING AMBIGUITIES

As organized anarchies, schools are also characterized by an ambiguous core task: *teaching and learning*. As will be addressed in Chapter 7, good teaching is more easily discussed than observed; it is much more an art than a precise science. The teaching and/or curricular approach that worked with one student may be ineffective with another. Students present certain variables that can be addressed only indirectly by teachers—if at all. Furthermore, and in spite of the best intentions and pedagogical skill, the causal links between what is taught and what is learned are not always known, making learning outcomes unpredictable. As we noted in the preceding chapters, the factory model doesn't actually fit too well for schools because of the uncertainty of teaching and learning linkages. Teachers also vary in the knowledge, skills, and dispositions they bring to the classroom—their pedagogical content knowledge—which we discuss at length in Chapter 7. Given that schools are about teaching and learning, the uncertainties that surround this core task present choices for teachers and administrators that lack clear success criteria. As a consequence, strategic decisions regarding curricular or pedagogical reform within schools are chancy. Specific teaching and learning issues may be addressed in some classrooms, but they will persist in others and new ones will undoubtedly emerge.

A Changing Cast of Characters

The third major characteristic of schools as organized anarchies is their consistent state of flux. Cohen et al. (1972) noted that organized anarchies are defined by the *fluid* participation of organizational members and constituents. As a result participants vary in the amount of time and effort they devote to different domains. This involvement varies across time. Teachers, leaders, and parents come and go from decision arenas and from the school itself. As students move through elementary school, they change so much their kindergarten teachers hardly recognize them and they essentially become different participants. Because students graduate or move to the next grade level, the cohort of students in high school from one year to the next changes dramatically. Over a 4-year period, there is a drastic turnover in the student body and households represented therein. Once their children have graduated, parents who were politically active in school governance, either as super-supporters, chronic-complainers or hovering-helicopters, pass from the scene. Teachers leave schools and teaching in exceedingly high numbers, particularly in challenged schools. Principals retire, resign, and accept new assignments. With each new election cycle, new board members emerge, while others step aside.

Flux is a staple of school life and the organizational environment in which it is embedded. The cumulative effect is the creation of organizational boundaries that are uncertain and changing, as noted in Chapter 2. The audiences and decision makers for any given decision "change capriciously" (Cohen et al., 1972, p. 1). This too introduces uncertainties into decision-making processes engaged by principals. Although the level of uncertainty varies across decisions, the effect created by fluid participation further defines the larger decision context principals face.

Thought Partner Conversation

Think of a significant decision made recently that affected your school or a school you know; for instance, the adoption of a new curricular program. Who were the primary decision makers who influenced this decision? Were they the same actors who led implementation of the decision, and if not, who were they? Who, then, is responsible and accountable for the outcome?

MANAGING UNCERTAINTY, AMBIGUITY, AND EQUIVOCALITY: RESPONSIBILITY WITHOUT CONTROL

Just *how* do these features justify the moniker of schools as *organized anarchies*? Why should you as a promising school leader know such things? To answer these questions, recall again what oxymorons convey: contradictions, cross-purposes or tensions of an entity or experience that are hidden or not initially apparent. With this in mind, let's examine the contradictions and/or tensions organized anarchy conveys about schools and the popular myths it challenges.

The first feature signaled by this oxymoron is that schools are *organized* and thus purposeful. Structure, order, certainty, and predictability are evident in schools. Even when the structure feels old fashioned, such as the factory model or the agrarian calendar, its familiarity makes it difficult to change. The structure of a school constitutes the means whereby the wide range of activities engaged by participants in and around the school are coordinated and controlled. Teachers, administrators, and students have discernable roles and responsibilities. They know where to be, when, and for how long. Classrooms are grouped around definable axes such as subject and grade-level cohorts. Policies and procedures defining the parameters of participant behavior also exist. In addition, there is a formal hierarchy of authority. Stephanie Wright has a sense of the rules that govern her behavior in her classroom, in her department, and on her team and the roles that she plays in each of these venues. Tyack and Cuban (1995) referred to these familiar structural characteristics as the grammar of schooling to convey the idea that they signal what people are supposed to do and how they are expected to act. Together structural characteristics emphasize a discernable level of order, certainty, and predictability in the school: there is *organization*.

Yet organized anarchy also highlights a contrary dynamic in schools, one that eludes even the best efforts to achieve the predictability organizing seeks to ensure: *processes that promote anarchy within the organization*. The three features of multiple and conflicting goals, core task ambiguity, and flux identified by Cohen et al. (1972) represent fundamental de-stabilizing processes in schools. These processes are not only perennial, but also elusive: aspects of them evade our best efforts to impose order on them. Thus, in the ongoing struggle between organization and anarchy, control, and chaos, Luke Skywalker and Darth Vader, there is an occasional sense among school leaders like Stephanie Wright that anarchy is clearly winning. Competing educational purposes infused into public education coupled with perpetual ambiguities regarding teaching and learning process *and* the coming-and-going of school participants and constituents present dynamics that potentially threaten order within the school. These conditions likewise inform the decisions principals are called on to make.

Thought Partner Conversation

To illustrate what we are talking about in a very small way, consider a lesson plan you made and implemented recently. How did it go? Were you able to implement the plan precisely as you envisioned it? Did you meet your objective, or did the objective change somewhat? What decisions did you make as you implemented the lesson to alter what you were doing, and why?

How Do Leaders Navigate in These Waters?

Tensions between organization and anarchy challenge the myth of leading and organizing as *hyper-rational* endeavors. In offering this observation, we are *not* suggesting that rationality and the pursuit of certainty are absent from these dual endeavors. Leadership and organizational structure are consequential in schools. Students learn and progress; teachers develop skills and grow; schools graduate cohorts of competent students prepared for the next level of instruction. Results such as these do not occur by chance or without intent. They are the product of focused leadership and deliberate organization. *Organizing* is an attempt to impose purpose, structure, order, and coordination on collaborative efforts where little or none exists. As Thompson (1967) and others note (Perrow, 1979; Weick, 1979), the existence of an organization is the visible fruit of ongoing efforts to address uncertainties that prevent people from effectively and efficiently realizing their goal(s).

What we *are* suggesting is the following. First, whether in reference to principals or teachers, human control over outcomes—and the activities that produce them—is *not* total. While many of the processes critical to school success can be controlled through organizing and leading, there are limits to such controls. Districts control which principals get hired. Principals structure incentives they use to motivate teachers. Teachers in turn control the inducements used to engage students in learning. But *total* control is not possible. The ways in which others receive our intentions to manage and help are varied and unpredictable. And, as we have argued in Chapter 2 and in this chapter, influences external to the school can alter or thwart our best intentions.

Thought Partner Conversation

Educators know all too well that there is only so much that a teacher can control in a classroom, or a principal in a school. Can you think of initiatives, policies, or procedures existing in your school or in schools in general that seem to ignore this reality?

Variable control is a feature of school life. Of those structural dimensions and organizational dynamics that promote learning, some are more conducive to leader control than others. As principal, you can do much to promote a sense of efficacy among the teachers in your school. Yet this is an indirect influence on the quality of teaching and learning that occurs in each classroom.

Thought Partner Conversation

What are school leaders' most impactful strategies to promote improvements in teaching and learning, and how would you characterize the nature of their impact—direct? Indirect?

Uncertainty generates a sense of being out of control. Uncertainties associated with the defining features of organized anarchies (i.e., multiple, competing, and abstract educational goals; the uncertainties of the teaching and learning process, and the fluid nature of student, educator, and constituent participation), create dynamics beyond the school that undermine control within. Many of these must be accepted as *givens* by school leaders. For example: the election of a new governor with an aggressive reform agenda; tight educational budgets at the state and district levels; impossible demands from community members who do not currently have children in the system; or the influx of non-English speaking students into the school. While school leaders can do little or nothing about the existence of these factors, they are responsible for managing their effects on teaching and learning. More specifically, their decisions must attend to the negative effects these potentially create for the school. The processes that promote anarchy in school organizations do so because of the uncertainties and ambiguities within and around schools that challenge the realization of instructional goals.

Together the ideas associated with organized anarchies point to the existence of uncertainties and ambiguities that define the context of principal work. Whether present in the decisions they make, the actions they plan, or the strategic responses they develop to shifting environmental demands, uncertainties and ambiguities exist. But what do these concepts mean? In what ways do they affect the decisions principals are called on to make?

Uncertain and *ambiguous* are distinct yet related terms. To these we add here a third, a synonym of ambiguous: *equivocal*. To define these terms, consider the following:

1. We do not know everyone in our neighborhoods.
2. We do not know how to convert salt water in to fresh, potable H_2O.
3. We do not know what matter exists beyond the smallest known sub-atomic entity (*quark*).
4. We do not know in advance how effective (if at all) a newly-hired math teacher fresh out of pre-service will be 5 years into the future.

While each of these four scenarios is currently uncertain, they are uncertain for different reasons. For example, in time it is possible to become acquainted with all those who live in our neighborhood. With a modicum of effort we can also learn the chemistry and mechanics of the desalination process. Given that knowledge about such things exists, these uncertainties are surmountable as existing data are collected and considered. It is *our* (not others') lack of information about the neighborhood and desalination process that accounts for the current deficit in our knowledge. The knowledge exists but we have yet to avail ourselves of it. Uncertainties of this type are reduced as existing data are collected. Increased certainty ensues as these data are analyzed.

The third uncertainty, however, differs qualitatively from the first two. Because such information cannot be found in the collective bank of human knowledge, we do not know what micro-matter exists beyond the *quark*. We don't know because *no one* knows. Regardless of how hard we search, no data exists anywhere for us to know. Such information lies beyond the existing frontiers of human knowledge.

The fourth scenario is also distinct. We are uncertain how effective a new math teacher will be 3 years from now for *temporal* reasons. While the data we have provide grounds for optimism—a high grade point average from a reputable institution, a substantive student teaching experience, strong recommendation from others, and a convincing, pre-hire teaching demonstration—teaching effectiveness is difficult to predict with certainty. This is because information needed to do so lies in the future. As data become available, confirming or disconfirming evidence will emerge. With it the level of uncertainty regarding his/her ability will decrease.

When outcomes cannot be known with more data, the situation is ambiguous. The concepts *ambiguous* and *equivocal* are indicative of the multiple meanings associated with decision contexts. For example, determining why an otherwise bright student performed poorly on an exam may be explained by one or more factors: (1) inadequate preparation on the student's part; (2) lack of motivation; (3) sickness that impedes clear thinking; (4) test anxiety; (5) distractions in the testing environment; and/or (6) other known and unknown factors. While explanations based on each are possible, no single factor can be identified and isolated with certainty a priori. The student's performance is open to multiple possible explanations. Determining which factor(s) account for this outcome and in what degree is thus problematic. For this reason, causes of poor performance are *ambiguous* [Latin: *ambiagere*—"to drive both ways"] or *equivocal* [Latin: *equivocare*—"to call equally"]. By "driving us in different directions" and "calling out to us equally," a definitive explanation of the student's performance is not possible without further investigation.

Thought Partner Conversation

Can you identify decisions you might have faced recently, or may be facing, that are affected by each of the above-mentioned factors? How do you plan to proceed to reduce uncertainty?

Circumstances that are ambiguous or equivocal contribute to the level of uncertainty that surrounds the decision-making process. Yet as illustrated above, additional data may reduce uncertainties. Clarifying the meaning of existing data reduces *ambiguity* or *equivocality*. However, an overwhelming amount or complex array of data create ambiguous and equivocal decision scenarios for school leaders. Such conditions speak to the existence of a tipping point beyond which the data to be analyzed exceed the cognitive capacity of the decision maker(s). In spite of this, principals and others still must make decisions. Realities such as these once again challenge hyper-rational views of leading and organizing that have historically dominated our collective thinking. In light of these realities, we suggest that decision-making uncertainty is a function of one or more factors: (1) an insufficient amount of data or information; (2) ambiguous or equivocal circumstances; (3) the existence of data or information, the complexity and/or volume of which, lie beyond the analytic ability the decision maker(s) to process.

RETHINKING ORGANIZATION AND DECISION RATIONALITY

As implied multiple times in this and previous chapters, the uncertainties presented by ambiguous or equivocal situations that define organized anarchies converge on the decision-making process. It is here that such features come into bold relief. These uncertainties not only challenge, but also force principals to temper the hyper-rational assumptions historically associated with decision making by scientific management. Non-rational features of leaders' lives further underscore the need for leaders to hone their cognitive capacity to read and assess the context in which decisions are made (Simon, 1976; Weick, 1979).

When used to describe decision making, *rationality* is the extent to which a series of choices and the actions that follow from them are strategically organized to realize pre-determined goals with maximum efficiency (Mannheim, 1950; Simon, 1976; Thompson, 1967). Because most of us have been socialized into the "scientific" thinking reflected in this definition, its logic is appealing. Yet a careful review of the normative assumptions on which it rests forces us to think twice about its validity. For this level of rationality to exist in an organization, there must be complete certainty: *no* unknowns, *no* ambiguous or equivocal data, and adequate resources. Furthermore, there must be a critical level of agreement on the purposes of the organization and the means used to pursue these purposes.

CAUSE AND EFFECT

An element of rationality that is worth considering is the notion of cause and effect. For a decision to be *rational* there is a presumption that we have considerable confidence about the causal relationship—that A causes B (in organizational terms that specific actions led to meeting agreed-upon goals). This is quite a challenge in education because there are so many and varied causes of most important outcomes such as student learning.

As you build your decision-making abilities, it may be helpful to consider: What are the requirements of a cause-and-effect claim? We know of three:

1. For A to cause B, it must come before B in time—until we master time travel, there is a temporal ordering.
2. For A to cause B, the two must be related or associated with each other, in statistical terms they must be correlated.
3. To be able to claim that A causes B, there must not be other existing factors that cause both A and B that would otherwise explain their relationship.

Source: Bauer and Brazer (2012)

In light of the characteristics of organized anarchies reviewed above, consider further the applicability of this definition for *school* organizations. To achieve this level of rationality in schools assumes that *the* purpose(s) of education and *the* most efficient means for achieving this purpose (i.e., complete knowledge and predictability of the: (1) teaching-learning process, and (2) the structures that support this process exists) are known, measurable at a high level of validity, and consensual to all.

Thought Partner Conversation

Thinking about school policies and practices, for instance discipline policies, to what extent are these based on the kinds of rationality defined above? What are some of the consequences of this? What are reasonable *alternatives*?

The assumptions above are important to consider before accepting them. Is this an accurate description of the school or district in which you work? Pause at this point and consider the percentage of decisions made by educational leaders that fit these restrictive parameters. Of the high-stakes decisions you've faced this week, which conform to these assumptions? What about the last *major* decision you made? Chances are few, if any, decisions conform to these assumptions.

For these reasons, our thinking about the decision-making process must be *tempered*. We must shift from a mindset oriented toward finding the best decision solution *for all times and places* to that of finding the best solution in light of the uncertainties which define most, if not all decision contexts (or often, the decision context facing us right now). Whereas the former mindset assumes omniscience, the latter does not. Simon (1976) labels these competing approaches to decision-making *optimizing* (complete knowledge of all decision parameters exists) and *satisficing* (complete knowledge does *not* exist, but a "good enough" choice may be made) respectively. This important categorical distinction underscores the variable nature of rationality. It also justifies the need to qualify what constitutes an "acceptable" decision solution or goal. In shifting from an optimizing to satisficing orientation, and in light of the variables that define the decision context, there is need for the leader to determine the criteria for a "workable" solution.

Thought Partner Conversation

Can you come up with examples of times you made consequential decisions that impacted either colleagues or students when you sought to *satisfice* rather than optimize? What characterized the situation that led you to choose to satisfice?

In making this cognitive shift, we are not suggesting that principals abandon the rational processes associated with sound decision making (Johnson & Kruse, 2009)—for example, defining with a reasonable level of precision the problem which prompts a decision as accurately as possible by attending to the relevant data at hand, developing alternative solutions to ameliorate this problem, and weighing alternatives with the intent of choosing the most viable option in light of available resources.

To the contrary, if possible the systematic search for a solution reflected in these processes should *never* be abandoned. Along with others, however, we do question the assumption of human omniscience that the scientific management literature imputes to rational decision processes. This assumption is specious. In the presence of multiple and conflicting goals and the absence of complete knowledge, decisions based on this approach are misguided at best. Frustration lies in their wake.

Thought Partner Conversation

Elsewhere we observe the prevalence of "best practices" guiding educational decision making. How is the claim of a practice being "best" similar to optimizing? Can a practice possibly be best for all students in all classes at all times?

The amount of information available for the decisions principals are called on to make, as well as the validity and reliability of these data, varies from decision to decision and across time. Rarely, if ever, is there a comprehensive level of information. Equally as rare is the complete absence of information. Most decisions faced by principals are made in contexts defined by varying degrees of certainty and uncertainty, and decision ambiguities remain. To be sure, such givens challenge the understanding of the decision-making process we have been taught. Yet we suggest that acceptance of them is one of many prerequisites for leader success.

CONFORMITY VERSUS VARIABILITY

One of the several sets of criteria that affect school leader decision making has to do with conformity or consistency versus variability. Leaders are often under a lot of pressure to ensure that practices are the same, or as same as they can be, for all students (or at least all students in a specific grade or group). There are many reasons for this, including issues associated with fairness and equity.

As you develop your decision-making capabilities, the role of conformity or consistency and the pressure for sameness is worth scrutiny. In unpredictable contexts characterized by many and competing goals and highly variable student needs, sameness may result in inefficiencies and inequities and reduce teachers' abilities to meet the needs of all learners.

The flip side of this, though, is the reality that extreme variability is chaotic and makes it very difficult for teachers to work together and for leaders to lead. In the extreme, everyone doing their own thing at their own pace would be any school leaders' worst nightmare.

This issue, we believe, is one of the most complex for leaders to negotiate, and bears careful attention. Striking a productive balance is one sign of a great leader.

Based on the description of the decision-making process outlined above, two important points are worth reiterating before we progress. First, uncertainty is *the* fundamental problem *for* organizations and *to which* organizing is a response. The act of organizing is in essence an attempt to impose order on disorder. Some strategies for organizing are more successful in this endeavor than others. Uncertainty stands in the way of the organization achieving its goals.

Second, *coping with uncertainty* is *the essence* of the administrative process. To be effective, educational leaders must be able to recognize and manage uncertainty in functional ways (Johnson, forthcoming). Both points underscore the importance of understanding the context in which decisions are made. These principles likewise emphasize the importance of possessing the capacity to read, navigate, and act on this context as a leader (Weick, 1979). It is to these foci that we now turn.

UNDERSTANDING THE DECISION CONTEXT

Interest in decision making in all types of organizations has resulted in a variety of explanations (*theories*) of how decisions are made. All can be classified into one of two categories: normative or descriptive explanations. Normative theories offer a description of how decisions *should be* made. The goal of those who develop them is *absolute* optimization: making the best decision, *period*. Such theories assume omniscience.

By contrast, descriptive explanations are grounded in observations of how leaders *actually* make decisions. These theories reject notions of complete knowledge in varying degrees. In so doing, they also recognize the limits of human cognition. Using the logic articulated above, these theories acknowledge the uncertainties presented by unknown, ambiguous, or equivocal data.

Because leaders and organizations vary along a number of dimensions, there are more descriptive than normative explanations of decision making (Johnson & Kruse, 2009). Our intent is not to review these theories here; this has been done elsewhere (e.g., Northouse, 2016; Stogdill, 1974; Yukl, 2016). Rather it is to explore a dominant feature of the decision-making process that all descriptive explanations assume: *a context*.

Thought Partner Conversation

Below we consider decision context as an important factor in leadership decision making. Before reading on, with a critical friend outline all of the elements that you would include in "context" for school leader decision making. What kinds of factors impact what you would consider as "context"?

Understanding Context

As noted above, *decision context* refers to that collective array of variables, facts, and circumstances that surround a given decision. Decisions arise from and are embedded in this context. Regardless of decision content, all decisions exist in a specific context. Because of the uncertainties presented by the ambiguities and equivocalities in it, decision context is *the* variable that complicates the decision-making process. The features inherent in the character of schools as organized anarchies are the source of many of these contextual uncertainties. This complexity not only varies across different types of decisions made in schools, but for similar decisions made in schools across time.

To illustrate the importance of context and the complexities it presents to the decision process, consider a familiar example from the classroom. Information is revealed and numbered sequentially in what follows. With each revelation, more data emerge about the decision context.

1. *A student comes to you in the middle of the period and asks if he can go to the restroom.*

   At first glance, this appears to be a rather simple, straightforward request. Although you wonder why the student didn't use the time between periods to answer the call of nature, you are well aware that emergencies do arise. Hence, you are sensitive to such requests. At the same time, past experiences with similar requests from other students prompt you to consider other contextual data:

2. *The class is taking a test.*

   This fact is of no small significance. It clarifies yet complicates the decision for you. Students were notified well in advance that this was test day. You've also made them aware of behavioral expectations associated with test-taking: no talking, books and notes closed and secured, write name on exam immediately upon receipt, eyes on your own work, and remain seated until all have completed the test. This request violates one of those expectations. Yet you remain uncertain as to the legitimacy of his request. Is it a genuine emergency or calculated ploy by the student? At this point, the information that exists to answer this question is equivocal. Additional contextual data provide a hint:

3. *Chuck does this at least every other day.*

   Ah hah! A measure of clarity appears to emerge. This behavior pattern sheds further light on the decision you face. But then again, maybe it does not. While it suggests one tentative explanation, it fails to exhaust all possible explanations regarding the sincerity and legitimacy of his request. Thus, ambiguity persists. It is complicated further by other, more temporal data. You've designed the exam in a way that requires students most or all of the period to complete. Time away from the desk means less time for Chuck to finish the test. It is also the last school day before Thanksgiving. There is little time to waste here, particularly in light of other contextual factors:

4. *He has a reputation in the school for being a discipline problem.*

   With this bit of information, decision closure appears imminent. After all, students with reputations for being "discipline problems" do such things—not occasionally but on a consistent basis. Chuck is no different. His request must therefore certainly be a plot to stall or perhaps cheat.

   It's shaping up to be an open-and-shut decision for you. Yet to deny his request at this point would be legally problematic. You see:

5. *Chuck has a documented medical condition.*

   Such data is a game-changer. In spite of his behavioral issues, to willfully ignore or unintentionally overlook this condition could create a medical emergency. Beyond this, your denial of his request could even result in a lawsuit against the school and/or your dismissal. On top of this is the fact that:

6. *Chuck's father is the superintendent of the district.*

   Not only does your decision have legal overtones, it has political ramifications as well. How might the superintendent respond should you deny his son's request?

Although we could explore other data and the implications these have for the decision you must make, our intent with this example is to: (1) illustrate how contextual ambiguities and unknowns create uncertainties for decision makers, even in the face of what initially appear to be straightforward decisions; (2) emphasize the importance of being aware of these contextual features and the implications they have for decision making; and (3) underscore the need for principals to develop the capacity to read and navigate the decision context in light of the uncertainties that exist.

Thought Partner Conversation

As we discuss the frameworks presented below to map decision context, consider a decision that may be facing you in school or in your professional career and practice using this tool—map the context. How does this help you as a decision maker?

MAPPING THE DECISION CONTEXT

Figures 3.1–3.4 provide heuristic frameworks for identifying and assessing uncertainties found in most decision contexts. While they do not exhaust all possible factors, the variable sets depicted in each provide useful dimensions for analyzing context. In one way or another, all are informed by the defining characteristics of schools as organized anarchies. Included in this are contextual variables related to: (1) *information*; (2) *logistics and capacity*; and (3) *political dynamics*. Many of these factors are discernable in the decision scenario with Chuck and his request to go to the restroom above.

Decisions rise and fall on the amount and quality of information available to leaders. Scarce, invalid, and unreliable data increase uncertainties in the decision context. Figure 3.1 identifies *informational* dimensions of the decision context. Much data may exist, but it may be irrelevant or invalid to the decision at hand; much *relevant* data may exist, but it may be unreliable for decision purposes. Each of these dimensions is presented as a continuum in Figure 3.1. The extremes are also labeled.

As referenced above, the *amount of information available for decision* can range from *none* to *exhaustive* with multiple levels in between. Decisions defined by the extremes are the exception rather than the rule. The amount of information available for most decisions lies somewhere in between. Effective decision making is a function of the leader's capacity to determine: (1) what information is needed to make a decision; (2) what data are present in the decision context; and (3) what data are absent.

Assumed and coupled with this is the extent to which the goal(s) of the decision— that *end/purpose* toward which the decision is directed—is *known* and the *criteria* for assessing the extent to which the decision realized this purpose(s) are *explicit*. Given that decisions are prompted by problems and/or opportunities, they are directed at resolving problems and/or exploiting opportunities. Leaders must also analyze the context in order to assess the extent to which consensus regarding ends and means does or does not exist. Given the character of schools as organized anarchies, consensus on decision goals and means should not be assumed by the leader (Cohen et al., 1972; Thompson, 1967).

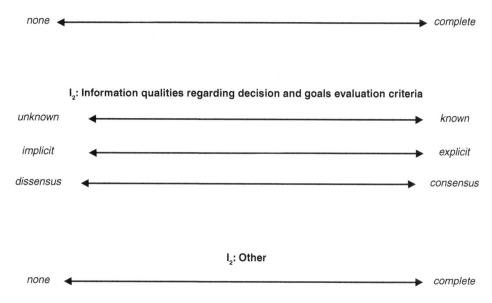

I_1: Amount of information available for decision

none ←————————————————————————————→ *complete*

I_2: Information qualities regarding decision and goals evaluation criteria

unknown ←————————————————————————————→ *known*

implicit ←————————————————————————————→ *explicit*

dissensus ←————————————————————————————→ *consensus*

I_2: Other

none ←————————————————————————————→ *complete*

FIGURE 3.1 Decision Context: Information Variables

Information regarding the risk associated with a decision may also be found in this context. Risk is conceptualized here along two related and variable dimensions: *probability* and *magnitude*. Whereas the former speaks to probability of choosing an alternative that adequately addresses the problem (or opportunity) to which the decision is a response, the latter is indicative of the magnitude of the decision's effect on the organization, be it positive or negative. Risky decisions are characterized by a low probability that leaders will choose an alternative that adequately solves an extensive, wide-ranging problem with negative effects. The presence or absence of key contextual data allows decision makers to assess the level of risk associated with a decision to greater or lesser degree. Figure 3.2 depicts the logic of determining decision risk along these two dimensions.

Related yet distinct from these data/information factors are those associated with decision-making capacity and logistics. These contextual variables are presented in Figure 3.3.

Decision-making capacity refers to the ability of the principal or leadership team to identify, collect, analyze, and as needed, generate the data required for decision. Although schools are data rich, many remain analysis poor. Much of this is due to inadequate analytic capacity that exists in the school. This too defines the context in which decisions are made. Even if this capacity exists, the willingness to engage in these essential cognitive activities and the incentives for doing so may be lacking.

Decision logistics likewise consist of multiple dimensions. Only a few are noted here. For example, decisions vary in the amount of time available to make them. Some are tightly linked and thus dictated by the schedule of the school day. Others involve more prolonged timelines. Reports of annual progress and the development of plans

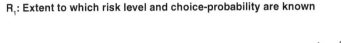

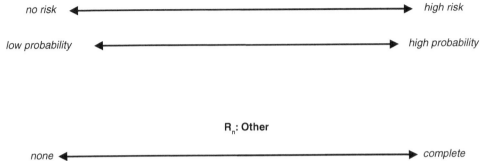

FIGURE 3.2 Decision Context: Risk Variables

for strategic school improvement require longer periods of time that may or may not be granted by district, state, or federal policy makers. Still, others emerge in the moment. Emergency situations that threaten human safety call for quick, immediate decisions.

Correlated with this and other contextual features are the costs associated with making a decision. Included are the costs associated with retrieving and analyzing decision data, the costs of coordinating multiple individuals, departments, or organizations, and the opportunity costs foregone in the neglect of other pressing decisions in and around the school. Whereas routine, predictable decisions tend to be less costly, major decisions typically require a greater and wider array of organizational resources of various kinds. Since both time and money are scarce resources in schools, more time and money spent here means less time and money spent there.

In addition to this are the logistical demands associated with the size of the decision-making body: the number of individuals or groups involved in the decision-making process. This number can range from one to many, from a single, site-based team to the voting citizens in a community or state. The collective profile of those involved may present additional logistical challenges. As the number and diversity of the decision-making body increase, the time needed for consensus building likewise increases. Smaller, more homogeneous decision-making bodies tend to be more efficient than larger, more diverse ones. Democratic decision making is more time and logistically intensive than its autocratic counterpart, and introduces much more uncertainty and ambiguity. Just as there are times and decisions when the context demands greater involvement by the principal, there are situations when it does not. The decision context often provides multiple cues to the discerning leader in this regard.

This examination of the challenges associated with coordinating the efforts of multiple individuals in the decision-making process provides a logical segue to the fourth and final variable-set found in most decision contexts: political dynamics. Realizing that more could be added to Figure 3.4, we examine what we consider to be the most essential political factors here. Given that each emphasizes a different aspect of the political stakes associated with the decision-making process, all are related.

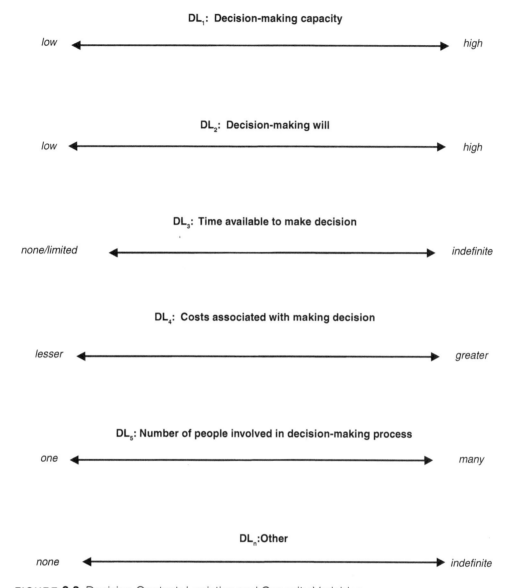

FIGURE 3.3 Decision Context: Logistics and Capacity Variables

The first political dynamic springs from the number of stakeholders associated with decisions made in the collective. A political stake is an interest. Be they individuals or groups, stakeholders have a vested interest in the outcome of a given decision: these interests are potentially "at stake" in the decision. Depending on the configuration of interests represented among stakeholders, these interests will be enhanced, maintained or diminished by the decision. Toward these ends it is not unusual to find competing stakeholders in the decision context—individuals and groups whose interests differ. The existence of multiple, diverse interests increases the probability of decision conflict for leaders.

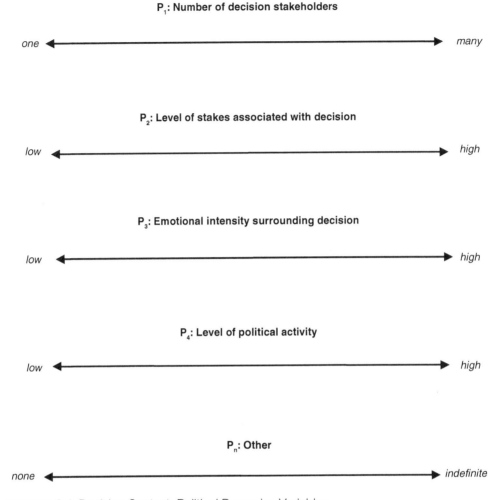

FIGURE 3.4 Decision Context: Political Dynamics Variables

Thought Partner Conversation

The discussion of stakeholders was broached a bit in Chapter 2, when we learned about open systems. Here, select a decision facing your school or district and make a list of the potential stakeholders who seek to influence the decision. In examining this list, try to figure out which stakeholders might form an alliance or *interest group* in order to enhance their influence.

Decisions faced by principals and other school leaders vary by the number of stakeholders affected by them. For example, the stakeholders affected by a decision to overlook a verbal argument between boys and girls during recess over who gets to use the playground basketball court first is far smaller than the number affected by a decision to add 30 minutes to the beginning and end of the school day. Stakeholders and decision-visibility co-vary. As the number of stakeholders increases, the visibility of the decision being made assumes a higher profile. More become aware of it. Greater visibility in turn exposes the leader to closer public scrutiny from a broader range of constituents.

Decision stakes also vary by degree. These range from low to high stakes, with multiple levels in between. The stakes associated with differentiated pay decisions based on (1) the principal's evaluation of classroom performance and (2) gains in student test scores over a 3-year period are much higher than decisions about which brand of custodial supplies to order. As with multiple stakeholders, high-stakes decisions have the effect of increased decision-visibility, close, sustained analysis of the external environment of the school, and increased conflict.

High-stakes decisions often evoke visceral responses from stakeholders, the cumulative effect of which is to increase the level of emotional intensity within the decision context. This political dimension is also depicted in Figure 3.4. Visceral issues in turn promote a militancy that can easily escalate into open, internecine conflict on multiple fronts. Ignoring this dynamic and its effect on the decision-making process can result in the loss of leader credibility. Principals do so at their own risk (Gamson, 1992; Johnson & Kruse, 2009; Malen, 1995).

Thought Partner Conversation

Consider a decision made by schools regularly—a students' eligibility for special education services. Make a list of the stakeholders involved in this decision, and consider how each might view the stakes involved. Be sure to include in your consideration both the parties that are directly involved and others that are affected.

Together the dynamics generated by the number of stakeholders, the importance of the stakes to them, and the level of emotional intensity, and the nuances associated with all three, determine the level of political activity surrounding a decision. Decisions defined by multiple stakeholders, high stakes, and intense emotions combine to create higher levels of political activity than those with fewer stakeholders and lower stakes. Much like insufficient information and complex decision logistics, these political dynamics introduce uncertainties to the decision context. These uncertainties in turn represent decision challenges that must be solved or managed in functional ways by the leader. Once recognized, puzzles provoke dissonance that seeks resolution (Dewey, 1910; Fetsinger, 1957). Leadership and organizing are about reducing the uncertainties presented by puzzles in order to achieve the purpose(s) identified for the organization. Leaders often have organizational puzzles to solve for which pieces are absent or altogether unknown to them. Nevertheless, this does not impede the never-ending quest for certainty in organizations.

RECAPITULATION AND CONCLUSION

A principal's duties are varied and far-flung. Whether performed in operational or strategic settings, these duties engage the leader's full spectrum of thought. Considered together, the ideas presented in this chapter represent the experientially familiar, yet unspoken aspects of school leadership that often go unaddressed. We offer them with the intent of adding yet another level of complexity to our collective thinking about the organizations in which leadership occurs. They do so by challenging the hyper-rational myths that guide the processes associated with these essential activities. In spite of their questionable validity, these myths are persistent. All pivot on faulty assumptions of human omniscience and the extensive control these implies.

As Cohen et al.'s (1972) incisive oxymoron reminds us, schools represent *organized anarchies*. On the one hand, schools reflect order and purpose: students learn, things get done, and progress is made. On the other hand, a modicum of disorder and anarchy can be discerned in them. There are processes and dynamics in schools that are subject to human control; there are also those that are not. It is in this sense that schools are both tamable and untamable for leaders. Cognitive limitations make definitive prediction, and the extensive control that follows from it, impossible. In sum, certainties and uncertainties define the essence of schools as formal organizations. They reflect order and disorder.

Uncertainty is thus *the* fundamental problem to which organizing is a response. It stands in the way of total control and predictability needed to achieve desired outcomes with complete certainty. It is for this reason that principals and other school leaders find themselves perpetually engaged in solving puzzles of various kinds. For some of these puzzles pieces are lacking; for others they are altogether unknown. Leaders often don't know what they don't know.

Successfully coping with uncertainty is the essence of school leadership. Although this uncertainty comes into bold relief around most organizational decisions, it is felt most forcefully by school leaders when stakes for decisions are especially high. For this reason, it behooves the principal and those she or he leads to develop the capacity to cope with this uncertainty in functional ways. But how is this done? How do schools as organizations *learn* this capacity? These questions are addressed in Chapter 4 using the conceptual framework of organizational learning.

EXERCISE 3.1 DISCUSSING GOALS AND AMBIGUITY

Gather with a partner or a small group to consider and discuss the following questions and prompts:

1. Based on what you know from your experience with life in schools, what are three to five (or more) goals implied or explicitly stated in the vignette about teacher leader Stephanie Wright that opens this chapter?

    •   In what ways are the goals you have listed aligned or complementary and in what ways are they divergent or contradictory?

2. Looking at the list of goals you created, come to consensus about their priority order.

    •   What criteria did you use to prioritize?

3. Compare your ordered list to at least one other group in your class to check for convergence and divergence.

   - What would you do with the similarities and differences of perspectives revealed in your list making and comparing across groups?
   - What are the implications for leading and managing schools?

EXERCISE 3.2 CATALOGUING ORGANIZATION AND ANARCHY

Think carefully about your school to identify sources of organizational stability and anarchy. The questions below ask you to consider the advantages and disadvantages of each.

1. What are three to five of the most prominent ways in which teaching and learning are organized in your school? It is ok to state the obvious.

   - In what ways to do these organizational features support or enhance teaching and learning?
   - In what ways do these organizational features impede or confuse teaching and learning?

2. What are three to five key features of *dis*organization in your school?

   - Are you or others in your school able to exploit any of these features? If so, how and to what end?

3. If you could *organize* one thing better or mitigate anarchy in one area in your school, what would it be?

   - If you could have *less* organization in one area, what would that be and why would it be attractive to you?

4. Share your conclusions with at least one other partner to learn varying perspectives on desired organization and tolerance for anarchy.

EXERCISE 3.3 UNCERTAINTY, AMBIGUITY, AND EQUIVOCALITY

Stephanie Wright is concerned about how HMMS fare in high school and beyond. She knows some things about their progress through HMMS and what happens to them in high school, but she doesn't know everything. Using what you know about schools and the transition from one educational setting to the next, talk with one or more partners about the following:

1. What could Stephanie *learn* through examining data?

   - Which data should she explore?
   - Is this kind of data available to you in your school?

2. What is puzzling about Stephanie's middle school students' transition to high school that doesn't have specific data that would reveal causes? In short, what is ambiguous about the situation?

   - What are one or two student achievement and progression mysteries that persist in your schools? What keeps them mysterious?

3. Sometimes we know that taking an action will produce an outcome, but we may not be sure which outcome it will produce—an equivocal situation.

   - Think of one action Stephanie might take, then brainstorm the possible different outcomes.

     - How should Stephanie decide when she doesn't know the exact path the decision will leader her on? How should she respond to equivocality?

MIDDLE SCHOOL PUZZLES

It should be clear by now that the many and varied dimensions of leading schools make them complex organizations that are challenging to read, let alone lead. Using the vignette that begins the chapter to understand a bit about teacher leader Stephanie Wright's world, we encourage you to use concepts from this chapter to work through two puzzles she faces.

Puzzle 1: What Happens in High School?

HMMS administrators, teachers, and families are proud of the strides the school has made over the past 10 years to improve the quality of education for all students. The success story that HMMS has come to represent is trumpeted in the local press and on the school's website as various state and regional awards for improvement and excellence have accumulated. But recently, Stephanie, the Mustangs team, and a few teachers on other teams have come to question the meaning of their apparent success after Stephanie explored the ways in which HMMS graduates participate in the life of Groveland High School. The high school seems outside the influence of HMMS faculty and administration, but nagging at Stephanie is a sense that they are missing something in the way in which they have prepared their students to enter high school.

1. If HMMS students are as well or better prepared than their peers from the two other middle schools that feed into Groveland High School, why aren't they better represented in advanced courses?

   - What factors might an emphasis on improved academic performance overlook?
   - What data might be missed by focusing on rising test scores?

2. What is uncertain, ambiguous, and or equivocal when students move from middle school where they have experienced success into high school, which is unknown to them?

- What might Stephanie and other teacher leaders to do mitigate the effects of the unknowns?

Puzzle 2: Reading the Decision Context

Sit down in Principal Schmidt's chair and imagine Stephanie coming to you and saying, "The participation data from the high school are terrible. Not only are HMMS kids not a large presence in honors and AP classes, they're not even participating in sports, music, or other activities. It's as though they're invisible at Groveland. That really makes me mad because we have a lot of great kids who have proven that they are as academically capable as any of those other kids at Groveland. This is outrageous and we have to do something about it. Our graduates are facing discrimination at the high school that is seriously damaging their futures!"

You are at least as concerned as Stephanie about this situation, but you also have the sense that you don't fully understand it. You are inspired by Stephanie's energy and vehemence, but it also makes you nervous. You face a host of decisions that cluster around this question: Should you encourage Stephanie and her colleagues to try to figure out what happens to HMMS graduates and do what they can to address the situation, or should HMMS just keep doing its good work and try to influence the high school to take the lead on addressing the disproportionate representation of HMMS students in their programs? Think through the four dimensions of decision context depicted in Figures 3.1–3.4:

1. What information do you have and what more might you be able to obtain?
2. If you publicize what is happening to HMMS graduates at Groveland by addressing the situation, what risks are you incurring?

- What, exactly, would you be risking?
- What criteria would you use to weigh the risks against potential benefits?

3. What HMMS characteristics present logistical strengths should you decide to address the problem as Stephanie has presented it to you?

- In what ways does the organization of schooling in your district present logistical hurdles for addressing the problem as Stephanie has presented it to you?

4. Thinking about the politics among teachers and administrators within and across schools, what are the most important factors that would influence your decision posed in the preamble to these puzzles?

- What are the most important stakes and how high are they likely to be?
- What is likely to be the degree of emotional intensity emanating from the decision you make?

REFERENCES

Bauer, S.C., & Brazer, S.D. (2012). *Using research to lead school improvement: Turning evidence into action.* Thousand Oaks, CA: Sage.

Bolman, L., & T. Deal. (2013). *Reframing organizations: Artistry, choice, and leadership* (5th ed.). San Francisco: Jossey-Bass.

Cohen, M.D., March, J.G., & Olsen, J.P. (1972). A garbage can model of organizational choice. *Administrative Science Quarterly, 17*(1) (March), 1–25.

Dewey, J. (1910). *How we think: A restatement of the relation of reflective thinking to the educative process.* Boston: D.C. Heath & Co.

Festinger, L. (1957). *A theory of cognitive dissonance.* Palo Alto, CA: Stanford University Press.

Gamson, W. (1992). *Talking politics.* London: Cambridge University Press.

Johnson, B.L., Jr. (forthcoming). Organizations, organizing, and schools: Accessing theoretical tools and models in organization theory. In M. Conley (Ed.), *The SAGE handbook of school organization.* Thousand Oaks, CA: Sage Publications.

Johnson, B.L., Jr., & Kruse, S. (2009). *Decision making for educational leaders: Underexamined dimensions and issues.* Albany, NY: SUNY Press.

Malen, B. (1995). The study of educational politics. In J. Scribner and D. Layton (Eds.), *The study of educational politics* (pp. 147–167). Washington, DC: The Palmer Press.

Mannheim, K. (1950). *Freedom, power, and democratic planning.* Oxford: Oxford University Press.

Meyer, J., & Rowan, B. (1977). Institutionalized organizations: Formal structure as myth and ceremony. *American Journal of Sociology, 83*(2), 340–363.

Northouse, P. (2016). *Leadership: Theory and practice* (7th ed.). Thousand Oaks, CA: Sage Publications.

Perrow, C. (1979). *Complex organizations: A critical essay* (2nd ed.). Glenview, IL: Scott, Foresman and Company.

Shakespeare, W. (2015). *Romeo and Juliet.* Overland Park, KA: Digireads.

Simon, H. (1976). *Administrative behavior: A study of decision-making processes in administrative organization* (2nd ed.). New York: Macmillan.

Stogdill, R. (1974). *Handbook of leadership: A survey of theory and research.* New York: Free Press.

Thompson, J.D. (1967). *Organizations in action.* New York: McGraw-Hill Publishing Co.

Tyack, D., & Cuban, L. (1995). *Tinkering toward utopia: A century of public school reform.* Cambridge, MA: Harvard University Press.

Weick, K.E. (1979). *The social psychology of organizing* (2nd ed.). New York: McGraw-Hill.

Yukl, G. (2016). *Leadership: Theory and practice* (7th ed.). Thousand Oaks, CA: Sage Publications.

CHAPTER 4

Organizational Learning

Anita Constant has been principal at Mariposa Elementary School for the past 9 years. She adores her school and feels a great sense of devotion to the low-income, predominantly Latino community. Mariposa was chaotic when Anita took over, but through her leadership the school has substantially increased parent involvement and won greater respect within the district. Mariposa is a well-run school with many non-profit supported programs intended to help the student population. One such program is ExEl—an intensive English language development curriculum designed for second language learners that comes with extensive professional development. Near the end of the academic year, Anita was hit with the news that after a 7-year partnership, ExEl is pulling out next year because of their dissatisfaction with implementation at Mariposa. Just as she learned this, Anita was reviewing student achievement data in math and ELA when she saw that no consistent improvement had been made over the past 5 years.[1]

IF YOU WANT TO LEAD, YOU HAVE TO LEARN

It seems natural that schools would be learning organizations that engage in organizational learning, but doing so is not easy. Real learning changes perspectives, making individuals uncomfortable. Organizational learning means changing the status quo, potentially making everyone uncomfortable. Consequently, leading learning of any type takes courage.

Great leaders are also leading learners. If leaders don't learn, then the learning in the organizations they lead is not likely to flourish. Good learners take risks when they learn and try out new ways to do things better. This means that leading learners learn how to fail, learn from their mistakes, and continuously improve what they do based on their previous experiences (Sahlberg, 2018, p. xi).

HOW DOES AN ORGANIZATION LEARN?

Organizations are not people, but they are made up of people. People can learn, but merely adding up their learning would not describe organizational learning. Organizational learning occurs when a school, for example, engages in a process of changing beliefs and practices in order to resolve long-standing, deep-seated performance weaknesses or failures (Argyris & Schon, 1978). The principal in the opening vignette should probably take a good hard look at why her apparently well-run school is not showing improvement in key areas, particularly with years of support in ELA. Where should she begin and how does her own learning transfer into organizational learning?

A good place to start is examining the difference between what a school or district wants for its students and present reality. In other words, we advocate collecting information that reveals the difference between learning goals and learning outcomes. We can assume that Principal Constant never intended for achievement levels to remain flat in her school. She is a responsible, dedicated educator and devoted to her students and their families, making such an outcome unsatisfactory. Given that she has invested a great deal in ExEl, she is probably particularly motivated to investigate why her aspirations for student achievement in ELA are far out of line with outcomes from the past five years.

When a particular gap has been identified and demonstrated with evidence, the next step is to understand *why* this gap exists. As we will discuss in Chapter 6, our preferred term for discovering why is root cause analysis (Preuss, 2007) because it is important to understand what *causes* the gap in order to address it. Principal Constant has discovered that her aspirations for student achievement are not being met, but without knowing why she doesn't know what strategy to employ to reverse the trend. Her situation is even more perplexing because she believes she has been implementing a valuable program for improving students' literacy skills. Why does it seem that the program is not having the desired effect?

When root causes are known, it becomes possible to write an action plan designed to implement a solution that mitigates or eliminates the root causes, thus removing the problem. Simple, right? Well, maybe not. We know in general that change is difficult. Organizational learning helps explain a large portion of this difficulty and presents some important choices to education leaders. In the rest of the chapter, we step through the major stages of organizational learning by engaging you in some thought exercises and illustrating specific steps with the Mariposa vignette and one other that looks at a problem faced by an individual student and his family.

Organizational learning is a theoretical construct that informs problem solving. Thus, organizational learning is an important theoretical transition from looking at schools as organizations into identifying what leaders do (Chapter 5) because a central leadership behavior is solving problems so that organizational improvement will happen. Most schools have areas in which their communities expect them to perform better. We argue that organizational learning provides a conceptual roadmap for improvement because of its foci on problem identification and mitigating or eliminating the reasons why problems exist to generate meaningful and lasting changes that, in the education context, improve teaching and learning. There are many tools for engaging in organizational learning that we will touch on in this chapter. More detailed issue-specific discussion can be found in a number of sources (e.g., Argyris, 1999; Argyris & Schon, 1978; Bauer & Brazer, 2012).

As you will learn in this chapter, organizational learning has some variations, and we present a limited number. We take the position, however, that aligns with Argyris and Schon (1974, 1978): organizational learning is most meaningful when it involves making change, and when that change leads to changing the status quo, it will last and help the organization improve. This is why we believe organizational learning is so important for prospective leaders to understand because leadership itself is manifest in change and improvement. Much of what we discuss here is complementary to your thinking about transformational leadership, the topic of Chapter 6.

Essential Questions

1. Why is focusing on performance gaps or challenges important?
2. How do root causes link to the emergent problems schools need to address?
3. What is required to change the status quo?

   • What is wrong with quick fixes that keep people mollified, if not fully satisfied?

4. What are the connections between organizational learning and organizational change and improvement?

IDENTIFYING GAPS

There are numerous ways in which schools' and districts' performance gaps emerge into public view. Sometimes these revelations are out of educators' control, such as when a parent sues the school district for not providing appropriate special education services or a popular online source publishes test score results as evidence of severe deficiencies in student learning. This kind of uncontrolled gap identification creates crises of varying magnitude and generates responses that may not be entirely productive. But, such difficulties for a school or district also create opportunities for more systematic gap analysis as a starting point for organizational improvement. Wise education leaders will have identified difficulties with how students with disabilities are treated in their systems or where teachers, schools, and administrators are struggling to provide high-quality educational experiences before such issues explode as crises. The ability to be forward thinking in this manner requires an inquiry stance. Recent publications explain how superintendents in a handful of diverse school districts have employed organizational learning-type strategies to address persistent achievement gaps (Smith et al., 2011; Smith & Brazer, 2016). What often happens when schools and districts are confronted with disappointing results, however, is quite the opposite and has two extremes—defensiveness and helplessness. Our intent in this chapter is to demonstrate powerful tactics for addressing performance gaps.

Knowing Aspirations

One way to think about a challenge facing a school or district is to compare aspirations to outcomes. Argyris and Schon (1978) identified aspirations as *espoused theories*—what we say we are trying to accomplish—and behaviors as indications of *theories-in-use*—those actions we take based on experience and beliefs that generate specific *outcomes*. Organizational learning begins when a gap between aspirations and outcomes has been identified.

Thought Partner Conversation

Discovering aspirations can be difficult. Does your school have a vision or mission statement? How prominently is it displayed? Are teachers, students, and parents aware of the vision or mission? How would you describe your school's aspirations for its students?

Knowing a school or district's aspirations can be challenging because of vague explicit statements about vision, mission, or goals. Ambiguity surrounding aspirations takes over because we are challenged to answer the question, "What is the purpose of school?" As we discussed in previous chapters, there are many purposes. We expect public schools to prepare students academically for something—for the next level of school, for career, for citizenship. And we also expect schools to shape students' values (but there can be controversy there) and behavior in ways that serve academic needs. With a range of purposes and goals, vision and mission statements tend to be broad to capture multiple interests. Here is a small sample of public statements from three actual school websites exemplifying the struggle to clarify a school's mission or vision (notice how the statements become more general as the schools increase in size and complexity):

Aspirations are embedded in these reasonably typical statements, but it is difficult to know the hoped-for outcomes when you see them. For Liberty Valley Elementary School, what does "academic excellence based on the diverse needs of our study body" look like in practice? What are the high academic and social standards to which Spencer Middle School aspires? How would I know if Webster High School successfully taught my son or daughter to be a lifelong learner? Certainly goals, objectives, and core values could be employed in these schools to support their vision or mission statements, but the point here is that specific intentions may not be obvious, they are probably numerous, and different aspirations may be in conflict with one another, helping to generate the kinds of organized anarchies we explored in Chapter 3. Yet, goals, objectives, and aspirations exist. They are the reasons why adults and children walk into schools every day to teach and learn.

Mining the actual vision and mission statements presented here demonstrates how they might be used in an initial stage of organizational learning. Liberty Elementary School and Spencer Middle School both contain reference to embracing their diverse student body. Although they express valuing diversity somewhat differently, one can easily infer that these two schools want all children to feel appreciated and respected no matter what

TABLE 4.1 Vision Statements for Different Schools and Levels[1]

Liberty Valley Elementary School	Spencer Middle School	Webster High School
Our entire community of learners accepts responsibility for success. We provide a warm, safe, orderly and trusting environment. We nurture and continually pursue academic excellence based on the diverse needs of our student body. Liberty Valley Elementary is a school where learning is expected and respected. We believe that every child deserves our best.	Spencer Middle School is an inclusive community of students, families, and educators engaged in achieving high academic and social standards with respect for diversity in a positive school climate.	The mission of Webster High School is to prepare students to become lifelong learners and contributing citizens.

1. Pseudonyms are used to disguise school identities.

their background or learning needs—that is an aspiration. How would we know the degree to which that aspiration is being achieved? We would need to collect data to know if a gap between aspirations and outcomes exists and, if it does, the nature of the gap.

Thought Partner Conversation

Locate your school's or work organization's mission and/or vision statement, and explore what aspirations these statements suggest. Are these aspirations shared by stakeholders? How do you gauge how well the organization is living up to these aspirations?

When schools aspire to use student diversity to advantage, we can safely assume that they want to create harmonious communities in which students with varying identities survive and thrive. Community building might help to make students happy and help motivate them to go to school. But the most important outcome is what students gain from attending school. Though certainly an imperfect measure, test scores of varying types indicate student success. Other indicators of school benefits could also be participation in special programs ranging from gifted education to instrumental music instruction. For Liberty and Spencer, the most important data to collect will likely be achievement and participation cross-tabulated with dimensions of diversity most important to them. Race is a common example. Central questions to kick off such an analysis would be: (1) Do students achieve at the various levels (often basic, proficient, and advanced) in proportion to their representation in the school? and (2) Do students of varying racial identities participate in school programs and activities in proportion to their representation in the student body?

DEFICITS VERSUS GAPS

The table below uses a few examples to differentiate between deficit thinking and gap analysis. Embedded in each statement is a challenge differently stated. Deficit statements tend to be personalized; gap statements invite further investigation.

Deficit Statement	Gap Statement
Students don't have the skills and knowledge needed for chemistry.	Student performance in chemistry falls below the standard for proficiency.
"Those parents" are not interested in their children's education.	An identifiable group of parents is not attending our parent education opportunities.
Teachers don't know how to differentiate instruction properly.	Our professional development to date does not appear to yield appropriate instructional differentiation.

The deficit statements seem to lead to a shoulder shrug and moving on in the same patterns. The gap statements target areas for organizational improvement.

Webster High School's statement is more general and therefore not as helpful for purposes of organizational learning. "Contributing citizens" is a particularly difficult concept to work with, but "lifelong learners" has promise. We would need to identify the characteristics of people who engage in lifelong learning to provide a working definition, then we could collect data to determine if those particular attributes were being fostered in the school and how. The degree to which data demonstrate that Webster is not able to instill lifelong learning behaviors in its students would help us to understand the gap between aspirations and outcomes.

> ### Thought Partner Conversation
>
> Above, we focus on mission and vision as statements of aspirations. What are some other sources of aspirations—how else might we know what your school or organization is committed to attaining? Talk a bit about what these are, and how you communicate them (and to whom).

We pause at this point to clarify two important ideas. First is the notion of gap analysis. Our position is that for a school or a district to improve, the difference between aspirations or goals and outcomes must be understood in order to engage in improvement work. This seems simple, but we find resistance to the idea of working on *problems*, as noted in the Preface, because doing so seems to be a negative activity. Problem identification has gotten something of a bad name as "deficit mindset." Yes, we're examining deficits, but with the *positive* intent of remedying them. Thus, identifying problems, challenges, or gaps presents opportunities for schools to improve and to do so from a foundation of their unique strengths. All change springs from recognition of a gap between the real and ideal—between where we aspire to be and where we actually are (Bauer & Brazer, 2012). To avoid examining gaps would create what Argyris and Schon (1978) called an *inhibitory loop* that obstructs organizational learning. It is difficult to remedy what is not examined, as we shall see in further discussion focused on organizational learning theory.

The second clarification is what we mean with respect to data. The most common conception of data is numbers, which are in fact an important kind of data. But we also value qualitative data. Data is defined as a group or body of facts or information, some of which might be statistics, but information may also be non-statistical (Random House, 1968). Quantitative data would be the number of days a particular student is absent. This tells you *what* happened. The reasons *why* absences happened would be qualitative data that include illness, family vacation, and "cutting class." In this book, we often use the term *evidence* to cover both quantitative and qualitative data, and we don't favor one over the other. Both are important for explaining phenomena such as the extent to which all students with diverse learning needs get the nurturing, support, and instruction they require to succeed in their elementary school.

A Gap in Special Education Services

Mitchell has a math disability and Attention Deficit Disorder. He has experienced substantial difficulty in his 8th grade pre-algebra class. His performance on homework, when he turns it in, is generally strong and so are his results on short quizzes. He has much greater difficulty with unit tests and end-of-semester exams, exercises in frustration for him. The consequence is that Mitchell cannot seem to achieve at a level higher than D+ or C–. Mitchell is a friendly young man who generally likes school and his teachers. He tends to be passive and avoid conflict. His IEP stipulates that he should be provided a setting in which he can take math assessments with unlimited time and minimal distractions.

Mitchell's mother's anger boiled over in early December after months of frustration with his math teacher who was not providing required accommodations. She had numerous meetings with the math teacher, with Mitchell's special education case manager, and with the AP in charge of special education. Everyone was always understanding and accommodating in meetings, but nothing changed. Two things kept happening over and over: Mitchell never took much more than the normally allotted time to complete his assessments and the teacher never provided a separate setting where he would be free from distractions. When confronted, the math teacher's and case manager's responses were that no one could force Mitchell to sit with his assessments longer than he wanted. The teacher also stated that there wasn't any place other than her classroom for him to take quizzes and tests. She was unwilling to meet him at lunch or after school to extend his time for assessments because doing so would be a violation of her duty hours in the collective bargaining agreement.

The Individual Default

It is easy to default to problem-solving tactics that come more naturally to most of us—thinking about a vignette like Mitchell's from the individual point of view. The problem is, it can be challenging to understand what others are thinking, particularly if we do not work with them frequently. We are willing to bet that you and your classmates might imagine the following perspectives:

MITCHELL: I'm no good at math and I hate it. I might have to go to summer school if my grades aren't good enough to get into Algebra I in high school.

MITCHELL'S MOTHER: I agreed to have Mitchell enrolled in special education after he was tested because I wanted the school to help him get better in math and perform better generally. This is a waste of time because his grades are as weak as ever and he is getting frustrated.

MITCHELL'S TEACHER: I can't make the kid sit there longer than he wants. The IEP makes no sense. How can you ask a student with ADD to sit longer for a test than students who don't have ADD? Someone wrote it up so that it's my responsibility to provide a quiet location, but my colleagues don't want him in the math office and I don't see why I should have to give up my off-duty time to accommodate one student.

MITCHELL'S SPECIAL EDUCATION CASE MANAGER: I don't understand why the math teacher refuses to follow Mitchell's IEP. The AP doesn't back me up on enforcing the terms of IEPs, so we often don't include accommodations that kids need but teachers won't follow.

THE ASSISTANT PRINCIPAL: Special education isn't working for Mitchell. We always struggle with this particular math teacher and the case manager always collapses in the face of teacher resistance. By the time I get involved everyone is angry and frozen into positions. The best I can hope for is to mollify the parent and pray for better student success.

Analyzing the situation from individual perspectives is important for the AP who has the most responsibility and authority to try to resolve Mitchell's situation before his angry mother complains to someone at the central office and hires a lawyer. He likely feels stuck because he has little power to compel adherence to the IEP. He can browbeat the math teacher, but he can't fire her or dock her pay. Would that help the teacher's relationship with Mitchell anyway? The AP has the following choices within his grasp:

- Move Mitchell in the second semester to a math teacher more willing to provide accommodations he needs.
- Work with the case manager to provide effective out-of-class assistance with math and provide the quiet space he needs to take his quizzes and tests.
- Seek input from Mitchell's mother so she feels part of the process and commits to the ultimate set of solutions.
- Hope that things get better if one or more of the above actions is taken.

Our imagined AP's thinking is an example of what is known in organizational learning as a Model I approach that yields *single-loop learning* (Argyris & Schon, 1974, 1978). In practice, this means accepting the status quo—all of the individuals continuing their current behaviors driven by their perspectives—and working from there to make life better for Mitchell in math class. Doing so, the AP appeases everyone in the situation so they will stop complaining and he can move on to the next urgent matter. Learning extends only as far as solving the immediate problem. This kind of Model I behavior is premised on defining goals and working to achieve them, winning instead of losing, minimizing conflict, and remaining rational (Argyris & Schon, 1974, 1978). These traits don't seem all bad and they have the effect of making some people happy, at least in the short run. Model I behavior sows the seeds of more and deeper problems down the road, however.

Think about this: If Mitchell is moved to a different math section, then the math teacher has learned that resistance to what appear to be unreasonable demands on behalf of passive students relieves her of an immediate problem, the case manager learns that the AP will ward off potential teacher-teacher conflict, and the parent learns that if she leans on the administration, they will do something potentially helpful in response. The receiving teacher may learn that success with special education students will result in more special education students in his classes. Take a minute or two to think about how things will go when in the next 6 to 12 months, if not sooner, the situation repeats itself with Mitchell or with another student.

Standing at the Crossroads

Thought Partner Conversation

A wise high school principal used to talk about what he "taught" parents, teachers, and students by his actions. Talk with a partner about unintended lessons you have witnessed from well-intended administrators' choices.

The principal in the first vignette and the AP in the second stand at a crossroads where their next move has major implications for their professional futures. Each has two essential choices: (1) accept how the school (and possibly the district) functions and "fix" the situation by appeasing some people, blaming a few, avoiding others, and shifting responsibility in hopes that students will be served, or (2) investigate ways in which individuals interact with their schools as systems to discover why these problems have emerged. The consequences of the first strategy can be severe and long lasting, though not immediately apparent. For example, the principal could blame teachers for not implementing the ExEl curriculum properly and evaluate them negatively to get their attention and hope they improve. Such a move may result in short-term improvement in ELA instruction but may also lead to long-term resentment and teacher attrition if the principal has overlooked teachers' sincere efforts and alternative causes of the problem. The AP, by stepping in to make unilateral decisions about how to address Mitchell's learning needs, becomes the owner of a problem that originated in the teacher's classroom when she neglected to implement the IEP as intended. The only behavior that is likely to change is his own.

DOUBLE-LOOP LEARNING TERMS

Translating theory to practice can be a challenge. The table below lists key terms used by Argyris and Schon (1978) alongside our working definitions that will help you use double-loop learning as a tool.

Double-Loop Term	Definition
Espoused theory	What organization members say they want to accomplish, often articulated in vision or mission statements. We are calling these *aspirations*.
Theory in use	The actions we actually take, which may or may not be consistent with the espoused theory. We are calling these *outcomes*. Outcomes are expressed in terms of quantitative and qualitative evidence.
Undiscussables	The issues we do not talk about, often including the misalignment between aspirations and outcomes.
Governing variables	Rules or operating procedures that maintain the status quo.

THINKING ORGANIZATIONALLY

Model I behaviors lead to learning, but not necessarily the kind we might be seeking. There are organizational dynamics at play in the vignette about stagnating achievement that led off the chapter and in Mitchell's case. We begin this section by considering the vignette about Mitchell to shift thinking about the individual actions people will take to thinking more organizationally. Argyris and Schon's Model II recognizes social dynamics in a manner that creates the potential for *double-loop learning*. Exercises 4.2 and 4.3 are intended to show you what this looks like in practice.

It is common for people to focus their problem solving on fixing people. For example, it is easy to see how Mitchell's math teacher is being difficult from the perspective of his mother. But, the math teacher works in an organization we call Mitchell's school and she is therefore subject to systemic influences on her behavior. Exercise 4.2 is intended to shift your attention away from individuals and toward the organization, and it begins with a search for evidence that reveals how the system or organization influences the people within it to take actions that appear to violate goals or objectives.

Organizational Learning Entry Points

Figure 4.1 is a graphical representation of organizational leaning. Aspirations for students are not aligned with how we actually work with students—i.e., outcomes are not meeting aspirations. The existence of this misalignment is shrouded in *undiscus-*

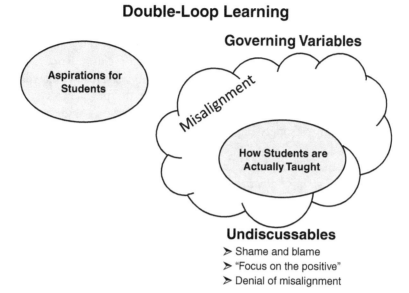

FIGURE 4.1 Organizational Learning in Schools

sables, examples of which we list on the figure. As the name suggests, an undiscussable is something that people do not talk about, such as an inability or unwillingness to differentiate instruction. Undiscussables are important because they often hide root causes for the existence of a gap. Opening them up for discussion may make some in a school upset because they protect the status quo (see, for example, Smith & Brazer, 2016). In the case of organizational learning, the status quo is represented by *governing variables*—the written and unwritten rules that everyone follows and that maintain the gap. Double-loop learning involves clearing away the cloud of undiscussables with forthright presentation of quantitative and qualitative evidence of the gap between aspirations and outcomes so that changing governing variables becomes possible. Changing the status quo with respect to instruction improves school performance in important and lasting ways. We demonstrate how this works through our use of vignettes and in the exercises at the end of this chapter.

Exercise 4.2 asks you first to explain a gap between aspirations and outcomes. Note that we are seeking evidence, not who was to blame. Evidence could come in the form of test scores, sample student work, teacher assignments, informal discussions, or observations. Thus, the problem is de-personalized to some extent and you begin to look elsewhere other than that this teacher or that teacher is not doing his or her job. Providing evidence of the gap may separate people from the problem in a manner that opens up inquiry, which is what you want if you are to resolve the larger problems (Fisher, Ury, & Patton, 2011). Most important, evidence moves the discussion from myth, rumor, and opinion into the arena of proof or disconfirmation, thereby laying important groundwork for agreement. The gap between aspirations and outcomes must be clearly described and supported by evidence to initiate organizational learning and move away from Model I behaviors and thinking. If no one is blamed at this point, then no one gets hurt.

Question 2 in Exercise 4.2 takes you into the realm of root causes (Bauer & Brazer, 2012; Preuss, 2007)—the reasons why the problem or gap exists. Root cause analysis is not part of the organizational learning framework, but is closely related. When we discover *why* problems occur, we will often find that the problem or gap was neglected for reasons that Argyris and Schon (1978) identify as undiscussables. Each vignette has one or more strongly implied undiscussables, bringing us to question 3 in Exercise 4.2.

There is evidence that the math teacher is pursuing personal goals that are at best not helpful to and at worst in conflict with Mitchell's learning goals. The math teacher makes a reasonable case that she shouldn't be required to anger her colleagues or violate the collective bargaining agreement, but at the same time she is not offering solutions. She appears instead to be striving to maintain control over her workday, to the possible detriment of Mitchell's capacity to learn and demonstrate what he has learned on assessments. What's more, while she may be aware that the IEP could not be followed under current circumstances, she did not raise this as an issue requiring attention—IEPs can and are often changed to accommodate the needs of both the teacher and the learner. This potential cause for the gap might be addressed by the AP but he did not do so in the vignette. (Did you address it in Exercise 4.1?) Most likely, no one would question the math teacher's integrity or motives in the name of treating teachers as professionals, making a potentially important root cause of Mitchell's struggle undiscussable in organizational learning terms (Argyris & Schon, 1974, 1978).

How is it possible that the ExEl program could be in place for 7 years yet not make a difference in student achievement? At least two potential explanations exist: (1) the ExEl program is ineffective; or (2) the ExEl program is not properly implemented. The second possibility most closely mirrors what happened in the real elementary school upon which the vignette is based. What our student learned in this case is that no one talked about the fact that teachers, for many reasons, were not actually implementing important features of the ExEl program. Instead, they showed the principal and others some ExEl strategies while they were in the classroom, but ignored ExEl when they were alone with students. Most important, no one talked about the fact that these teacher behaviors were occurring and everyone behaved as though the program was implemented as intended. The achievement data demonstrated otherwise, but this too was ignored until a crisis occurred and the program was under threat of being eliminated. Silence about ExEl's realities is a classic case of an undiscussable. No one talking about the fact that no one acknowledged poor implementation made the undiscussable self-sealing; i.e., impossible to discuss (Argyris & Schon, 1978).

Question 4 in Exercise 4.2 asks you to assess an attempt the principal at Mitchell's school might make to open up undiscussables. Most of us might be reluctant to try this approach because we want to avoid conflict. It is embarrassing to acknowledge neglect or malfeasance with respect to an important learning problem. Defensive strategies kick in whenever undiscussables are approached because they protect individual interests, such as the math teacher's apparent need to control how she spends her time at the expense of individual student needs.

The glue that binds schools and districts to an inability to address performance gaps and the undiscussables that insulate them is governing variables, the written and unwritten rules and norms that control behavior (Argyris & Schon, 1978). The elementary teachers expected to implement ExEl operated on the unwritten norm that they needed to show the principal and visitors to the school ExEl when those adults entered their classrooms. Another important norm, however, was that other teaching and learning strategies were more important or fit better with teachers' skill sets (inadequate ExEl professional development was a contributing factor) and therefore crowded out ExEl in classroom teaching when there was no apparent need to pay attention to this specialized literacy program.

When you went through Exercise 4.2 you were guided to address organizational questions rather than blame individuals. To solve problems requires those involved to adopt and maintain an inquiry stance about both individual and organizational features of a challenge or gap. This is easier to do when shame and blame are not part of the discussion.

Redefining the Problem and its Root Causes

How does Principal Constant know that ExEl can actually deliver on its promises? We have no way of answering this question from the vignette, but it is often true that districts buy programs for their schools expecting implementation without having solid proof that the program is effective in their context. One reason for this is that leaders are pressured by time constraints and tradition to have answers—solutions— even before they fully understand the problem. Solutions sometimes precede full awareness of the problem, making commitment on the part of implementers problematic at best. The outcome of disappointing achievement in ELA could be a systemic problem rooted in a poorly conceived curriculum, rather than the fault of incompetent or recalcitrant individual teachers. We should note, however, that ExEl published results of improved ELA outcomes in other schools.

In the actual case, teachers were reluctant to implement because they didn't *know how* to implement ExEl appropriately, and this was complicated by the fact that in their ignorance they thought they did know how to use the program. They chose not to implement completely because they didn't believe the program was effective, despite published results, and they did not want to waste precious instructional time. Investigation by our student revealed evidence that ExEl professional development had only been partially completed over the years and the follow-on support the non-profit expected from the school never materialized. Hence, teachers' false beliefs that they fully understood ExEl and its capabilities led them to put on a show for the principal and others but never really implement the program as intended. There is a strong argument to be made that the principal got the outcomes she deserved because the teachers were inadequately supported in their efforts to use the program she advocated. Recall our discussions in Chapter 1 and Herzberg's admonition that individuals are unlikely to be motivated if they do not need to feel skilled and/or they do not have the opportunity to enact these skills. Thus two alternative root causes of flat-lined ELA performance emerge: (1) teachers were not adequately prepared to implement ExEl, and (2) teachers made choices about how to use class time based on their belief that ExEl was ineffective, despite evidence to the contrary in other schools. The only way the principal might have understood the effect of these root causes is if she engaged in learning about and finding evidence for their existence and importance.

The factor that cemented the ExEl problem in place for so long was the fact that it was undiscussable until our student's master's program project revealed to the principal what she discovered from observations and interviews (evidence). Teachers did not openly discuss their dissatisfaction with ExEl because they knew it was important to the principal that the school function as a demonstration site. The principal made her reputation on the basis of connecting with her community and did not talk about disappointing achievement results. To have admitted these and numerous other truths would have resulted in admitting to ineffectiveness or even malfeasance of one sort or another, which is very difficult to do. Thus, everyone behaved as though ExEl was a program that made a difference and no one talked about the fact that no one mentioned what was really going on in classrooms and with student achievement. The undiscussables were self-sealing.

If the AP working with Mitchell and his mother wanted to solve the larger issue of proper implementation of IEP's, he would need to move out of single-loop learning by addressing root cause issues similar to the ExEl vignette. These begin with "why?" questions and the search for evidence that supports answers. Why isn't Mitchell progressing even after he qualified for special education services? Why is it so hard for the math teacher to differentiate instruction so that the math curriculum is accessible to Mitchell and students like him? Why is the math teacher so reluctant to provide extra time for assessments? Why does the case manager have such a hard time getting other teachers to cooperate? Why does the AP allow IEP requirements to be ignored? By asking these kinds of questions, it is possible to uncover root causes of a deeper problem of which Mitchell's plight is merely a symptom. In summary, what evidence can be found that special education services may be inadequate for students with disabilities?

Answers to the why questions are likely to be both individual and systemic. Here are some possibilities:

1. Students may engage in negative learning behaviors that are motivated by affective factors not addressed in the IEP or the classroom.
2. High school teachers face 150 or more students a day or throughout the week and are therefore challenged to keep track of the specifics of 10–25 special education IEP's depending on how many special education students they have in their classes.
3. Mitchell's teacher may not *know how* to differentiate for Mitchell's needs. There may be no one at school who does, or no opportunity to share that information with the teacher in a meaningful way.
4. Case managers are colleagues, not supervisors, putting them in the position of having responsibility for their students' goal achievement without authority to enforce the terms of an IEP.

5. The administration trusts only a handful of content teachers across the spectrum of the high school to teach students with disabilities effectively. They hand-schedule special education students into these teachers' sections, sometimes overwhelming them and isolating the rest of the faculty from understanding these students' needs. Teaching effectiveness suffers in the classrooms of overwhelmed teachers and ineffectiveness is revealed when students with disabilities show up in other teachers' classrooms.

6. The AP has too many responsibilities and emergencies to monitor IEP implementation adequately.

What would you do about root causes such as these? Work your way through Exercise 4.3 to find out.

Identifying Key Governing Variables

Recall that governing variables are the written and unwritten rules organizations follow to complete their work (Argyris & Schon, 1978). They are the mechanisms by which the status quo is maintained. Consequently, changing governing variables is critical to changing and improving organizational performance. In the Mariposa Elementary School case, there are two central governing variables that bear further discussion: (1) the principal's need to promote Mariposa as a demonstration site for ExEl, and (2) adoption of multiple simultaneous initiatives that leaves insufficient time and resources for building teacher capacity to employ ExEl techniques. These are interrelated, but we will address them one at a time for clarity purposes.

The principal staked her reputation as an instructional leader on adopting ExEl, which had a strong research base demonstrating its effectiveness. It was important to her own professional story of turning Mariposa around from a school that families avoided to one that they embraced. In addition to the community support and appreciation of the school she successfully engendered, she sought academic legitimacy by adopting and showcasing the school's use of ExEl. It was the showcasing procedure that was the greatest contributing factor to teachers' reluctance to speak up about their inability or unwillingness to implement ExEl completely despite the fact that they were not receiving adequate professional development. The inappropriateness of setting up Mariposa as an exemplary ExEl site was undiscussable because doing so was of great importance to both the principal and the sponsoring non-profit who were building their reputations based on ExEl implementation. A result of inability or unwillingness to acknowledge that Mariposa's outcomes were not meeting aspirations is that systematic assessment—i.e., data collection and analysis—of ExEl's implementation was missing. A crisis hit when the long-term, flat-lined student achievement data could no longer be ignored.

Mariposa's principal also engaged in a number of initiatives that our student perceived as causing innovation fatigue. The district in which Mariposa is located serves a large low-income population and is therefore under-resourced. This affects Mariposa such that supporting numerous initiatives to the extent required to achieve full implementation is not possible. The unwritten rule affecting ExEl became something such as, "We don't have time for all that professional development and we cannot pay for teacher substitutes, so we will provide as much time as we can and rely on the non-profit to give teachers the materials they need." This was a compromise that didn't work, but it wasn't recognized as such at least until the crisis was upon the principal when the non-profit said they would pull out.

For Mariposa to improve student performance in ELA, these and probably other governing variables would need to change. The principal could try to renegotiate her agreement with the non-profit to release the constraints of existing governing variables. At least initially she would have to concede that Mariposa should not be a demonstration site because they needed to regroup to get on track with ExEl. To address the second governing variable of too many initiatives, the principal could decide to focus on ExEl exclusively until she, the teachers, and the non-profit could agree that it was fully implemented as intended. There is, of course, another alternative. Mariposa's principal could address the governing variable that keeps ExEl at her school by deciding that, despite other evidence, this program simply does not work for her teachers and students. This kind of thinking could lead her to end participation in ExEl and focus on other, more promising initiatives.

ORGANIZATIONAL LEARNING AS A LEADERSHIP STRATEGY

Up to this point, we have relied primarily on Argyris and Schon's classic work in organizational learning to explain what it is and how it works. In the interest of building your portfolio of leadership strategies, we want to inform you about other strands within this field and explain how they align with and where they diverge from Argyris and Schon.

Routines as Learning Mechanisms

Levitt and March (1988) wrote about organizational learning from a perspective very different from Argyris and Schon. They examined *organizational routines* as depersonalized mechanisms for teaching people how to behave within organizations. Routines that appear to work are preserved and those that appear to fail are modified or discarded. Their argument is grounded in two premises important to our understanding of organizational learning: (1) human behavior is routine in nature and (2) behavior is governed not by a logic of consequences but by a logic of appropriateness. We address each of these premises, describe more recent conceptual modifications, explain what they look like in practice, and demonstrate how they relate to the Argyris and Schon model of organizational learning.

Human behavior is routine. March and Simon (1993) and Simon (1993) wrote for large portions of their careers about humans' need to routinize behavior to address limited capacity to choose the best option and to make decisions more generally. Routines simplify and accelerate decision-making processes, helping people to work more efficiently. The relationship to organizational learning is that routines capture organizational beliefs about how to accomplish goals and objectives and serve as communication avenues for how work is to be done. Teachers, for example, learn that they should use attention-getting mechanisms such as, "Clap once if you can hear my voice." An added benefit is that routines sustain desirable organizational behavior because they supersede individuals. Thus, the organization survives intact even when important people leave, and newcomers are more easily socialized into the appropriate ways to conduct themselves in our school.

Routines can change, Levitt and March (1988) claim, when there is a rich pool of alternative routines and when there is willingness within the organization to search for alternatives. An education example is middle school science. Routines are captured in the curriculum and accepted strategies for teaching it. Using eighth grade physical science as an example, it would be possible to have a predominantly conceptual curriculum intended to prepare students for high school physics that is taught in lecture format with support from a textbook. Suppose that the science faculty discuss the excruciating boredom students experience over 180 days of school and their desire to have their students more actively engaged in a subject the teachers enjoy. There are many curricula and teaching strategies available to these teachers that would change their classes into laboratories that could allow for deeper inquiry through problem-based learning or other strategies. The search for new routines would be spurred by motivation to improve the experiences of teachers and students in physical science classrooms.

Those with experience in schools might be thinking that our description of middle school science teachers doesn't consider constraints that state standards and district requirements impose on teachers. And it doesn't consider that teachers may be complacent or in denial about students' reactions to their curriculum and instruction. Levitt and March (1988) accounted for these factors by noting that routines are sustained when the motivation for search is low, either from satisfaction with the status quo or a lack of alternatives. From Levitt and March's perspective routines that are sustained support the status quo and new ones have the potential to change the status quo. Routines both embody past learning and contain potential for future learning. Organizations preserve learning in the form of routines in the following way:

> The experiential lessons of history are captured by routines in a way that makes the lessons, but not the history, accessible to organizations and organizational members who have not themselves experienced the history. Routines are transmitted through socialization, education, imitation, professionalization, [and] personnel movement. … They are recorded in a collective memory that is often coherent but is sometimes jumbled, that often endures but is sometimes lost. They change as a result of experience within a community of other learning organizations. These changes depend on interpretations of history …
>
> (Levitt & March, 1988, p. 320)

They perceived future learning as fraught with problems, but not necessarily worse than non-learning.

> [L]essons of history as encoded in routines are an important basis for the intelligence of organizations.… If we calibrate the imperfections of learning by the

imperfections of its competitors, it is possible to see a role for routine-based, history-dependent, target-oriented organizational learning. To be effective, however, the design of learning organizations must recognize the difficulties of the process and in particular the extent to which intelligence in learning is often frustrated, and the extent to which the comprehension of history may involve slow rather than fast adaptation, imprecise rather than precise responses to experience, and abrupt rather than incremental changes.

(Levitt & March, 1988, p. 336)

The de-personalized nature of seeing organizational learning through the lens of routines, at least as presented by Levitt and March, might lead to a conclusion that there is little role for leadership in organizational learning. But initiative is required for the search for alternative routines, as are resources such as information, training, and opportunities to learn. What might start such a search connects back to our discussion of recognizing gaps between the real and ideal, i.e., identifying underperformance in relation to aspirations. Levitt and March (1988) recognize that organizational weakness or failure might not be readily perceived, thus preserving the status quo, however leaders engaged in critical examination of performance vis-à-vis aspirations may well initiate action. Similar to Argyris and Schon, Levitt and March argue that organizational learning takes place when adaptive change occurs, but routines in and of themselves may or may not lead to organizational learning. At least three important outcomes seem possible: (1) nothing is changed and nothing is learned, (2) a gap is identified and routines are slightly modified to address the gap—Model I learning in Argyris and Schon's (1978) terms, or (3) fundamental routines change so that change governing variables (again from Argyris and Schon) and the status quo change. Levitt and March conceptualize an important reason for the persistence of undiscussables (though they do not use that term) that inhibit organizational learning as they address individual motivation.

Logic of consequences versus logic of appropriateness. The term *logic of consequence* suggests that decisions are made based on criteria related to optimizing outcomes. A logic of consequences leads to individuals pursuing the best outcome—often described as "value maximizing"—as they go about their work. Teachers, for example, will teach in the most effective ways possible in order to maximize student learning. Admirable and rational though it may seem to behave in a manner consistent with a logic of consequences, doing so is not easy, may not be possible, or may not even be desirable. A central problem, particularly in education, is that the value we strive to maximize is not always clear and the means to achieving it may be unknown or out of reach. Think about the difficulty of defining and putting into practice concepts such as an "inclusive community" or "lifelong learners" from the vision statements presented earlier in this chapter. Even in the simpler case of teaching physical properties, knowing the value maximizing way of doing so is made difficult by the fact that teachers have varying capacities to teach students with a range of needs across multiple contexts—weaknesses in our understanding of the technical core of schooling discussed in Chapter 3.

When uncertain how to value maximize, individuals will turn to behaving in a manner acceptable to the organization within a *logic of appropriateness*, meaning that decisions will be made using criteria associated with whether the decision is appropriate in the context and under the circumstances. For a physical science teacher this might look like meeting all classes on time every day with a written lesson plan that he or she is able to follow in a reasonably well-controlled classroom. Anyone would recognize these as the behaviors of a competent teacher, but none of them are wholly predictive of student learning because what matters most is how the teacher interacts with students, what is taught, and how it is taught. This activity internal to the classroom may be value maximizing, but it isn't necessarily so. Why not?

As we discussed in Chapter 2, legitimacy—both for the individual and for the organization—governs appropriateness. Teachers seek legitimacy, recognition that what they are doing is at least acceptable if not exceptional, by teaching content in a manner that their school and district directs. If they deviate from the curriculum or teach with outlandish strategies not recognized as "best practice," they risk losing legitimacy, which for probationary teachers may result in being let go at the end of the year. Fundamental concerns about keeping a job and being rewarded for good practice motivate pursuit of individual legitimacy. The school and district do the same on an organizational level, never wishing to stray too far from common conceptions of what schools and districts should be doing and what they should look like. DiMaggio and Powell (1983) explained these tendencies to maintain a status quo and the reasons why organizations of a similar type (e.g., all schools and districts) look so similar. The search for legitimacy, they said, resulted in organizational isomorphism.

An important connection to Argyris and Schon at this point is the observation that pursuit of logics of appropriateness probably will not move the organization toward improvement precisely because they do not lead to value maximization. It is easier not to talk about such non-rational behavior than it is to open up the undiscussable of doing the same thing poorly year after year despite disappointing outcomes simply because the behavior is what is expected. A good example would be the pursuit of higher test scores through drill-and-kill methods focused on test preparation. Such a method is usually discussed in terms of focusing on standards in a rigorous manner designed to prepare students for college despite the fact that proficiency at performing the same operation repeatedly is not highly valued in most higher education settings. Furthermore, K–12 standards are not well aligned with college expectations (Venezia, Kirst, & Antonio, 2003), but who talks about that?

Flexible routines. Feldman and Pentland (2003) and Spillane (2012) have taken a less mechanistic approach to routine enactment compared to Levitt and March and reintroduced greater volition for individuals. Using non-educational and educational settings, these authors found that individuals first understand routines as they believe they were intended. That is, a principal might think, "The district will send me a monthly budget report and require me to report back and certify that I am not over-spending any of my accounts." This is the *ostensive* or articulated routine (Feldman & Pentland, 2003). The principal recognizes the importance of budget control and budget monitoring and does her best to follow this routine. She quickly discovers, however, that district information is usually 3 months out of date and in a form that is very difficult to decipher. She therefore decides to put her secretary to work creating a school-based system to keep track of departmental spending in real time. Her *performative* routine (Feldman & Pentland, 2003)—the modified routine she actually follows—allows her to meet district expectations for ensuring proper budget management, actually improving upon the ostensive routine and giving the district office the information it requires. It is interesting to note that what we have just described is Model I behavior that mitigates the immediate problem but does not address systemic inadequacies in budget recordkeeping and reporting.

Routines for Stasis and for Change

The type of bending or flexing of routines described here shows the potential for organizational learning through the use of routines. This chapter's vignettes demonstrate how routines can either prevent or support organizational learning.

Principal Constant at Mariposa Elementary School required routines in support of ExEl. Her teachers modified or ignored these ostensive routines and performed some of them only when others were observing. Thus the teachers' routines were in opposition to what the principal intended, but teachers maintained legitimacy in the eyes of the principal by signaling their implementation of ExEl at the appropriate moments. This behavior resulted in a sustained period of stasis when all appeared to be well until the non-profit announced its intention to remove ExEl support from Mariposa. The situation as it exists, however, is filled with potential for new routines.

Mitchell's middle school AP in charge of special education faces a daily diet of poorly implemented IEPs and unhappy students, parents, and teachers. The vignette seems to indicate that ostensive routines are either ignored or changed so much in practice that IEPs lose their meaning and special education services are weakened by what occurs in content classrooms. Frustrated though everyone appears to be, the performative aspects of existing routines align to sustain the undesirable status quo. The teacher is the linchpin and she demonstrates no motivation to search for more effective routines. The case manager and the AP seem likely to want to make change but have not yet voiced creative means for doing so.

Fostering a Learning Organization

The concept of a learning organization was popularized by Senge from the 1990s and into the current era (e.g., Senge, 1990/2006; Senge et al., 2012). Research focused on the idea is contained in an edited volume intended to explain the characteristics of schools and districts characterized by fertile learning environments (Leithwood & Louis, 1998). Following our lengthy discussion of organizational learning, one may wonder how it differs from the concept of a learning organization. Do learning organizations achieve organizational learning? With apologies for the repetitive use of terms arranged in different orders, we conclude that fostering adult learning within schools and districts is a necessary but not a sufficient condition for achieving organizational learning.

Although Senge borrowed heavily from Argyris and Schon, he and his co-authors de-emphasized markers of organizational learning such as changed governing variables or adoption of new routines at the organizational level when they intended to demonstrate to schools how to become learning organizations (Senge et al., 2012).

Leithwood and Louis (1998) stake out a position as editors that is much closer to Argyris and Schon (1978), Levitt and March (1998), Feldman and Pentland (2003), and Spillane (2012) in that they write in terms of learning within schools driving systemic change. Their contributors, in contrast, vary from the systemic change connection, as does Senge et al., by focusing on evidence of teacher learning (e.g., Ben-Peretz & Schonmann, 1998; Louis & Kruse, 1998). Our own research has demonstrated that teacher learning alone rarely drives whole-school changes; i.e., changes in governing variables (Van Lare, Brazer, Bauer, & Smith, 2013). It is up to leadership to translate teacher learning into systemic changes and improvements at the school and district levels.

CONCLUSION

Argyris and Schon (1978, p. 147) emphasized that they had great difficulty identifying cases in which organizational learning was occurring as they envisioned it.

> As mentioned at the outset, we have not been able to find in our experience or to draw from the literature descriptions of [Model II] learning systems with the degree of concreteness that was possible for Model [I]. Nor can we depend on the reader to fill in our gaps with his or her own knowledge because we predict that few, if any, readers have observed organizations that double-loop learn.

We are thus in the delicate position of advocating leadership behavior in support of organizational learning when we are unable to provide numerous exemplars to guide aspiring leaders. We hope to inspire you to show others the way toward organizational learning by applying the concepts presented in this chapter. In the meantime, there are glimpses of organizational learning in action that have been published (Brazer, Rich, & Ross, 2010; Smith & Brazer, 2016) and our consulting work is generating cases that may look like organizational learning when they come to fruition. For now, we ask that you keep organizational learning in mind as you read about additional perspectives on leadership in the chapters that follow.

EXERCISE 4.1 WHAT'S WRONG? PART I

Think about the vignette with Mitchell, the student with a math disability. Use your experience to diagnose a gap between aspirations and outcomes on a *personal* level by briefly answering the question, "What's wrong?" from the following five perspectives:

Mitchell the student:
Mitchell's mother:
Mitchell's math teacher:
Mitchell's special education case manager:
The AP:

Share your answers with one or more classmates and discuss the ways in which your answers are in agreement and where you differ. Pay particular attention to the differences between the people named above and between you and your classmates because people have a hard time solving problems when they don't agree on what the problem is.

EXERCISE 4.2 WHAT'S WRONG? PART II

Assume that Mitchell's school aspires to have students with disabilities achieve at a level comparable to the majority population. In other words, they are trying to narrow the achievement gap for special education students. First individually, then with one or more partners, answer the following questions based on Mitchell's situation.

1. What evidence do you have (or could you gather) that a particular goal or aspiration is not being met?
2. Knowing what you do special education, what would you predict are the reasons why Mitchell's school is not yet meeting their achievement gap aspirations? What evidence might support your predictions?
3. How would you characterize communication that has likely taken place regarding the performance gap Mitchell seems to represent?
4. Put yourself in the shoes of the principal of Mitchell's school and explain why you might or might not want to say one of the following:

   - To the middle school IEP team: "The IEP must be written such that it serves the educational best interests of the student. Once that has been accomplished, it is the responsibility of all involved—classroom teacher, case manager, student, parent, and administration—to ensure that the spirit of the IEP is being met. This is clearly not happening in Mitchell's case. If this is how we serve all of our students with disabilities, we will never succeed in narrowing or closing the achievement gap they experience."

After you have articulated your own answers, share with your partners. Discuss and possibly resolve any inconsistencies that surface.

EXERCISE 4.3 GOING TO THE ROOT OF THE PROBLEM

Use Worksheet D to map out your thinking about the six potential root causes listed above. Fill in the cells alone or with a partner. Discuss disagreements and blanks. Can you come to agreement on an approach to address each root cause? Would you choose *not* to address one or more of the root causes? Why?

Working through Worksheet D, you may have noticed that root causes can be intertwined. Root causes 2 and 5 are mutually reinforcing because it is often true that teachers who are effective with special education students get higher proportions of

WORKSHEET D

Root Cause	Evidence	Effect(s)	Why Undiscussable?	Leadership Response
1. Student behavior				
2. Teacher overload				
3. Teacher capability				
4. Case manager authority				
5. Distribution of special education students				
6. Administrative overload				

them in their classes. (The same can be said for students with other special instructional needs and/or behavior challenges.) Causes 2 and 3 also interrelate because if certain teachers have limited ability to differentiate instruction, then they will quickly become overloaded and resort to preservation techniques such as those employed by Mitchell's teacher. Enhancing case manager authority may get more compliance from teachers, but with the other root causes in place doing so may make little difference in terms of student outcomes.

PUZZLING THROUGH A COURSE FOR ORGANIZATIONAL LEARNING

If we asked you at this point to flesh out organizational learning for Mariposa Elementary School or Mitchell's special education program, we would be asking for you to write fiction because you do not have access to the evidence necessary to think through organizational learning stemming from the vignettes. We thus depart from puzzles in other chapters and ask you to put together puzzle pieces from your own school as you apply organizational learning concepts to a potential improvement effort. First, answer these questions:

1. What is one problem of practice (i.e., gap between aspirations and outcomes) you believe your school should address?

   - What evidence for this gap is already public?
   - What evidence might you collect and analyze?

2. Why does the problem you have identified exist, and why does it persist?

    • What evidence of root causes is already public and what you might you collect and analyze?
    • Can you describe undiscussables that prevent any of these root causes from being made public?

3. Which governing variables in your school cause the problem you have identified to continue?

    • Are these the same as the root causes you identified? How are they different and/or how do they overlap?

After you have answered the above questions, sit down in your principal's chair (metaphorically, of course) and complete Worksheet E. You should not feel obligated to fill in every cell, and you might want to expand the table.

WORKSHEET E

Organizational Learning Item	Evidence	Undiscussables	Risk Assessment
Gap			
Root cause 1			
Root cause 2			
Root cause 3			
Governing variable 1			
Governing variable 2			
Governing variable 3			

If you were principal in your school, would you address the gap you have identified? If so, when and over what period of time? If not, why not? What are the most immediate or important consequences stemming from the choice you would make?

NOTE

1. We wish to acknowledge Allyson Voss from whose capstone project required for the Stanford University Graduate School of Education Policy, Organization, and Leadership Studies program this vignette is taken. Pseudonyms are used.

REFERENCES

Argyris, C. (1999). *Organizational learning* (2nd ed.). Malden, MA: Blackwell Publishing.

Argyris, C., & Schon, D. (1974). *Theory in practice: Increasing professional effectiveness.* San Francisco: Jossey-Bass.

Argyris, C., & Schon, D. (1978). *Organizational learning: A theory of action perspective.* Reading, MA: Addison-Wesley Publishing Company.

Bauer, S.C., & Brazer, S.D. (2012). *Using research to lead school improvement: Turning evidence into action.* Thousand Oaks, CA: Sage Publications.

Ben-Peretz, M., & Schonmann, S. (1998). Informal learning communities and their effects. In K. Leithwood and K. Louis (Eds.), *Organizational learning in schools* (pp. 47–66). Lisse, Netherlands: Swets & Zeitlinger.

Brazer, S.D., Rich, W., & Ross, S. (2010). Collaborative strategic decision making in school districts. *Journal of Educational Administration, 48*(2), 196–217.

DiMaggio, P., & Powell, W. (1983). The iron cage re-visited: Institutional isomorphism and collective rationality in organizational fields. *American Sociological Review, 48*(2), 147–160.

Feldman, M.S., & Pentland, B.T. (2003). Reconceptualizing organizational routines as a source of flexibility and change. *Administrative Science Quarterly, 48*(1), 94–118.

Fisher, R., Ury, W., & Patton, B. (2011). *Getting to yes: Negotiating agreement without giving in.* New York: Penguin Books.

Leithwood, K., & Louis, K. (1998). *Organizational learning in schools.* Lisse, Netherlands: Swets & Zeitlinger.

Levitt, B., & March, J.G. (1988). Organizational learning. *Annual Review of Sociology, 14,* 319–340.

Louis, K., & Kruse, S. (1998). Creating community in reform: Images of organizational learning in inner-city schools. In K. Leithwood and K. Louis (Eds.), *Organizational learning in schools* (pp. 17–46). Lisse, Netherlands: Swets & Zeitlinger.

March, J.G., & Simon, H.A. (1993). *Organizations.* Cambridge, MA: Blackwell.

Preuss, P. (2007). *School leader's guide to root cause analysis: Using data to dissolve problems.* Larchmont, NY: Eye on Education.

Random House (1968). *The Random House dictionary of the English language: College edition.* New York: Random House.

Sahlberg, P. (2018). *FinnishED leadership: Four big, inexpensive ideas to transform education.* Thousand Oaks, CA: Corwin.

Senge, P. (1990/2006). *The fifth discipline: The art and practice of the learning organization.* New York: Doubleday.

Senge, P., Cambrone-McCabe, N., Lucas, T., Smith, B., Dutton, J., & Kleiner, A. (2012). *Schools that learn: A fifth discipline fieldbook for educators, parents, and everyone who cares about education.* New York: Crown Business.

Simon, H. (1993). Decision making: Rational, nonrational, and irrational. *Educational Administration Quarterly, 29,* 392–411.

Smith, R., & Brazer, S.D. (2016). *Striving for equity: District leadership for narrowing opportunity and achievement gaps.* Cambridge, MA: Harvard Education Press.

Smith, R., Crawley, A., Robinson, C., Cotman, T., Swaim, M., & Strand, P. (2011). *Gaining on the gap: Changing hearts, minds, and practice.* Lanham, MD: Rowman & Littlefield.

Spillane, J.P. (2012). Data in practice: Conceptualizing the data-based decision making phenomena. *American Journal of Education, 118*(2), 113–141.

Van Lare, M., Brazer, S., Bauer, S., & Smith, R. (2013). Professional learning communities using evidence: Examining teacher learning and organizational learning. In S. Conley and B. Cooper (Eds.), *Moving from teacher isolation to teacher collaboration: Enhancing professionalism and school quality* (pp. 157–182). Lanham, MD: Rowman and Littlefield.

Venezia, A., Kirst, M.W., & Antonio, A.L. (2003). *Betraying the college dream: How disconnected K–12 and postsecondary education systems undermine student aspirations.* Stanford, CA: The Bridge Project.

CHAPTER **5**

What Do Leaders Do?

"I like the first candidate, Eve" Judy, a math teacher, chimed in. *"She was perky, intelligent, and so well spoken. She answered every one of our questions without much hesitation and rose to the occasion during what must have been a very stressful interview."* Inwardly, Fazia, a seasoned AP, rolled her eyes as she listened to the search panel de-briefing interviews with the three finalists for the AP opening at Huerta High School. The candidate Judy just spoke about couldn't manage her way out of a paper bag, in Fazia's opinion, and that would place a burden on her and the other continuing AP who is close to retirement. Eve's answers were all over the place. Mostly, Fazia wondered how a resume, a short visit, and answers to some canned and heavily neutered interview questions would help the panel know whom to hire. She was also quite concerned that the principal was quiet as the seven-member team reviewed the applicants. This decision was critical to what Fazia's work life on this administrative team would look like for the next several years.

"Look," Jerry, the social studies department chair chimed in, *"The first gentleman, Adam, has a resume to die for. So much experience—department head, football coach, lots of special education experience, designing and delivering professional development, curriculum writing, and test item development. And a very collaborative style, from all indications. Notice how many of his experiences involved working as part of a team? He seems to have been very involved as a team leader at his previous school."*

Jenny, a physics teacher and former union representative, remarked, *"Yeah, but what I noticed was that he never seemed to be in charge of anything, he seemed to always defer to the team. Even when he referenced being a head coach he stressed how much credit his assistant coaches and team captains had for their winning seasons. Did he give any indication that he is capable of making a tough decision and being accountable for it? And he seems to shy away from conflict, even in his answers to our questions. I don't think he's tough enough to handle the job here."*

"What about Dr. Able?" added Joshua, the special education department chair. *"First of all, the fact that he has a doctorate should suggest something about his dispositions toward learning—he demonstrated through his actions that he is a lifelong learner."*

With uncharacteristic energy, Judy jumped out of her seat and countered: *"Oh, come on! What does that really show? That he has a lot of book learning. What about actual talent? I didn't get a sense of his capabilities, his innate abilities."*

"Now wait a second, Judy," Joshua retorted. "There's a lot more to Dr. Able. He gave us a couple of examples of times he led a group collaboratively, and also some occasions when he jumped in to correct his teacher team's course when they seemed to be going astray. He was quite directive, almost commanding. That's not just book learning. That's a natural born leader."

Mark, who had been silent until now, raised a curious question: "Who said we're looking for a leader, anyway? We already have a principal, and the buck stops with him. The last thing we need is a strong-minded person to upset the apple-cart, you know?"

Now Fazia rolled her eyes for all to see, fidgeting in her seat, feeling as though the panel was getting nowhere. Conclusions seemed to be that Eve, the first candidate, has some desirable abilities; Adam is collaborative in his actions; and Dr. Able has both a credential and, it seemed, the ability to be either collaborative or directive, depending on the situation. Each of these candidates has something to offer, and this last question about whether the panel was seeking a leader made Fazia crazy. Of course they were seeking a leader, didn't they see that she herself led collaboratively within her curriculum and instruction sphere? How many times a week did teachers come to her with questions about district-mandated curriculum and standardized testing? They didn't want someone to take over for the principal, but they sure did need a lot of leaders to make a school like Huerta successful. Fazia was desperate to hear from Dr. North, the principal. What did he make of each of these candidates? Is he looking for a strong candidate with a mind of his or her own, or someone who would follow orders and manage well? And why did he sit idly by letting them prattle on without some direction?

Thought Partner Conversation

Suppose Fazia and Dr. North bumped into each other in the office later and debriefed about the search committee meeting. What do you imagine the conversation would have been like? What would their take-aways from the meeting be?

INTRODUCTION

In the opening vignette, a search team is wandering around the question of how to determine which job candidate might be the most suitable AP. Panel members seem to disagree about criteria: Is education and/or experience critical? Do key players on the administrative team come with a certain set of traits or inborn qualities? Do APs require the ability to be flexible and adapt to different situations? Is the school looking for someone to follow Dr. North's orders or a leader, and if so, what does that even mean?

It is no wonder that the group is having some difficulty. If any member of the group had engaged in an in-depth study of the question of what makes a leader a leader, she or he could be equally confused. This should not be surprising—we would hardly expect consensus on the meaning of any number of constructs we use as a shorthand for signifying a complex aspect of human conditions (for instance, satisfaction, intelligence, or well-being). Finding a clear and agreed-upon definition of leadership has vexed scholars for decades (Rost, 1991). James Macgregor Burns (1978), one of the most prominent leadership theorists, concluded: "Leadership is one of the most observed and least understood phenomena on earth" (p. 2). Warren Bennis (1959), an equally prolific and astute scholar on leadership and management practice, wrote:

> Of all the hazy and confounding areas in social psychology, leadership theory undoubtedly contends for top nomination. And, ironically, probably more has been written and less is known about leadership than any other topic in the behavioral sciences. Always, it seems, the concept of leadership eludes us or turns up in another form to taunt us again with its slipperiness and complexity. So we have invented an endless proliferation of terms to deal with it: leadership, power, status, authority, rank, prestige, influence, control, manipulation, domination, and so forth, and still the concept is not sufficiently defined.
>
> (pp. 259–260)

Ongoing confusion, ambiguity, and disagreement about what constitutes leadership and who is actually leading whom requires our readers to figure out for themselves how they wish to lead within a particular context defined by the level of schooling (elementary, middle, or high school; or district office), the student population served, history of educational performance, and numerous other factors. We subscribe neither to the view that leadership qualities are completely inborn nor that there are defined steps anyone can take to arrive at a capacity to lead. Instead, our perspective is that each of us is imbued with certain dispositions—character traits—that align with specific contexts and can be enhanced or mitigated through specific leadership practices.

Thought Partner Conversation

Before we begin to explore the scholarly ideas informing the concepts of leadership and leading, discuss what they mean to you with your critical friend. What is leadership? Who are leaders? How do you know an effective leader when you see one?

Northouse (2019) reports that "in the past 60 years, as many as 65 different classification systems have been developed to define the dimensions of leadership" (p. 5); some focus on personality characteristics, some on group process, others on behaviors, and still others on the dimensions and uses of power.

Why do we bother seeking a consensus on the meaning of leadership? Bennis (1959) observes:

> The issues involved in studies of leadership have plagued man since the beginnings of intellectual discourse. The study of leadership raises the fundamental

issues that every group, organization, nation, and group of nations has to resolve or at least struggle with: Why do people subordinate themselves? What are the sources of power? How and why do leaders arise? Why do leaders lead? What is the function of the leader? … [T]hese questions, because of their complexity and value-laden potency, stubbornly resist a final answer.

(p. 261)

Aside from the importance of questions related to leadership from an organizational or functionalist perspective, Rost (1991) believes that leadership has taken on a symbolic, almost mythological, status in our culture. "It helps people explain effectiveness and concomitantly allows them to celebrate the people who achieve that effectiveness; the lack of leadership helps them explain ineffectiveness and concomitantly allows them to blame certain people for that ineffectiveness" (p. 8).

Rost (1991) goes on to bemoan the fact that leadership studies, texts, and speeches have a tendency to recount in ritualistic fashion the litany of traditions that have emerged and subsequently faded away with regard to our understanding of leadership. The twentieth century witnessed the Great Man theory, group theory, trait theory, behavior theory, contingency theory, and excellence theory. "The dialectic and reversals of emphases in this area," Bennis (1959) writes, "very nearly rival the tortuous twists and turns of child-rearing practices, and one can paraphrase Gertrude Stein by saying, 'a leader is a follower is a leader'" (p. 260).

Thought Partner Conversation

Discuss with a critical friend the number of different ways the word "leader" is used in everyday communication and the different kinds of leaders you encounter in a given week. What are the common threads that connect the various actors and/or their roles that might help you capture what it is we mean by "leader?"

With apologies to Rost and despite the persistent difficulties in understanding what leadership is, in this chapter we review some of the primary traditions that explain leaders and leadership, for two reasons: First, understanding these perspectives elucidates our present conceptualization of leadership and helps explain how the field has evolved. Second, it is our contention that aspects of each of the so-called "outdated" perspectives lingers in our treatment of leadership and, sometimes, in our policies and practices. There are nuggets of wisdom worth retaining in each of the perspectives we review, regardless of the field having moved on from them. We believe, further, that even if there is no single consensus definition of leadership, there is vast agreement on several core principles that are vitally important for school leadership aspirants and in-service leaders to know and understand. We will close the chapter with these.

Uncertainty about what we mean by "leadership" is evident in the interview panel that wasn't readily able to agree on who best would fill the AP vacancy at Huerta High School. Thinking about the primary traditions in viewing leaders and leadership as you make your way through this chapter is intended to help you think more clearly about appropriate leadership for an administrative team. Understanding multiple leadership perspectives informs your conceptualization of leadership and helps you understand where education leadership has progressed as a field. The organizational culture that suffuses schools and districts demands leadership in various forms. We believe, further, that even if there is no single consensus definition of leadership, the Huerta interview panel would be better served if they understood what leadership is and the kind of person they seek to fill the AP role.

Essential Questions

1. How do various conceptions of leadership shape contemporary beliefs about what leaders should do?
2. What do leaders actually do?
3. How should contemporary school leaders lead?
4. How do context and personal dispositions intersect in leadership behaviors?

FROM TRAITS TO TRANSFORMATION

It is almost certainly true that humans have been fascinated with and tried to understand leadership since we slithered out of the muck and began to congregate in groups. No doubt, as well, there are philosophies, historical accounts, and written and oral lore that we could include in a historical review of how we perceive and define leadership. For the present, however, we limit ourselves to the primary views of leadership as presented in systematic study of the phenomenon over the past century and a quarter or so. We are illustrative, not exhaustive, in our review. Our selection is meant to allow you to gain a feel for the trends and progress in academic study of leadership as a foundation for understanding where we are as a field and how the study of leadership, writ large, informs theory and research on school leadership, the focus of Part II.

Before beginning our review, we emphasize that the various theory sets we outline here are very much reflective of what was going on in society at the time, testament to the influence of culture and the organizational environments predominant during each theory's heyday. We do not claim to be historians, but will comment briefly on the context of each theoretical tradition to set the tone and enable you to reflect on how circumstances influence thought on who leaders are and what effective leaders do.

Thought Partner Conversation

We will start our journey through leadership theories with the trait theories, the idea that leaders are leaders because they possess certain characteristics or traits. What do you think about this simple notion? Are there traits you associate with effective leaders? Why?

Great Man and Trait Theories

Traditional notions of leadership tended to focus on the person of the leader, that is, the single individual who was in command (Pearce & Conger, 2010). The earliest of the perspectives we include here, the so-called Great Man theories emerged in the mid-1800s during a period of urbanization, industrialization, and in the United States, successive waves of immigration as the New World spread west and grew rapidly in population, economic strength, and complexity. Farming and craft industries were being supplanted by manufacturing and transportation, industries that fueled growth and took advantage of the rich natural resources that were abundant in newly settled territories in the Western Hemisphere and in colonies ruled by imperial powers. In the United States especially, wealth was increasingly concentrated in the hands of a select few, the Robber Barons—Morgan, Vanderbilt, Rockefeller, and Carnegie, to name but a few. As the industrial revolution raged on and the select few emerged as economic and political leaders, social scientists began to ask: What was it about these "great men" that accounted for their position and power?

A GREAT MAN?

The Great Man theory is alive and well in education, along with its sexist overtones. Brazer served as principal in the long shadow of Robert "Buck" Armstrong.* Eighteen years passed between Buck and Brazer, but faculty never stopped talking about Buck. At 6 foot 5 inches and over 250 pounds, he was an imposing man who was legendary for maintaining order and quality for 10 years. Those were the glory days, so the stories went, of winning football teams and state track champions. Buck was "in charge." The implications of these stories included the notion that a potentially unruly high school needed a *man* in charge who could overwhelm anyone in his path. What was easily forgotten was that the student body was far more homogeneous (predominantly white, Asian, and affluent) in Buck's day and that part of his legacy was a decline in the high school's reputation for quality not long after he left. Subsequent weak leadership and a more complicated student body left many faculty yearning for the "good old days" of Buck's leadership.

* A pseudonym.

Although Pearce and Conger (2010) rightly observed that throughout the 1800s theories of management featuring a command-and-control sort of leadership were almost commonplace, many attribute the emergence of the Great Man perspective to historian Thomas Carlyle (Cumming, 2004). As Spector (2016, p. 250) observed:

> In leadership discourse, the Great Man theory—an assertion that certain individuals, certain men, are gifts from God placed on earth to provide the lightning needed to uplift human existence—is associated mainly with Thomas Carlyle. For good reason. In the spring of 1840, Carlyle delivered a series of six public lectures

on the role played by heroes in shaping the arc of history. The following year, those lectures were brought together in a single volume entitled On Heroes, Hero-Worship, and the Heroic in History, and the Great Man theory was born.

In reality, Carlyle was more philosopher than theorist, and his perspective less a well-postulated theory based on rigorous research than a statement of faith (Spector, 2016). Nor was the Great Man perspective universally well received in its time. The sociologist, Herbert Spencer, called it childish and simplistic, noting that the so-called great men were as much products of their environment as they were leaders within it: "Before he [the great man] can remake his society his society must make him" (Spencer, 1901, p. 31).

From an academic perspective, the Great Man theory is insupportable. Ulysses S. Grant was a contemporary of Spencer's and helps to prove his point. His career was fraught with extreme highs and lows, such as incomparable bravery during the Mexican–American War, humiliation in 1850s peace time, gradual vindication during the Civil War, and limited success during perhaps the most corrupt presidency in history (Chernow, 2017). Was Grant a Great Man, a drunkard, or a naïve puppet manipulated by unscrupulous politicians? He was all of these and more as he encountered different circumstances, rendering the Great Man theory useless no matter how much some may yearn for larger-than-life leaders. Nevertheless, the Great Man perspective ushered in the systematic study of a key question: Are leaders born or made? Is a leader a leader because of some set of inborn qualities or characteristics? Were these the things that set the leader apart from ordinary mortals?

Thought Partner Conversation

Nature versus nurture is of course a classic debate. "Are leaders born or made" is a staple of the genre. Nonetheless, who hasn't uttered the phrase "natural born leader" about someone? Stepping back from the debate, discuss the ways "Great Man" type thinking persists today, and what effect this has on how schools and school systems work.

Trait theories took up these questions in the early years of the twentieth century, combining some of the tenets of the Great Man paradigm with trends emerging in psychological measurement (Short & Greer, 1997). From a trait perspective, leaders are individuals with certain inborn qualities, and leadership is a one-direction, command-and-control process whereby followers naturally accede to the wisdom and superior qualities of the leader. Stogdill (1948), in a review of studies to date, noted five categories of traits that tended to emerge as prime candidates as ingredients to clarify leadership's puzzle:

- *Capacity* (intelligence, alertness, verbal facility, originality, judgment).
- *Achievement* (scholarship, knowledge, athletic accomplishments).
- *Responsibility* (dependability, initiative, persistence, aggressiveness, self-confidence, desire to excel).

- *Participation* (activity, sociability, cooperation, adaptability, humor).
- *Status* (socio-economic position, popularity).

Decades later, Stogdill (1974) identified both traits and skills that were thought to be critical to effective leadership, illustrated in Table 5.1.

Northouse (2019) summarized that five attributes appear to form a consensus from among the many traits identified in various studies and reviews: intelligence, self-confidence, determination, integrity, and sociability. He goes on to point out that quite recently, psychologists have lent some support to the notion that leaders possess certain personality traits, with extroversion being the most important factor, followed by conscientiousness, openness, and low neuroticism.

The trait approach is both intuitively appealing and straightforward. Who can argue with the notion that effective leaders ought to be intelligent, self-confident, etc.? The criticisms of this perspective, though, cast a long shadow: First, adherents to the trait

TABLE 5.1 Stogdill's Traits and Skills

Traits	Skills
• Adaptable to situations	• Clever (intelligent)
• Alert to social environment	• Conceptually skilled
• Ambitious and achievement-orientated	• Creative
• Assertive	• Diplomatic and tactful
• Cooperative	• Fluent in speaking
• Decisive	• Knowledgeable about group task
• Dependable	• Organized (administrative ability)
• Dominant (desire to influence others)	• Persuasive
• Energetic (high activity level)	• Socially skilled
• Persistent	
• Self-confident	
• Tolerant of stress	
• Willing to assume responsibility	

approach seem to be saying that leaders are born and that individuals without these inherent traits can never become leaders. You either have it, or too bad. Second, the trait perspective suggests that individuals who possess these traits would be leaders in any context—a great general can lead a school system, for example, by virtue of possessing key leadership attributes. Third, decades of research has revealed dozens—maybe hundreds—of traits that are purported to be candidates for the leadership recipe, including many contradictory attributes. Even if this were not the case, do we believe that all effective leaders must possess all significant attributes to be truly effective? How likely is this? Finally, the trait approach has an inherent logical flaw: Even if research could come up with a set of compelling attributes that most effective leaders possess, that does not mean that possession of these characteristics *caused* *them* to become great leaders. Trait theory treats the attributes as necessary conditions, but does not tell us how these conditions generate effective leaders. Thus, from this perspective, leaders are born and not made, and we don't really know why.

As Stogdill (1948) concluded decades ago, "A person does not become a leader by virtue of the possession of some combination of traits, but the pattern of personal characteristics of the leader must bear some relevant relationship to the characteristics, activities, and goals of the followers" (p. 64). Even with its limitations, we must admit that the trait perspective lives on in our management and organizational practice, for instance, as teams go about reviewing potential candidates as in the chapter's opening vignette. Our personnel practices and day-to-day work experiences demonstrate that we often act as if leaders are individuals with particular (inborn) traits; we use personality inventories and other instruments to discover these traits and factor our findings into decision making. At the broadest level, this is probably human nature. In our investigations of leadership, however, the trait approach receded in importance by the middle of the twentieth century as scholars and management gurus began to focus instead on leadership behaviors.

Behavior/Style Theories

Even during the Great Man theories heyday, notable authorities and students of leadership questioned their command-and-control assumptions. Mary Parker Follett, among others, introduced concepts more aligned with what present-day theorists would call shared leadership, focusing on the notion that workers should follow the leader with the most knowledge or expertise associated with a task rather than the individual with positional authority (Pearce & Conger, 2010). The notion that leaders are born, and not made, and the overtly sexist and classist nature of these theories were increasingly out-of-sync with the times, as well.

The kind of thinking represented by Follett and others illuminates a fundamental problem for the AP interview panel vignette. The group faces two important sources of uncertainty: (1) What kind of expertise does the school require on its administrative team as it is currently constituted? and (2) Who will be best suited to assert that expertise at the appropriate moments while being a good team player? These kinds of questions are important when choosing individuals for leadership positions in school systems—superintendents, site administrators, department heads and grade-level leaders, and Parent–Teacher Association presidents. But questions such as these are not always the focus of discussion because latent beliefs about what constitutes "strong" leadership or affective impressions take over.

THE PERFECT CANDIDATE?

An assumption that leadership can be learned has great potential to change the focus of the interview panel's deliberations.

In the vignette, everyone argues about who brings the most important traits—demonstrated decisive leadership, scholarship, charisma, etc. A trait not mentioned is the ability to take and use feedback—the ability and willingness to learn—because no one is yet thinking about how each of the candidates might grow in the position once they understand the context and expectations.

Fazia might be more interested in a candidate who could be her collaborator rather than one who comes in with pre-conceived notions about what teachers and students need from him or her.

Most important, the principal might see a candidate's capacity for *learning on the job and improving leadership skills over time* as a powerful lever for improving the effectiveness of his administrative team. It would still be difficult to determine which candidate is the most likely to respond well to coaching, but hiring for that quality might lead to a better outcome over the long run.

Prior to World War II, the assembly line and scientific management brought unheard-of efficiencies and productivity on a scale never before known, but increasingly workers and their advocates bemoaned turning workers into automatons, long hours, and the resulting alienation present in ever-larger industrial concerns. Labor reforms, including limitations on child labor and passage of statutes that enabled unionization, were indicators of increasing concerns about worker's rights and the role of leadership in promoting at least a reasonable quality of work life. During the war years, social scientists were put to work to find ways to increase productivity to bolster the war effort. So dramatic were the resources applied and the efforts rendered that Kurt Lewin (1947) wrote in the first issue of the first volume of the journal *Human Relations*: "One of the byproducts of World War II of which society is hardly aware is the new stage of development which the social sciences have reached. This development indeed may prove to be as revolutionary at the atom bomb" (p. 5). During the post-war years, pressures to better understand the leader's role in bolstering productivity continued as efforts were underway to rebuild war-ravaged lands, Cold War concerns mushroomed, and business grew in an effort to satisfy an explosion in consumer demand for goods and services that were not available during the war, fueled by the baby boom. In this context, the study of leadership and leaders' roles in the workplace blossomed.

In the immediate post-war years, two sets of studies at two prominent American universities took center stage in reinventing our conception of leadership, replacing the focus on individual traits to one on behavior or leadership style. This shift is revolutionary because these theorists opened the door to the possibility that leadership behavior *can be and is learned*. The focus on what leaders do, rather than who leaders are, stands in sharp contrast to the earlier Great Man and trait theories, and spawned a robust and long-term research agenda that continues to this day.

Leadership researchers and scholars working on the behavior theories posited that leadership can be characterized as either people-focused or task-focused. Scholars associated with the Ohio State studies developed the Leaders Behavior Description Questionnaire, or LBDQ, to measure the degree to which a leader emphasizes *initiating structure* (task-oriented behavior) or *consideration* (people-oriented behavior). These were considered two separate dimensions, and hence were measured separately. In other words, a person could be high or low in consideration, and high or low in task or structure orientation (Stogdill, 1974). Scholars at the University of Michigan used the terms *employee orientation* and *production orientation*. Initially, scholars at Michigan viewed the orientations as opposite ends of a single continuum, but based on empirical results they modified this view later to operationalize the two orientations as separate (Northouse, 2019). These perspectives embraced the notion that leadership can be taught. Later theorists looked for regularities and patterns that could be learned by current and prospective leaders through education and training. Blake and Mouton (1964, 1978), for example, developed the *Managerial Grid* based on the hypothesis that style originates in leader's *concern for people* and their *concern for results*. Hersey and Blanchard (1969 a & b) proposed that leadership style varies based on their degree of *directive behavior* and *supportive behavior*, further modified by attributes of the situation, namely the developmental or maturity level of followers.

In terms of the major contributions of the behavior or style theories, Northouse (2019) reminds us that these theorists provide us with the simple yet profound realization that whenever a leader leads, she or he is employing some behavioral strategy to influence followers, and that these styles may be characterized as either tending toward consideration or to task, or to both. "Whenever leadership occurs, the leader is acting out both task and relationship behaviors; the key to being an effective leader rests on how the leader balances these two behaviors. Together they form the core of the leadership process" (p. 81).

People orientation or task orientation—and all combinations in between—seem likely to be embedded in individuals' experiences and how they interpret them. Panel member Judy says, "*I like the first candidate, Eve. She was perky, intelligent, and so well spoken. She answered every one of our questions without much hesitation and rose to the occasion during what must have been a very stressful interview.*" Judy picks up on the personal or relational style she saw in Eve. Fazia starts to get frustrated because she is less interested in the candidates' interpersonal relations skills and more interested in their ability to pull their weight on the administrative team. Jerry reveals more of a task orientation when he emphasizes his favorite candidates' accomplishments with a nod toward collaboration: "*The first gentleman, Adam, has a resume to die for. So much experience—department head, football coach, lots of special education experience, designing and delivering professional development, curriculum writing and test item development. And a very collaborative style, from all indications.*" Followers' expectations of leadership behavior can have an effect on who gets hired into leadership positions and for what reasons. This is why candidates for leadership roles frequently feel as though interview panels expect them walk on water. It is challenging for most of us to be personable while being highly productive.

The style theories provided a marked contrast with most prior work on leadership by moving away from inborn characteristics of the individual leader to a focus on what leaders do, prompting the question of whether particular styles better suited certain work environments and challenges. A robust and long-lasting research program showed, for instance, that under most circumstances, high levels of consideration or employee involvement in work was beneficial (Northouse, 2019), but in work settings characterized by highly routine and repetitive tasks, this was not the case. Situations such as this require clear direction and task specification, and giving the employee voice has little bearing on their work. This research supports notions of teacher leadership and involvement in decision making in schools, since school work settings are epitomized by many and sometimes unclear goals and the nature of work is quite varied. The leader cannot pre-determine task specification or judge beforehand the best teaching behavior to use at any specific point in time with any specific group of students; the teacher must use his or her judgment. (Recall McGregor's claims about Theory X and Theory Y from Chapter 1 and our application to education as knowledge work.)

Thought Partner Conversation

The research cited in this section highlights the fact that technology—how work is conducted—matters in terms of the type of leadership that seems to work best. When the technology is varied, uncertain, or rapidly changing, consideration and employee involvement are critical. What are some of the reasons for this? Does the conclusion make sense? What are the implications for the work of the teacher and school leader?

In addition to spawning a robust research program, the style theories produced a wealth of activity and helped professionalize—perhaps even legitimize—the leadership development field. If leaders are made and not born, the question follows regarding how to train and develop leaders. The 1960s, in particular, saw the growth of consulting and training firms, the blossoming of leadership development programs within college and university settings, and the emergence of associations devoted to human resource and leadership development issues.

The style theories were not without problems, however. First, critics pointed out that work in this tradition could not settle on the definition of a "best" form of leadership, i.e., the search for a "best" style proved fruitless. Research failed to establish that style predicts performance outcomes or even outcomes such as employee satisfaction with any consistency (Northouse, 2019). Second, focusing on leader behaviors, even when accounting for some element of the situation, ignores followers' preferences and needs. Finally, it deserves to be mentioned that even if research showed that a supportive style was correlated with high productivity, it is entirely possible that the cause-and-effect direction of this relationship could go either way, that is, supportive leadership behavior might engender productivity or a highly productive work setting might stimulate supportive leadership.

Perhaps the most telling flaw in the behavioral approach to understanding leadership is also its virtue, namely its simplicity. Although the mark of any good theory is the ability to focus attention by reducing complexity of social phenomena the theory is trying to explain, the behavioral theories proved incapable of satisfactorily explaining leadership because they ignored followers and accounted for little, if anything, about the leadership context. While we continue to understand and explain various aspects of leadership based on the task/consideration dimensions, the style theories gave way to a set of perspectives that are by their very nature designed to incorporate greater complexity, namely contingency theories.

> **Thought Partner Conversation**
>
> The behavioral theories are criticized because they fail to account for elements of the work context. The implication is that in some contexts, an otherwise effective style (for instance one that was high in consideration) would not work. Can you come up with examples of circumstances in which the context would dictate an effective leader to act quite differently than he or she normally would?

As panelists in the vignette debated various candidates' virtues, their statements imagined them in various situations, facing a range of contingencies or challenges. Assumptions they made about each of the candidates based on limited information caused them to draw conclusions about their leadership potential. Their inconclusive debate illustrates that context matters and yet what the school will demand of any of these people in the future is difficult to predict. What they may need most of all is an AP who can think on her or his feet and adapt to present circumstances.

Contingency Theories

The 1960s was a decade of hope, change, and questioning, certainly in the United States and arguably across the globe. As Nobel Laureate Bob Dylan foretold in 1964, *the times they were a' changin'*. The Cold War was in full swing, a hot war was widening and deepening in Southeast Asia, and social change was on the agenda in the form of Great Society legislation and the Civil Rights movement. In industrial settings, wildcat strikes and other union actions were challenging workplace norms in support of worker rights. In education, teachers' unions were emerging in large, urban settings, and the National Education Association began to question its reason for being and remake itself as force. Baby boomers were flocking to college campuses as degree-seeking became more of a norm rather than an exception, and although hierarchy still reigned within the boardrooms and on the shop floors of most organizations, questioning authority was the rule of the day. It can also be argued that the 1960s and early 1970s saw a willingness to confront, if not embrace complexity and an unwillingness to accept simple answers to complex questions or adherence to "the ways it has always been done." It is amid these broad, societal trends that contingency theories of leadership were offered.

Thought Partner Conversation

This is the first instance in which we bring up the notion of followers as an important part of leadership. It seems odd to include followers in our conception of leading, doesn't it? In what ways might followers be a part of the definition of "leadership"?

From a contingency perspective, what makes an effective leader? The hallmark answer is this: *it all depends*. Contingency theory is a leader-match approach (Fiedler & Chemers, 1974), meaning that what defines an effective leader depends on the match between some attributes of that leader and some attributes of either the situation, followers (the group), or both. Contingency theorists both built on and went beyond the behavioral theorists' notion that leaders are either task or people oriented, and added *contingencies* to account for attributes of the context in which leaders act. This was a huge leap forward in two respects: first, for the first time the importance of context is front-and-center. No longer could we assume that anyone with certain traits or behaviors would be an effective leader in any situation or workplace. Second, attributes of followers began to be recognized as important. While contingency theorists did not quite define followers as a part of leadership itself, at least these perspectives considered the existence of followers and reckoned that they matter in how leaders lead.

You may be wondering: What were the major contingencies introduced by theorists to refine and improve our understanding of leadership? Within the answer to this question lies both the strengths and weaknesses of the contingency theorists. There were many models offered and tested, and little consensus on which contingencies matter most. Vroom and Yetton (1973) generated a theory in which attributes of decision making were factored into the leadership equation; House and colleagues (House, 1971; House & Mitchell, 1974) put forth the Path–Goal theory in which attributes of the leader, subordinate, and work setting are considered, postulating "a set of general recommendations based on the characteristics of followers and tasks for how leaders should act in various situations if they want to be effective" (Northouse, 2019, pp. 126–127). Hersey and Blanchard's (1969 a & b) work, which we introduced earlier because of its close affinity with behavioral theories, is considered by some to be better characterized as a contingency theory than a behavioral one.

Fiedler's (1967, 1978) contingency theory is perhaps the best known and certainly the most widely studied of the models offered in this tradition. Like the behavioral theories, Fiedler characterized leadership styles as tending to being either task or goal oriented, or relationship oriented. Fiedler created the Least Preferred Co-worker (LPC) survey to measure style, with individuals scoring high on this instrument judged as relationship oriented. Three factors of the situation were then used as contingencies: leader–member relations (are leaders liked and respected?); task structure (is the task highly structured/routine?); and position power (does the leader have authority to get the job done?). Ayman, Chemers and Fiedler (1995) summarize:

> The model predicts that a leader's effectiveness is based on two main factors: a leader's attributes, referred to as task or relationship motivational orientation ... and a leader's situational control. ... The model predicts that leaders who have a

task motivational orientation compared to those who have a relationship orientation or motivation will be more successful in high- and low-control situations. Relationship oriented leaders compared to task-oriented leaders will be more effective in moderate control situations. A leader is designated as "in match" in situations where the model predicts high group performance and "out of match" in situations of low group performance.

(p. 148; citations omitted)

Among the advantages of this model is the fact that it has generated a great deal of empirical study over a considerable timeframe (Northouse, 2019), including research that supports some of its major hypotheses (e.g., Chemers, Rice, Sundstrom & Butler, 1975; Graham, 1973; Green & Nebeker, 1978), and the model has been refined and extended over time (Ayman, Chemers & Fiedler, 1995). In fact, as compared with many theories offered to describe and explain effective leadership, the fact that Fiedler's work is based on years of empirical work distinguishes it (Campbell, 1968). Consideration and measurement of separate elements of the model—its contingencies—also separates it from other theories and enables both conceptual and methodological advances.

"BUCK" ARMSTRONG RECONSIDERED

Buck's principalship lasted from 1965–1975. By all accounts he was successful. The community was happy with his homogenous high school, sports teams were winning, and graduates were attending college in large proportions.

What if Buck had returned in 1985? The high school in the lowest-income part of the school district closed in 1981 and the student body and faculty divided between the district's two remaining high schools. Students of color (many of whom did not speak English as their first language) now made up nearly half of the student body. They and the teachers who followed them to Buck's school were not easily accepted into the school community. Within-school segregation quickly emerged as the "original" students and their teachers met in more advanced classes and the "new" students and teachers coped with learning difficulties and limiting assumptions about what both could achieve. How would Buck have fared in this new reality?

Of course, Fiedler's contingency theory has received its share of criticism (see, for example, Mitchell, Biglan, Oncken, & Fiedler, 1970). While its predictive nature offers certain advantages, the theory does not fully explain the primary finding that low-LPC (task-oriented) leaders seem to be more effective in high- or low-control situations, while relationship-oriented leaders seem to be most effective in moderate control circumstances (Northouse, 2019). House and Aditya (1997) observe that while experimental work generally supports the theory, field research yields inconsistent support, which is also true of contingency theories as a group. The empirical measures used within Fiedler's theory, such as the LPC, have been questioned methodologically. It is unclear, as well, whether leaders can alter their style or how leaders adapt when aspects of the situation change; the notion that a "match" is preferable and leads to more effective leadership does not help organizations understand how such a match can best be accomplished.

This latter criticism may be unfair; it seems to ask more of the theory than it was set out to accomplish. Yet, it exposes the main criticism of contingency theories as a group: they tend to be overly complex and difficult for practitioners to understand and manipulate in practice. Taken as a whole, just as the many trait theories explored dozens or hundreds of traits as possibly important to effective leadership, across the contingency theories there are many and different hypotheses about which contingencies are important. As Perrow (1986) concluded:

> One is tempted to say that the research on leadership has left us with the clear view that things are far more complicated and "contingent" than we initially believed and that, in fact, they are so complicated and contingent that it may not be worth our while to spin out more and more categories and qualifications.
>
> (p. 92)

He goes on to question: should we be designing situations to fit leaders, or train leaders to fit situations, and must leadership change each and every time the task or context alters appreciably? While the notion that "it depends" is an advance, it would be helpful to have some agreement upon what contingencies seem most important in a variety of circumstances. "At the extremes," Perrow (1986) concludes, "we can be fairly confident in identifying good or bad leaders, but for most situations we will probably have little to say" (p. 92).

Thought Partner Conversation

The entire notion of contingencies implies that people can and do change their behavior or style based on characteristics of the context and puzzle they are engaged in solving. What do you think about that notion? What implication does this have for the notion of differentiating instruction?

Political Models of Leadership

Through the 1970s and 1980s, the pace of change continued as social norms were commonly challenged. As the Vietnam War came to an end, the Watergate scandal heightened our questioning of politics as usual and, perhaps, signaled that things are not always the way they seem on the surface. By the mid-1970s the US auto industry, a symbol of American economic power and dominance on the world scene, was seemingly—if not actually—being overtaken by imports, especially those from Japan. We began to be fascinated with principles of total quality management and quality circles as explanations for the successes of firms such as Toyota and Datsun (now Nissan). Leadership, it seemed, might be greatest when shared. Setting high standards, asking line workers to identify production problems when they occurred, and then empowering them to help solve these problems became synonymous with manufacturing success. As the US faced new and not-so-new economic challenges, publication of *A Nation at Risk* in 1983 (National Commission on Excellence in Education, 1983) marked the beginning of an unprecedented, prolonged re-examination of education systems and, as we will explore in Part II, a focus on the role of school leaders as critical components in school improvement and reform.

In this context, scholarly work on leadership took a sharp turn away from what Foster (1986) called *psychological models* that focused on the person of the leader or the leadership context (e.g., trait, style, and contingency models), to a much greater concern with leadership as a process and the relationship between leaders and followers. "Political models" acknowledged that leadership is an influence relationship between leaders and followers, in which someone (the leader) is exerting influence to try to induce and motivate others to act in a particular way (follow). The accumulation and exercise of power (influence) is central to this relationship, with both leaders and followers exerting some degree of influence. Leadership, rather than being a unidimensional, command-and-control act of the leader, is recast as involving more than one party. "To understand the nature of leadership," Burns (1978) wrote, "requires understanding the essence of power, for leadership is a special form of power" (p. 10). He goes on to assert that power itself is relational, and that its exercise involves the pursuit of goals or purposes (intentions). Burns (1978) summarized:

> Leadership over human beings is exercised when persons with certain motives and purposes mobilize, in competition or conflict with others, institutional, political, psychological, and other resources so as to arouse, engage, and satisfy the motives of followers.
>
> (p. 294)

Hence, from a political perspective leadership is a purposeful relationship in which leaders and followers exert power in order to motivate and convince each other to seek and/or accomplish certain shared or complementary ends. Acknowledgment of the political nature of this relationship is accentuated by including the notion that this influence relationship occurs as parties engage resources *in competition or conflict with others*. Since resources are limited, action sought to satisfy leaders' and followers' goals and needs involves the exercise of power over the allocation and use of critical resources, i.e., politics (Salancik & Pfeffer, 1977).

The most prominent and influential of the political models, and indeed one of the most popular conceptions of leadership still, is *transformational leadership*. Though the term was used previously (Northouse, 2019), the concept took off with the publication of Burns' *Leadership* in 1978 and the subsequent work of Bass and his colleagues (Bass, 1985; Bass & Avolio, 1994; Bass & Ruggio, 2006). Since the popularization of this conception of leadership, it is the standard against which all other work is measured and has become a mainstay in work on leadership in schools (see Chapter 6).

Burns' (1978) formulation of transactional and transforming leadership (now more commonly referred to as transformational leadership) provided the foundation of this work. For Burns, "transactional leadership takes place when one person takes the initiative in making contact with others for purpose of an exchange of valued things" (Hickman, 2010, p. 64). An employee hired for wages in exchange for providing work is a classic example of such a transaction. In contrast, transforming leadership "occurs when one or more persons engage with others in such a way that leaders and followers raise one another to higher levels of motivation and morality" (Hickman, 2010, p. 64). Embedded in the latter notion is the centrality of leadership in promoting and supporting change, especially change that uplifts. "It is concerned with emotions, values, ethics, standards, and long-term goals. It includes assessing followers' motives, satisfying their needs, and treating them as full human beings" (Northouse, 2019, p. 163).

Bass extended and refined Burns' work with a particular focus on leadership in work situations. Bass (1985) proposed a theory and methods for measuring transformational leadership, and this work was refined by Bass and his colleagues in the *Full Range Model* of leadership development in which transformational, transactional, and laissez-faire leadership are proposed as a continuum. Bass and Avolio (1994) explain:

> *Transformational* leadership is seen when leaders:
> - stimulate interest among colleagues and followers to view their work from new perspectives;
> - generate awareness of the mission or vision of the team and organization;
> - develop colleagues and followers to higher levels of ability and potential; and
> - motivate colleagues and followers to look beyond their own interests toward those that will benefit the group.
>
> (p. 2)

Transformational leaders, they go on to say, "motivate others to do more than they originally intended and often even more than they thought possible" (p. 3). As in Burns' theory, transactional leadership involves an exchange between leaders and followers: "This exchange is based on the leader discussing with others what is required and specifying the conditions and rewards these others will receive if they fulfill those requirements" (p. 3). The Full Range theory postulates seven factors that describe these forms of leadership, four describing transformational leadership; two involving transactional leadership; and one involving laissez-faire (or non-) leadership. Each of these factors is measured in the Multifactor Leadership Questionnaire (MLQ; Bass & Avolio, 1995), and it is hypothesized that leaders who are transformational are both more active and effective, whereas laissez-faire leaders are most passive and ineffective.

Although an exhaustive exploration of the Full Range theory and accompanying research is beyond the scope of this chapter, it should be clear how this conception of leadership differs from prior work, and how the notion of transforming or transformational leadership takes us beyond the so-called psychological models. First, political models such as transformational leadership are relational in orientation; leadership includes and involves both leaders and followers. "Because the process incorporates both the followers' and the leaders' needs, leadership is not the sole responsibility of a leader but emerges from the interplay between leaders and followers" (Northouse, 2019, p. 179). Second, transformational leadership stresses the leader's role in change and improvement, both from an interpersonal and from an organizational standpoint, and an associated concept—vision—has become a central part of leadership as a result. Burns' (1978) work added a moral component to this, but regardless of the presence of a higher purpose, transformational leadership is intended to be uplifting (Bass & Avolio, 1994). Third, at least in terms of the Full Range theory, the model allows us to explore a range of types of leadership activity and, perhaps, to better understand the distinction between actions that might be described as "management" and those that truly involve leadership. Finally, the amount and quality of research on transformational leadership, and some generally promising support for many of the predictions associated with the theory, suggests that transformational leadership may in fact be an effective form of leadership (Northouse, 2019).

Critics of transformational leadership as a concept, and the various explications of the theory, note first that the theory does not say much about what one does to become a transformational leader. Indeed, especially when compared to previous theories, there is little if any description of what leadership behaviors might lead to transformational outcomes. Some have noted that within transformational leadership theory some of the assumptions of the Great Man theories are represented (Lee, 2014), at least insofar as the transformational leader image promotes a sense of infallibility and an almost heroic image (Yukl, 1999). Similarly, not all change or transformation is necessarily effective or worthwhile; in application, it seems safe to say that much organizational change and reform has been launched in the name of transformational leadership, regardless of need. Critics note that the theory lacks conceptual clarity (Lee, 2014; Northouse, 2019), and others have assailed research using the MLQ on methodological grounds.

TRANSFORMATIONAL SCHOOL LEADERSHIP

The concept of transformational leadership has been enormously popular over the past 40 years, possibly because it invests great potential power in the leader astute enough to exercise it. School leaders seem particularly enamored with the concept.

But, does it really "work"? Robinson, Lloyd, and Rowe (2008) analyzed more than 20 research articles purporting to measure the effects of transformational leadership as compared to IL on student test score outcomes. They found that transformational leadership has a positive effect, but that the effect of IL is more than four times greater. The authors' meta-analysis raises many questions, and it ought to make prospective leaders such as yourselves think about where your energy should be directed.

We explore these concepts in much greater detail in Part II of this book.

As we shall see in the next chapter of this book, the concept of transformational leadership has been embraced by educational researchers and scholars; definitions and operationalizations of the model have been put forth and used fruitfully to explore what we mean by "effective school leadership." Before we move on to our chapters focusing squarely on conceptions of effective school leadership, starting with transformational and extending to instructional and distributed leadership, we conclude this chapter by asking: what have we learned from theory and research on leadership to date?

LESSONS LEARNED: IS THERE A CONSENSUS?

We started this chapter with a bit of a false promise, or perhaps better said, a less-than-valid goal: to arrive at a single, consensus definition of *leadership*. An omnibus definition of leadership is often presented as the Holy Grail of management studies, which generates much consternation related to the field's inability to arrive at a satisfactory definition. We would be disingenuous if we were to suggest to you that we have arrived at any stronger conclusion. Further (and this is the deception to which we admit), such a goal is both improbable and unnecessary. As social scientists and students of organization, we confess that we seek to gain understanding, not outright certainty, of the complex constructs that we use to define the real-world phenomena we study. Our goal here is to share with you the trends and broad ideas that best embody where we have arrived as a field so that you too may understand different ways of defining and, ultimately, practicing leadership. Seeing these multiple perspectives helps to demonstrate how members of the interview panel in the opening vignette talk past each other because each expresses a different belief about what leadership is.

Defining leadership is, and will remain, contested terrain, and there are problems with all of the perspectives we presented individually and as a set of ideas. As Rost (1991) aptly summarized:

> Analyzed individually or in toto, these leadership theories have been (1) structural-functionalist, (2) management-oriented, (3) personalistic in focusing only on the leader, (4) goal-achievement dominated, (5) self-interested and individualistic in outlook, (6) male-oriented, (7) utilitarian and materialistic in ethical perspective, and (8) rationalistic, technocratic, linear, quantitative, and scientific in language and methodology.
>
> (p. 27)

As we reviewed decades of work, we observed continual confusion on even the most lasting questions confronting the field, for instance, the difference between leadership and management. We were amused and a bit perplexed to find that the first paper featured in the book, *Harvard business review on leadership* (1990), is Mintzberg's "The manager's job: Folklore and fact," a terrific paper but one that deals not one bit with leaders, leading, or leadership. (Mercifully, the next chapter, Kotter's "What leaders really do," tackles the question of how management and leadership differ. Management, Kotter asserts, involves coping with the complexity within large-scale organization; leadership, in contrast, involves coping with change. These are complementary but different social processes, both essential to organizational success.) We encourage you to be critical in your reading of this and other material that claims an understanding that is both meaningful and generalizable to the real-world puzzles leaders confront.

All theories have strengths and inevitably accentuate some sliver of the realities of leadership; likewise, all ignore some of the ambiguities and complexities of the phenomenon as it is practiced in the day-to-day of organizational life. With these caveats in mind, we assert that there is considerable consensus on certain attributes of what we commonly call "effective leadership," and this consensus set of ideas is exactly what we present in this summary—not as immutable or irrefutable laws of leadership, but rather as broad conceptions that help us understand the phenomenon we call "leadership."

Rost (1991) suggests a definition of leadership that we believe represents well where the field has arrived by the beginning of the twenty-first century: "Leadership is an influence relationship among leaders and followers who intend real changes that reflect their mutual purposes" (p. 102). He goes on to explain that this definition relies on four key elements, which we find incorporate the primary consensus of ideas represented in the scholarly study of leadership today:

- leadership is relational and depends on both leaders and followers;
- parties to this relationship seek to influence one another;
- parties to the relationship intend real change; and
- this change seeks to meet their mutual purposes (which either pre-exist or emerge).

(Rost, 1991, p. 104)

We now flesh out each of these four statements.

1. *Leadership is relational*; it involves both leader(s) and follower(s).
   As Katz and Kahn (1966/1978) remind us, "Leadership is a relational concept implying two terms: the influencing agent and the person influenced. Without followers there can be no leader" (p. 300). Though many of the theories postulated over the past century and a half focus on attributes of the person called "leader" and/or leader behavior, contemporary treatises agree that while a *leader* may be an individual person, *leadership* is a social process. Hickman (2010) explains why:

   > The fast pace and rapidly changing environment in which new era or postindustrial organizations function requires leadership that is substantially different from Max Weber's solitary executive at the top of the bureaucratic hierarchy. Organizations require leadership that is fluid, not simply positional, dispersed rather than centralized, and agile not inflexible. ... A single leader or leadership team rarely has enough knowledge, information, expertise, or ability to understand and respond quickly, effectively, and ethically to the dynamic changes in the environment and adapt or transform the organization and its participants.

   (p. x)

2. *Leadership is political.* The relationship between leader(s) and follower(s) involves the exercise of power.

    This is suggested in the definition offered by Katz and Kahn, above, with their reference to influence. Natemeyer and Hersey (2011) state this even more clearly: "Leadership is generally defined as the process of influencing the activities of others toward the accomplishment of goals" (p. 305). While various theories may differ on whether the power relationship between leader and follower is one characterized by "power over" versus "power with," there is little debate in contemporary leadership thought that the relationship between leader and follower is about influence, i.e., the ability of one party (the leader) to induce and/or motivate another (the follower) to act.

3. *Leadership involves meeting leaders' and followers' needs.*

    The change or transformation involved in the leadership relationship involves seeking out, defining, and working to meet the mutual or complementary needs of both parties to the relationship. Leadership is purposeful. An additional concept that is included here and that builds on the transformational nature of the relationship is that part of the leadership process is creating a shared vision of what is possible, a vision that is elevating and motivating. Leadership deals with such things as organizational values, commitment, beliefs about what is important, and crafting a culture that supports shared values that incorporate and reinforce the organization's reason for being and facilitates the pursuit of shared purposes. Primary functions of leadership, furthermore, are problem solving and decision making in service of organizational improvement and meeting the mutual and reinforcing needs of leaders and followers. This problem solving and decision making is strategic in nature, not merely operational; it involves moving individuals, groups, and the organization forward.

4. *Leadership involves promoting change and improvement*; it involves pursuit of a high (perhaps moral) purpose.

    The leader's primary role is to bring about change of a lasting nature, change that somehow furthers the goals of the organization, its members, its client(s), and/or the community at large. In this sense, Rost (1991) adds, leadership is intentional: "The word intend means that the leaders and followers purposefully desire certain changes in an organization and/or society" (p. 114). Further, these changes are substantial, not fleeting, or superficial. One distinguishing characteristic between leadership and management is that the former is concerned with change or improvement, whereas the latter relates more to maintaining the status quo and seeking efficiencies in its pursuit.

LEADING SCHOOLS

Suppose we return, now, to the opening vignette. In our search team's conversation, we observed various underlying conceptions of leadership—some focused on traits, some on style, some on the ability to act differently based on contingencies, and some were interested in change, vision, and transformation. In the background, the question also came up about what role the principal, as a school leader, should play in this process. Is she or he behaving as a laissez-faire leader, abdicating to the group, or is she or he sharing leadership with others so that members of the group can influence the decision?

As we conclude Part I, we want to emphasize why we have focused so intensively on organizations. In a word, context. There is no place to lead except within an organization. If leadership is fundamentally about influence relationships between leaders and followers, all those people need to be located somewhere—physically and/or virtually—in order to engage in influential processes. A critical aspect of leadership is understanding organization and organizing, and as we are sure you have surmised, theorists' and researchers' thinking about leadership and leading, and about organizations and organizing, are intertwined.

In the second part of this book, we transition to a focus on leading schools, first by focusing on the three models of school leadership most mentioned in the literature and researched by scholars and practitioners alike: transformational leadership, IL, and distributed leadership. It deserves to be mentioned before we start that part of the journey that it is our perspective that all three are united by their adherence to the four points outlined above—that leadership is relational, political, about meeting the needs of stakeholders, and about change and improvement. In particular, what sometimes gets lost in the various accounts of leadership theories as applied to schools and districts is the central concern with bringing about positive, lasting change. An enormous part of our interest in understanding leadership is to appreciate its role in *school change and improvement*; each of the three most prominent leadership theories deals with this question from different, but overlapping perspectives, and each provides an important clue about becoming a successful change agent (see Figure 5.1). Each suggests a focus on related, but different puzzles as well. And each builds on the foundational material covered in Part I.

FIGURE 5.1 Three Types of School Leadership that Focus on Leading Change

EXERCISE 5.1 LEADERSHIP TRAITS

Consider the opening vignette and discuss the following questions with a partner.

1. Which of the five traits (intelligence, self-confidence, determination, integrity, and sociability) are important to each of the panel members?

    •   Did the panelists converge on any particular trait(s)?

2. If you were a believer in the Great Man theory, trait theory, or some combination of the two, how might that make the process of choosing an AP candidate difficult or impossible?

EXERCISE 5.2 PONDERING THE IDEA OF "FIT"

Contingency theories, by considering "match" are aligned with a more contemporary notion of "fit," the idea that people bring skills, knowledge, and dispositions into a specific situation in which they may or may not be a good fit. Fit is hard to determine, however. Discuss the following questions with one or two partners:

1. Assume your school is looking for a new principal:

    •   What sort of person would be a good fit?
    •   What skills, knowledge, and/or dispositions would communicate to you that this person is a good fit?

2. How might bias play into your ideas about who is a good fit for your school?

    •   Does race or ethnicity play a role in our default beliefs about fit? How about gender?
    •   Should a leader always start out well aligned with the norms and expectations of the school community, or is it important to have a leader whose perspective differs, at least on some dimensions?

3. Finally, draft a job description for that position. Include each of the following: Job title; job responsibilities; required characteristics of the successful candidate; preferred characteristics of the successful candidate; minimum education.

EXERCISE 5.3 YOUR LEADERSHIP PLATFORM

Imagine for the moment that you are an applicant for the AP position at Huerta High School, and Dr. North contacted you with the following request: Could you please provide a short statement (less than 600 words) that summarizes your beliefs about effective leadership? Write your leadership platform of beliefs for the search committee, and share yours with a few critical friends to compare what you each believe.

PUZZLED ABOUT WHO SHOULD GET THE JOB

The interview panel that was bogged down in a directionless discussion is interrupted by Dr. North, the principal who finally speaks:

All of you are talking about what you think and what you want. We need to refocus on what is best for this school at this time and on this team. Our most pressing issue as a school is that, despite our best efforts and noticeable improvement in student achievement, we have flat-lined in the past couple of years. More concerning, the overall student experience at Huerta is very different if you are white and affluent as compared to black or Latino and/or low income. We will be much better off with someone who can bring us fresh ideas and energy for these critical issues. The second area where we need to focus is strengthening the administrative team. The way I see it, my role is largely working with the school community writ large to keep the main issues front-and-center and to stay connected to the various constituencies—students, teachers, parents, and staff. Fazia does the heavy lifting on helping departments keep curriculum current and rigorous while managing the various forms of assessment. Steve is the AP with the most experience, but he is not on this panel because he is close to retirement and has been largely focused on keeping the athletics department in line and making sure the school plant and equipment are taken in working order.

Dr. North decided to bring you in as a human resources consultant. He is a good leader, but he cannot take care of all of the school's needs by himself. Fazia is strong but feeling overwhelmed at times. Make a choice:

- Choose one of the candidates described at the beginning who seems like the best fit and explain why in detail (you may want to add some [fictional] information to what you learned in the vignette), or
- Recommend reopening the search.

   o If you choose this option, you must describe for Principal North and the panel the characteristics they should be seeking in the candidates they interview.

REFERENCES

Ayman, R., Chemers, M., & Fiedler, F. (1995). The contingency model of leadership effectiveness: Its levels of analysis. *Leadership Quarterly, 6*(2), 147–167.

Bass, B. (1985). *Leadership and performance beyond expectations.* New York: Free Press.

Bass, B., & Avolio, B. (1994). *Improving organizational effectiveness through transformational leadership.* Thousand Oaks, CA: Sage.

Bass, B., & Avolio, B. (1995). *Multifactor leadership questionnaire for research.* Menlo Park, CA: Mind Garden.

Bass, B., & Ruggio, R. (2006). *Transformational leadership* (2nd ed.). Mahwah, NJ: Lawrence Erlebaum.

Bennis, W. (1959). Leadership theory and administrative behavior: The problem of authority. *Administrative Science Quarterly, 4*(3), 259–301.

Blake, R., & Mouton, J. (1964). *The managerial grid*. Houston: Gulf Publishing Co.

Blake, R., & Mouton, J. (1978). *The new managerial grid*. Houston: Gulf Publishing Co.

Burns, J. (1978). *Leadership*. New York: Harper and Row.

Campbell, R. (1968). A review of: *A theory of leadership effectiveness* by Fred E. Fiedler. *Administrative Science Quarterly, 13*(2), 344–348.

Chemers, M., Rice, R., Sundstrom, E., & Butler, W. (1975). Leader esteem for the least preferred co-worker score, training, and effectiveness: An experimental examination. *Journal of Personality and Social Psychology, 31*(3), 401–409.

Chernow, R. (2017). *Grant*. New York: Penguin Press.

Cumming, M. (2004). *The Carlyle encyclopedia*. Vancouver: Fairleigh Dickinson University Press.

Fiedler, F. (1967). *A theory of leadership effectiveness*. New York: McGraw-Hill.

Fiedler, F. (1978). The contingency model and the dynamics of the leadership process. In L. Berkowitz (Ed.), *Advances in Experimental Social Psychology* (Vol. 11, pp. 59–96). New York: Academic Press.

Fiedler, F., & Chemers, M. (1974). *Leadership and effective management*. Glenview, IL: Scott, Foresman.

Foster, W.P. (1986). *Paradigms and promises: New approaches to educational administration*. Amherst, NY: Prometheus Books.

Graham, W. (1973). Leader behavior, esteem for the least preferred co-worker, and group performance. *Journal of Social Psychology, 90*(1), 59–66.

Green, S., & Nebeker, D. (1977). The effects of situational factors and leadership style on leader behavior. *Organizational Behavior and Human Performance, 19*(2), 368–377.

Hersey, P., & Blanchard, K. (1969a). *Management of organizational behavior—utilizing human resources*. Englewood Cliffs, NJ: Prentice Hall.

Hersey, P., & Blanchard, K. (1969b). Life cycle theory of leadership. *Training and Development Journal, 23*(5), 26–34.

Hickman, G. (Ed.) (2010). *Leading organizations: Perspective for a new era*. Los Angeles: Sage.

House, R.J. (1971). A path-goal theory of leader effectiveness. *Administrative Science Quarterly, 16*(3), 321–339.

House, R., & Aditya, R. (1997). The social scientific study of leadership: Quo vadis? *Journal of Management, 23*(3), 409–473.

House, R.J., & Mitchell, T.R. (1974). Path-goal theory of leadership. *Contemporary Business, 3*(4), 81–98.

Katz, D., & Kahn, R. (1966/1978). *The social psychology of organizations* (2nd ed.). New York: Wiley.

Kotter, J. (1990). What leaders really do. In *Harvard Business Review on Leadership* (pp. 37–60). Boston: Harvard Business School Press.

Lee, M. (2014). Transformational leadership: Is it time for a recall? *International Journal of Management and Applied Research, 1*(1), 17–29.

Lewin, K. (1947). Frontiers in group dynamics: Concept, method and reality in social science; social equilibria and social. *Human Relations, 1*(1), 5–40.

Mintzberg, H. (1990). The manager's job: Folklore and fact. In *Harvard Business Review on Leadership* (pp. 1–36). Boston: Harvard Business School Press.

Mitchell, T., Biglan, A., Oncken, G., & Fiedler, F. (1970). The Contingency Model: Criticism and suggestions. *Academy of Management Journal, 13*(3), 253–267.

Natemeyer, W., & Hersey, P. (2011). *Classics of organizational behavior* (4th ed.). Lake Grove, IL: Waveland Press.

National Commission on Excellence in Education (1983). *A Nation at Risk: The imperative for educational reform*. Washington, DC: US Department of Education.

Northouse, P. (2019). *Leadership* (8th ed.). Thousand Oaks, CA: Sage.

Pearce, C., & Conger, J. (2010). All those years ago: The historical underpinnings of shared leadership. In G. Hickman (Ed.), *Leading organizations: Perspective for a new era* (2nd ed., pp. 167–180). Thousand Oaks, CA: Sage Publications.

Perrow, C. (1986). *Complex organizations: A critical essay* (3rd ed.). New York: McGraw-Hill.

Robinson, V., Lloyd, C., & Rowe, K. (2008). The impact of leadership on student outcomes: An analysis of the differential effects of leadership types. *Educational Administration Quarterly, 44*(5), 635–674.

Rost, J. (1991). *Leadership for the twenty-first century.* Westport, CT: Praeger.

Salancik, G., & Pfeffer, J. (1977). Who gets power—and how they hold onto it: A strategic contingency model of power. *Organizational Dynamics, 5*(3), 3–21.

Short, P & Greer, J. (1997). *Leadership in empowered schools.* Englewood, NJ: Prentice Hall.

Spector, A. (2016). Carlyle, Freud, and the Great Man Theory more fully considered. *Leadership, 12*(2), 250–260.

Spencer, H. (1901). *The study of sociology.* New York: Appleton & Company.

Stogdill, R. (1948). Personal factors associated with leadership: A survey of the literature. *Journal of Psychology, 26*(1), 35–71.

Stogdill, R.M. (1974). *Handbook of leadership: A survey of the literature.* New York: Free Press.

Vroom, V., & Yetton, P. (1973). *Leadership and decision-making.* Pittsburgh: University of Pittsburgh Press.

Yukl, G. (1999). An evaluation of conceptual weakness in transformational and charismatic leadership theories. *Leadership Quarterly, 10*(2), 285–305.

PART 2

Leading Schools

Part I's focus on organizations prepares the reader to understand different choices leaders make in response to organizational goals and imperatives. Part II addresses the specifics of three main leadership theories to provide prospective leaders with tactics and strategies for making change in schools that leads to improved performance. Chapter 6 begins Part II with a comprehensive discussion of one of the most popular leadership models: transformational leadership. Although often set up in publications in opposition to IL, we see the two as complementary. Thus, IL is introduced briefly in Chapter 6 and addressed comprehensively in Chapter 7. Chapter 8 elaborates extensively on the concept of shared or collaborative leadership touched on in Chapters 6 and 7. We use the construct of distributed leadership as the most contemporary—and perhaps the most complicated—means of understanding how and why leaders choose to share influence and agency with others.

Through these chapters readers will see how various leadership strategies fit different kinds of problems and contexts. The challenges and questions we pose in the form of vignettes, exercises, puzzles, and discussion devices give readers opportunities to test their evolving sense of good leadership and reflect on the theories and research they find most useful.

Pronouncements about what leaders *should* do are common but theory and research about what they *actually* do is more valuable for our purposes. The final chapter that closes the book examines what leaders in schools and districts *actually* do as a filter for thinking about how they might do their jobs *better*. As should be clear at this point, there is no one set of leadership best practices. Understanding various leadership behaviors and their consequences in a range of contexts informs leadership choices readers will make in their future positions.

We hope that you will approach Part II in an integrative manner, building from and adding onto what you read and remember from earlier chapters. The puzzle that concludes Chapter 8 is an opportunity for you to showcase all of your thinking about organizations, leadership, and working within and shaping complex interpersonal dynamics. The summary we provide in Chapter 9 connects you back to leadership as practice, not dismissing theory but rather reminding us that the role of our excursion has been to build your knowledge and understanding of the complex phenomenon we call leadership so that you can do great things in schools. Enjoy the journey toward school leadership.

CHAPTER 6

Transformational Leadership and Change

The beginning of the school year always brought a bit of excitement, though as Terry Sipulski left her office on her way to the opening faculty meeting she also had a strong sense of déjà vu. This was hardly her first rodeo. A veteran of 27 years, the past 12 as principal of Madison High School, Terry had seen a lot and had worked through many complex situations. But here she was again, opening the school year with an announced change mandated by the district office—a change she had learned about only a few days ago, but that was required to be implemented this fall. She knew what she would hear from her staff, and empathized, even as she put on her game face for the meeting.

As Terry got to the part of the agenda that included the newly announced, required change to the grading system, she braced herself. There had been very little, if any, discussion about the "no zero" policy that requires that no grades under 50 percent be given for any assignment. "So," one teacher said, "Even if a kid totally ignores the assignment, I gotta give her a 50?" No, Terry explained, "the policy requires that if a student hands something in, however poorly done, that signals that the student made a good faith effort, and should get a grade between 50 and 100. If a student totally ignores the assignment, of course that's a different story." Terry thought to herself, though, what does this even mean? We have virtually no guidance about what a "good faith effort" is.

"Why do we need this change, anyway?" several teachers added to the general grumble prevalent in the room. "Whose idea was this?" "What did the union have to say about this change?" "Were there teachers, students, or even parents involved in discussing this?" On and on this went, until Terry put her hand up and said, simply, "I hear you, but the fact is that this is a mandate. We have to do it. From here forward, nothing below a 50 unless you can document that the student has truly made no effort to complete an assignment."

Later that week, at a meeting of the school's department chairs, several additional issues came up having to do with the implementation of the new policy, and it was clear that even this seemingly simple change was going to have ripple effects. Implementation, it seems, is a lot more complicated than anyone thought. For instance, one teacher asked, "What do we do about multiple-part assignments when a student hands in the first part but not the second? Is that a 50, or a partial 50, or a zero, or what?" Frankly, Terry had no idea. Nor was she prepared with any suggestions. She hated when the school system mandated changes that weren't thought-out or shared fully with the schools. It was much worse when whole new programs were introduced without much input, but even this seemingly marginal policy adjustment, she believed, was an example of change management gone bad.

Thought Partner Conversation

Can you recall a situation in your work experience like the one described in the opening vignette? What was the change, who initiated it, and how successful was it? Looking back, how might the change experience have been improved?

WHAT IS LEADERSHIP?

"Leadership is all about *organizational improvement*; more specifically, it is all about establishing widely agreed upon and worthwhile directions for the organization and doing whatever it takes to prod and support people to move in those directions. My generic definition of leadership—not just effective leadership—is very simple, then; it is all about direction and influence. Stability is the goal of what is often called 'management.' Improvement is the goal of leadership" (Leithwood, 2006, p. 180, emphasis added).

INTRODUCTION

It is no exaggeration to say that a primary responsibility of all school leaders, whatever their title, involves initiating and managing change. The considerable investment in public education—which exceeded $630 billion in the US during the last year for which such data are available (USDoE, 2017) is but one explanation for the call for continuous improvement. The pressure to change is exacerbated by the increasing heat of local, state, and federal political demands. High-stakes accountability policies, international comparisons of school quality, and ever-changing pronouncements about what represents "best practices" create demands for the adoption of various innovations. Most important, your work as a leader affects the futures of a generation of children and young adults who walk through the school's doors, a responsibility educators worldwide take quite seriously. Leaders are at the forefront of improvement efforts—as Leithwood (2006) explains, "As far as I am aware, there is not a single documented case of a school successfully turning around its student achievement trajectory in the absence of talented leadership" (p. 182). Louis, Leithwood, Wahlstrom, and Anderson (2010) point out that amid the many stakeholders who have an impact on school outcomes, "educators in leadership positions are uniquely well positioned to ensure the necessary synergy" (p. 9). Whether from a dollars-and-cents perspective, policy pressure, or as a moral obligation, it is clear that *if you aspire to school leadership, you are in the school improvement business.*

We introduced the general idea of transformational leadership in Chapter 5, noting its roots in the business and management literature. The concept centers on the notion that leaders influence followers to pursue something greater than themselves, to strive for an ambitious vision, and to seek improvement. "Transformational leadership," Avolio (1999) writes, "involves motivating others to do more than they originally intended and often even more than they thought possible" (p. 41). Some overall characteristics associated with transformational leadership (TL), according to Avolio (1999), include the notion that transformational leaders inspire and develop followers; that they stress shared values and an uplifting vision of what is possible, and that they "stimulate challenge, as opposed to suppressing it when it arises" (p. 34). Transformational leaders, from this perspective, are motivated by the desire to achieve ambitious outcomes. They are keen listeners, are aware of the need to be role models, and seek to move themselves and others beyond self-interest. Bass (1999) summarizes:

> The interests of the organization and its members need to be aligned. Such is a task for the transformational leader. In contrast to the transactional leader who practices contingent reinforcement of followers, the transformational leader inspires, intellectually stimulates, and is individually considerate of them.
>
> (p. 9)

Although transformational leadership is not solely concerned with fostering change, among the various conceptualizations of leadership it is the most concerned with improvement as a goal of collective action. The generic meaning of transformational leadership, Leithwood (1993) asserts, derives from the definition of "transform," that is, leadership practices that foster growth or change related to both practice and the motivation to improve. A logical outcome is that scholars and practitioners soon adopted it as a way of understanding the leader's role in school reform (Urick & Bowers, 2014). In the present policy environment—and in the US since the publication of *A Nation at Risk* in 1983 (National Commission on Excellence in Education, 1983)—leaders must focus their work on improving teaching and learning; transformational leadership uniquely suits this focus (Leithwood, 1992). "The popularization of transformational leadership theory in educational leadership cannot be understood apart from the current, change-oriented educational policy environment, which emphasizes restructuring and transformation to meet twenty-first century schooling requirements" (Berkovich, 2016, p. 609). Our emphasis on transformational leadership in the process of leading change appears in a modified version of Figure 5.1 (see Figure 6.1).

We review the concept of transformational leadership *as applied to schools*, beginning with a brief exploration of the meaning of TL, including what research suggests about the impact of TL on school outcomes. We also offer a brief discussion of the differences and similarities between IL—the focus of Chapter 7—and TL as two prominent school leadership models potentially focused on school improvement. Building from more academic perspectives, we will explore two fundamental transformational leadership practices: vision building and managing change.

FIGURE 6.1 Emphasizing Transformational Leadership for Leading Change

Essential Questions
1. How does transformational leadership define the relationship between leaders and followers?
2. How is transformational leadership practiced in schools?
3. How does change happen?
4. Why is transformational leadership so closely associated with change?

Thought Partner Conversation

The term "transformation" means more than just change—to transform something is to change it so fundamentally that it is difficult, perhaps impossible, to return to the previous state of being. Can you think of a change in your personal life or work experience that was so fundamental and comprehensive? Discuss what the change was, how it came about, what the goals were, and what you experienced that transformed you or your organization.

THE MEANING OF TRANSFORMATIONAL LEADERSHIP IN SCHOOLS

Bush (2017) claims that transformational leadership is "among the most enduring of the many leadership models" (p. 563) that offers a recommendation for school leadership—*a normative model*—focusing on the ways leaders influence others to become committed to school goals and motivated to engage in organizational improvement efforts. TL's emphasis on motivations and aspirations of organization members builds from the descriptive and analytical power of the human relations theories discussed in Chapter 1 and complements organizational learning's emphasis (Chapter 4) on analysis of organizational performance. Organizational learning and transformational leadership focus squarely on making meaningful change. Leithwood and Jantzi (2006) suggested that TL is the *ideal leadership style* for principals of schools considering substantial reform since change management is a central skill of transformational leaders.

Several reviews affirm TL's inclusion among a select few dominant leadership models in the educational leadership literature. For example, Leithwood and Duke (1998) identified 20 different educational leadership concepts represented in articles in prominent journals, with IL, leadership styles, and transformational leadership as the most mentioned. Hallinger and Heck (1998) found that IL studies dominated the literature through the 1980s, whereas the field turned to transformational leadership as the most prominent model in the 1990s. More recently, Bush and Glover (2014) identify nine leadership models that seem to be prevalent in education, among them IL (the subject of Chapter 7), transformational leadership, and teacher leadership. Berkovich (2017) notes that a systematic review of published research in general management studies on leadership from 2000 to 2012 finds transformational leadership to be the most prevalent model employed. But in education leadership, TL is not as dominant; it is a distant second in prevalence to IL in published work between 1990 and 2016. Day, Gu, and Sammons (2016) and Gumus, Bellibas, Esen, and Gumus (2018) concur that instructional and transformational leadership are the most widespread models invoked in research on educational leadership.

Bush (2011) categorizes transformational leadership as among the collegial models of leadership and organization, which "include all those theories which emphasize that power and decision-making should be shared among some or all members of the organization" (p. 72), although TL is presented as separate and distinct from *participative leadership* and *distributed leadership*. Marion and Gonzales (2014) associate TL with change writ large, de-emphasizing participation or leader–follower relations. Yet, the concepts of shared leadership and/or distributing leadership are never far behind applications of transforming or transformational leadership. For example, Urick and Bowers (2014) observe:

> Transformational leadership restructures and prepares schools for an increase in shared leadership with improved opportunities for innovation and change. Principals who are transformational leaders offer teachers a climate with a mission, professional growth, and a sense of community. Transformational leadership is focused on developing people and the organization, which improves outcomes.
>
> (p. 100, citations omitted)

In a later work, Bush (2017) explains that TL focuses primarily on the process by which leaders influence staff and stakeholders to become committed to school goals. Gumus et al. (2018) position transformational leadership as the counterpoint to managerial, top-down leadership.

Something that vexed Principal Sipulski to the point of distraction was that the district office was always preaching various forms of shared decision making as a means of cultivating faculty "buy-in" to school improvement efforts. Terry thought of herself as aligned with principles of participative management, shared decision making, and distributed leadership (see Chapter 8), but tried to take them a step further. Her intent was to involve the faculty in crafting major initiatives so that they would be committed to what they helped create, not merely "bought-in" to someone else's good idea. Every time the district handed down a mandate such as the "nothing-below-a-50" rule, they undermined her attempts to be a transformational leader fostering continuous improvement. Somehow, when she made these arguments in management team meetings, they fell on deaf ears with rationales about how urgent the particular mandate at hand was. Terry came to view one of her biggest leadership challenges as keeping her school on course with the initiatives that were generating improved student outcomes while minimizing the effects of district mandates. Doing so stretched her loyalties in different directions.

Thought Partner Conversation

Discuss the transformational leaders you have witnessed or worked with in your professional career. In what ways would you call them transformational? What about them as leaders would you most want to emulate in your own leadership practice, and why?

It should be clear from the above accounting that pinning down a definition of TL as applied to school leadership is confounded by the existence of a number of conceptualizations of school leadership that have similar and often overlapping attributes. Resulting confusion is mitigated by a select number of *characterizations* and *operationalizations* of the concept that tend to dominate the research literature, notably the work of Ken Leithwood and his various co-authors (Leithwood, 2005; Ninkovic & Floric, 2018; Stewart, 2006; Urick & Bowers, 2014).

Leithwood and colleagues took the work of Burns, Bass, and other theorists focusing on the business world "as a point of departure" for their work on TL in schools (Geijsel, Sleegers, Leithwood, & Jantzi, 2003, p. 230), which generated literally dozens of studies on the definition and impact of TL as applied to school leadership. Since their earliest work, formulations of TL have become refined and increasingly elaborate as research has progressed and been incorporated into subsequent work. Over time, publications shifted from broad ideas of the nature of TL to describing what transformational leaders *actually* do to improve schools (Leithwood & Jantzi, 2005). We rely on Leithwood to depict how researchers have developed the notion of TL as applied to schools.

In an earlier writing, Leithwood (1992) conceived of TL as involving three goals: helping school staff develop and maintain a collaborative school culture; fostering teacher development; and helping staff solve problems together. Leaders, he wrote, are in continuous pursuit of these goals. These relate to a claim Leithwood (2005) made over a decade later, namely:

> All transformational approaches to leadership emphasize emotions and values and share in common the fundamental aim of fostering capacity development and

higher levels of personal commitment to organizational goals on the part of leaders' colleagues. Increased capacities and commitments are assumed to result in extra effort and greater productivity.

(p. 9)

Leithwood and Duke (1998) summarize a more detailed conceptualization of TL offered by Leithwood and colleagues in the early nineties, involving eight dimensions (though it should be noted that this same model has been described as including anywhere from five to nine dimensions; see for example, Leithwood & Jantzi, 1997, 2000; Stewart, 2006; Urick & Bowers, 2014; Yu, Leithwood & Jantzi, 2002). Transformational leaders are concerned most with:

1. building school vision;
2. establishing school goals;
3. providing intellectual stimulation;
4. offering individualized support;
5. modeling best practices and important organizational values;
6. demonstrating high performance expectations;
7. creating a productive school culture; and
8. developing structures to foster participation in school decisions.

(Leithwood & Duke, 1998, p. 36)

Thought Partner Conversation

From among the eight characteristics depicted in the list above, which do you most associate with your conception of a transformational leader, and why? Are there any you would tend to omit from the list?

These dimensions, in turn, relate to specific leadership practices, which Leithwood and Steinbach (1995) associate with problem-solving processes employed by leaders to promote organizational change and improvement.

By the late 1990s, Leithwood's conceptual definition of TL encompassed three broad dimensions (Yu, Leithwood & Jantzi, 2002) or "superordinate categories of leadership practices" (Geijsel et al., 2003, p. 230): setting directions; developing people; and redesigning the organization. Shortly after the turn of the century, a fourth category found its way into the model: managing the instructional program (see, for instance, Leithwood, 2006). These four *superordinate categories*, in turn, relate to a number of leadership practices that were both conceptually and operationally defined for research purposes. These include the following, noted in parentheses (Leithwood, 2006):

- Setting direction (building a shared vision, setting goals to guide action, holding high performance expectations).
- Developing people (intellectual stimulation, individual consideration, modeling values and practices).

- Redesigning the organization (building and maintaining collaborative cultures, creating and maintaining structures, productive relationships with parents and larger community).
- Managing the instructional program (staffing the program, providing instructional support, monitoring school activity, buffering staff from distractions to their work).

(pp. 189–194)

In more recent work (Leithwood & Sun, 2012), managing the instructional program transitions to *improving the instructional program*, which continues to be associated with the above-mentioned behaviors. It is worth noting that this latter category emerged at a time when a good portion of Leithwood's scholarly writing focused directly on the question of how school leaders impact student learning. Whereas setting direction, developing people, and redesigning the organization might apply generically to leaders in any setting, *managing or improving the instructional program* applies uniquely to school contexts and, hence, is more likely to apply to improving student performance and achievement. The inclusion of this category might also serve to address questions and comparisons about the difference between TL and IL, a topic of scholarly research and speculation for some time (which we will review a bit later in this chapter).

> ### Thought Partner Conversation
>
> The transformational leadership behaviors associated with the four major categories listed above are illustrative, not inclusive of everything that might be mentioned. What would you add as essential behaviors for transformational school leaders, and why?

While springing initially from the more business-focused work of scholars such as Burns and Bass, Leithwood's model of TL emerged and was refined based on empirical research conducted in schools over decades in a wide variety of settings. Regardless of the iteration of this model, it embodies hypotheses about how school leaders impact student learning, primarily through their ability to influence the motivation, commitment, and behaviors of teachers. Ninkovic and Floric (2018) note that the first component, setting direction, tends to denote leaders' impact on the teaching staff as a whole, as does redesigning the organization, whereas developing people involves action directed at individuals and/or groups, as would improving the instructional program. The specificity and delineation of transformational leadership behaviors (TLB's)—actual leadership practices—sets this work apart from other publications on transformational leadership or, indeed, many other models depicting school leadership (Leithwood & Jantzi, 2006).

   The specificity of the model also suggests something important about who leaders might be as well as how they influence improvement. Much of the early work on TL in business settings seemed to reflect the underlying notion that transformational leaders are exceptional, rare, or reflecting the heroic form of leadership (Leithwood & Jantzi, 2006). When we step back and look at the evolution of the concept in education, it seems that our sense of transformational leadership *behaviors* is less about dramatic behaviors that only sporadically happen than an articulation of sound leadership and management practice. Contemporary views of who leaders are in schools and the distribution of leadership (see Chapter 8) that is purported to contribute to school improvement implies that anyone might develop and exhibit TLBs. In fact, our hopes for sustained school improvement depend on widespread initiative (leadership) throughout schools. Of course, an assertion that distributed TL is essential only makes sense if TLBs are known to influence important outcomes positively, a question we turn to in the next section.

Principal Sipulski had a hard time calming down after answering a barrage of questions about how to handle student assignments that might yield less than 50 percent of the total credit. When she did, she asked herself, "Is there any way to turn this annoying mandate into something positive for students and for the school?" She thinks the basic intention is good—students who are at least trying should not get saddled with failure that leads to defeat. Most teachers would agree with that sentiment. The trick, it seems, is to get teachers to focus on commonly shared values, such as supporting students to do their best and keep improving, instead of on a mandate that seems to undercut teachers' professional judgment in communicating students' academic progress. The other professional being undercut was Principal Sipulski herself. She needed to find a way to reassert her leadership with respect to students' academic progress.

RESEARCH ON TRANSFORMATIONAL LEADERSHIP IN SCHOOLS

Researchers have set out to determine whether there is empirical evidence to support the notion that transformational leadership affects a variety of important outcomes in schools. These include, but are certainly not limited to such things as collective teaching efficacy (Ninkovic & Floric, 2018), teacher job satisfaction (Tesfaw, 2014), student engagement (Leithwood & Jantzi, 2000), organizational citizenship behavior (Nasra & Heilbrunn, 2016), teachers' social capital (Minckler, 2014), and even teachers' adoption of instructional technologies (Vermeulen, van Acker, Kreijns, & van Buuren 2015). The lion's share of these studies employ Leithwood's conceptual (and often operational) definition of TL, sometimes seeking to tease out which TLB's contribute most to outcomes of interest. For instance, Ninkovic´ and Floric (2018) find that setting direction and developing people have the greatest impact on collective teacher efficacy. Day, Gu, and Sammons (2016) find that TLB's associated with setting directions and restructuring the organization are critical in initiating schools' improvement efforts, raising expectations, and providing structures to promote collaborative work among teachers.

An Important Purpose for Transformational Leadership

The highest value outcome of research on school leadership, however, is whether TL (or any other leadership model) influences student learning. The prevalence of papers that deal with the impact of TL on mediating variables—characteristics of teachers and/or the school setting—is testament to the complexity of the question. Although some research has attempted to determine a direct link between school leadership and student outcomes, overwhelmingly scholars conclude that school leaders mostly affect student learning indirectly through a complex set of relationships. That is, leaders have indirect effects on student learning because of the nature of their work—they exert their influence on members of the school community and/or school conditions (Hallinger & Heck, 1998; Leithwood, 2005). As Leithwood (2006) summarizes:

> Mostly leaders contribute to student learning indirectly, through their influence on other people or features of their organizations. We can think of this as a chain of variables effectively joining the actions of leaders to the learning of students. This indirect influence of leaders on students should be self-evident by simply reminding ourselves about how leaders of all but the smallest districts and schools spend the bulk of their time and who they spend it with—whether successful or not.
>
> (p. 182)

$P = f(M, A, S)$

Leithwood (2006) summarizes years of empirical work with the observation—in equation form—that teacher performance (P) is a function of teacher motivation (M), teacher skill and abilities (A), and characteristics of the work setting (S).

Leaders affect teaching behavior—what teachers actually do—by engaging in transformational leadership behaviors falling into the categories presented earlier: setting direction, developing people, redesigning the organization, and improving the instructional program.

How these four critical behaviors are expressed in practice depends on such things as the nature of the puzzle of the moment; human, fiscal, and social resources available; leader–member relations; and other characteristics of the situation and individuals involved.

The four areas of TLBs outlined earlier are the primary ways school leaders influence teacher performance in practice. "Leaders' contributions to student learning ... depend a great deal on their judicious choice of what parts of their organization on which to spend high-priority time and attention how they spend their time and what they focus on influencing" (p. 182). Accordingly, understanding the influence of TL on student outcomes is accomplished primarily by modeling the causal chain that links leaders' impact on a variety of mechanisms through which leaders might improve teaching practices, teacher motivation, or aspects of the school environment, in turn influencing student learning (Ninkovic & Floric, 2018).

Consistent with this perspective, in a review of studies conducted from 1996–2005, Leithwood and Jantzi (2005) found support for the relationship between TL and student engagement and achievement, with the impact of TL on perceptions of improvement characterized as large whereas the relationship between TL and direct measures of student outcomes "quite promising though limited in amount" (p. 193). In a meta-analysis of unpublished studies, Leithwood and Sun (2012) found substantial support for the impact of TL on school conditions, with a more modest and indirect impact on student achievement (though the impact on math achievement was more pronounced). Chin (2007) also reviewed unpublished studies from the US and Taiwan, and found that TL practices have significant effects on student achievement, though many studies reviewed relied on a narrow conceptualization of TL, limiting the ability to draw conclusions across studies.

Overall, the evidence seems compelling that leaders who engage in TLBs generally have a positive effect on a number of teacher emotions or perceptions (e.g., self-efficacy, commitment), which impact motivation and effort and consequently elements of teaching practice, thereby affecting student engagement and achievement (Berkovich & Eyal, 2017; Leithwood & Jantzi, 2000). Research affirms that TL is linked to greater teacher motivation, commitment, and effort (Berkovich & Eyal, 2017; Leithwood & Jantzi, 1999) and on teachers' classroom practices (Leithwood & Jantzi, 2006). Geijsel et al., 2003 and others (e.g., Yu, Leithwood, & Jantzi, 2002) provide empirical support for the notion that TLBs affect dimensions of teacher commitment and effort, noting the importance of vision building and intellectual stimulation among the various TL practices. Thoonen et al. (2011) show that a combination of TL practices appears to stimulate teacher professional learning and motivation (again, including vision building, providing individualized support, and providing intellectual stimulation), and Moolenaar, Daly, and Sleegers (2010) found that leaders' engagement in TLBs is positively associated with innovation.

Thought Partner Conversation

Think about a change you've experienced that you believe led to positive outcomes in terms of student learning. What TLBs did leaders use to influence this change, and how did these influence teaching practice?

INEVITABLE CRITICISMS

Though support for transformational leadership as a model has been widespread and the preponderance of empirical evidence supports the relationships between TLBs and a variety of important outcomes, the concept is not universally praised. For instance, Bush and Glover (2014) note that while the concept of TL stresses the importance of values, *whose values* are stressed has been a source of contention. This line of argument asserts that the default answer has been policy makers, government agencies, and school system leaders, i.e., people at the zenith of the education hierarchy. From this perspective, the voice of followers in the leadership process becomes muted. While TL stresses the commitment to organizational goals and change capacities of all—and the concept of "extra effort" is often mentioned—the top-down nature of this equation seems contrary to the spirit of the theory. Indeed, Burns' (1978) initial conception of transforming leadership begins with leaders tapping into the motivations, aspirations, and value of *followers*, not policy elites. Otherwise, TL may be seen as a means of controlling teachers (Bush, 2017).

From a research perspective, Berkovich (2016) also notes that TL has become something of a catch-all label for all sorts of behaviors and approaches linked primarily by their focus on change. This "lack of empirical distinctiveness" (p. 611) is problematic, in that it is hard to determine whether TL is different from other types of leadership such as participative or distributed leadership, or how such models are related. A bit of a cottage industry has emerged around determining which conception of leadership is most promising or explanatory in predicting various outcomes.

LEADERSHIP FOCUSED ON INSTRUCTION

The most prominent debate regarding leadership influence on student outcomes has focused on the relative merit of transformational leadership as compared with IL, two concepts that have traded places in prominence in research on school leadership effects for several decades. The debate was fueled most recently by Robinson, Lloyd, and Rowe (2008), who in a much-cited paper reanalyzed research on the two models and concluded that the mean effect size of TL on student outcomes is dwarfed by the impact of IL (ES = .11 versus .42), with 10 of 11 empirical studies of TL effects showing only a weak impact.

Bush (2014) observes that IL and TL differ in important respects. IL is primarily about leadership behavior that seeks to influence teaching and learning (Bush & Glover, 2014). Based on the preceding discussion, we might call this an emphasis on direct or first-order change seeking to impact learning (Hallinger, 2003). For example, Stewart (2006) states that instructional leaders focus on school goals, curriculum, and instruction, rather than the improvement of school conditions. Shatzer, Caldarella, Hallarm, and Brown (2014) claim that instructional leaders are more transactional than transformational, more focused and directive than visionary and inspiring. TL, in contrast, emphasizes how leaders influence followers by motivating or inspiring commitment and pursuit of organizational goals. This is most likely to have a second order influence on student learning by encouraging changes in mediating variables. Day, Gu, and Sammons (2016) write:

> While transformational leadership has traditionally emphasized vision and inspiration, focusing on establishing structures and cultures that enhance the quality of teaching and learning, setting directions, developing people, and (re)designing the organization, instructional leadership is said to emphasize above all else the importance of establishing clear educational goals, planning the curriculum, and evaluating teachers and teaching. It sees the leaders' prime focus as responsibility for promoting better measurable outcomes for students, emphasizing the importance of enhancing the quality of classroom teaching and learning.
>
> (p. 224)

Marks and Printy (2003) note that as a theory with its genesis in business, many conceptions of TL lack a specific educational emphasis. Even when applied to school settings,

TL models may tell us more about leader–staff relations than the impact of leadership on student outcomes (Robinson, Lloyd, & Rowe, 2008), or as Schatzer et al. (2014) put it, TL may be thought of as a more general theory that is less likely to demonstrate direct effects on specific behaviors. All told, these observations affirm the complex and indirect nature of the relationship outlined earlier between TLBs and student outcomes.

FIVE DIMENSIONS OF INSTRUCTIONAL LEADERSHIP

- Establishing goals and expectations
- Resourcing strategically
- Ensuring quality teaching
- Leading teacher learning and development
- Ensuring an orderly and safe environment

Source: Robinson, Lloyd, and Rowe (2008)

The difference between transformational leadership and IL is hardly crystal clear. Hallinger (2003) points out that when researchers measure TL and IL, they typically include behaviors that are similar if not identical, such as creating a shared vision, having high expectations, and providing intellectual stimulation. The five concepts associated with IL in the Robinson, Lloyd, and Rowe (2008) study (see box) appear to overlap with most operationalizations of TL, at least the most recent ones emphasizing TLBs in schools. Hallinger and Heck (1998) point out that TL models emphasize the organization's capacity to improve, not specifically in relation to enhancing curriculum and instruction, which is the central focus of IL models. Similarly Leithwood (1993) argues that IL models tend to focus on change within the classroom, whereas the TL framework may be more suited to understanding school-wide reforms that may involve much broader concerns (such as equity and social justice). Hallinger (2003) stresses that IL models tend to emphasize change that is initiated and coordinated by the leader rather than involving shared decision making, which may also distinguish the models. And yet, Marks and Printy (2003) and Urick and Bowers (2014), among others, found measures of TL and IL to be highly correlated, raising questions related to whether the constructs are indeed distinctly different empirically.

A BAG OF TOOLS

The discussion of different conceptions of leadership can easily turn into a competition of ideas: Which is better, transformational leadership or IL? We do not wish to set one leadership theory against another. Rather, we aspire to show you the various characteristics of transformational leadership (this chapter), IL (Chapter 7), and distributed leadership (Chapter 8), as well as their major critiques, so that you have a variety of tools at your disposal. We leave it to you, the prospective leader, to determine which tool or combination of tools best fits your hand in a given situation at a specific point in time.

Finding Meaning for Prospective Leaders

Our review of the various manifestations of TL and how it differs from and over-laps with IL reminds us of Leithwood's (2006) caution that "leadership by adjective is a growth industry" (p. 177), and Hallinger's (2003) that many uses of terms such as instructional and transformational leadership are at best sloganistic. Yet, the discussion prompts our attention to several important lessons we students of school leadership would be wise to remember. We have portrayed the debate carried out in the literature as if either IL or TL is important, as if these are competing ideas that somehow exclude the other. As Day, Gu, and Sammons (2016) observe, this relies on a rigid distinction between the underlying ideas behind the two models, as if effective leaders require only one or a small set of practices and can ignore others. Effective leadership, they write, "includes both a focus on the internal states of organizational members that are critical to their performance and classroom instruction" (p. 225). We might also observe that any instructional leader, however laser-focused on teaching and learning, will inevitably support instructional change by engaging in TLBs such as developing people (providing professional development, evaluating teaching) and redesigning the organization (organizing teacher teams, grouping teachers and students). The largest proportion of changes school leaders promote tend (we hope) to involve improving the instructional program.

Though it seems unlikely that we will drop modifiers such as transformational or instructional when we speak of school leadership, increasingly the research literature has focused less on getting the labels right and more on understanding the complex nuances of what school leaders do that has a positive impact on schools as organizations. Integrative models have been suggested (Day, Gu, & Sammons, 2016; Leithwood & Sun, 2012; Marks and Printy, 2003; Urick & Bowers, 2014) that affirm the reality that leaders in schools are neither solely focused on transformation nor instruction; they need to be both, and more. As Day, Gu, and Sammons (2016) concluded in their study of leaders committed to school improvement, successful leaders "combined and accumulated both transformational and IL strategies within, through, and across each developmental phase of their schools' long-term improvement" (p. 251). This work suggests, perhaps, that rather than considering TL and IL as separate leadership styles, we might view IL as a type of transformational approach that focuses more narrowly on teaching and learning processes in schools. It is what transformational school leaders do when they intentionally seek to improve instruction, i.e., when they focus on changing the technical core (Leithwood & Sun, 2012).

When TL and IL are considered together, we are able to answer an important "for what?" question. Transforming teaching and learning such that student, school, and district performance improve is the ideal—the highest value outcome as we termed it earlier in this chapter—for the dedicated principal and superintendent. Implied here is a belief in continuous improvement, which begins with an interest in leading change.

> **Thought Partner Conversation**
>
> With a critical friend (or two), consider a change that you experienced in your school that was wildly successful (or, if you prefer, a total disaster). What characteristics of the situation, leadership, people involved, etc., most contributed to this outcome? If you were leading a change like this in the future, what would you do differently, and why?

LEADING CHANGE

At the outset of this chapter, we claimed that leading change is central to all that leaders do, and that in today's environment for schools the pressure for change has never been more acute. The heart of the transformational leadership model is the notion that effective leaders encourage and support continuous improvement; the IL construct focuses this change on teaching and learning processes in schools, but it, too, stresses change. The TLBs discussed earlier provide some hints about what leaders need to do in their practice to be effective at leading change, and we have indicated throughout the preceding chapters about various organizational perspectives strategies that may help us understand and lead change, especially when we wrote about organizational learning in Chapter 4.

There is, of course, an enormous literature on innovation and change in organizations; it is a topic with deep and wide roots in organizational development and leadership studies. Likewise, there has been a great deal of work on school improvement with a range of processes suggested in both the scholarly and practitioner literature. Some related concepts, such as professional learning communities and shared decision making, are discussed elsewhere in this volume. For the remainder of this chapter we would like to return to some of the ideas introduced in Chapter 4 and share thinking that we find too often neglected, especially in the many how-to treatises on improving schools. Although we just dip our toes in a very deep pool, this material is critical to understand if you are to lead school improvement.

> **Thought Partner Conversation**
>
> Return to this chapter's vignette in which Terry Sipulski is introducing a planned change to her faculty at an opening faculty meeting. What would you do if you were in her shoes to support the district mandate as a loyal team member and promote change within a faculty who is likely feeling that Terry's collaborative values have been undermined?

CHANGE AS THREE STEPS (CATS)

Although we will not engage in an exhaustive review of the many theories and models related to changing organizations, we have found that a foundational concept embodied in many, if not most work on *planned change* in organizations is exceedingly useful to understand as a leader. This idea, *change as three steps* (CATS), is generally attributed to one of the founders of social psychology, Kurt Lewin (Burnes, 2004; Cummings, Bridgman, & Brown, 2016; Higgs & Rowland, 2005; Weisbord, 2012), who devoted a substantial portion of his life's work to understanding organizational and social change (Burnes & Bargal, 2017). Lewin's contributions to the body of knowledge on change are vast, including work on the value of shared governance and employee participation (group dynamics); the analysis of environmental forces related to change (field theory); and the role of experimentation in promoting organizational learning (action research). Although there is evidence that Lewin saw the planned approach to change as involving group dynamics, field theory, and action research as an interconnected system (Burnes, 2004), we focus here on one of his key ideas: CATS.

In his work, Lewin postulated that change—or better put, *planned change*—occurs in three steps or phases (Burnes, 2004; Weisbord, 2012), depicted in Figure 6.2:

1. Change begins with *unfreezing*. Imagine that we as individuals and groups begin the change process in a sort of equilibrium; for change to occur, we must abandon our current ways of doing and thinking, breaking with this equilibrium, i.e., *unfreeze*. In organizational life, this is associated with letting go of existing policies, practices, and beliefs. It is unlikely participants will be willing to do this unless they feel a need for change or experience a gap between the real and the ideal, between how things are and how we would like them to be. In Chapter 4's discussion of organizational learning, we discussed this as a gap between aspirations and outcomes. Letting go of tried-and-true ways of thinking and doing can be frightening; we need a compelling reason for doing so. Lewin recognized that with change comes potentially powerful psychological and emotional baggage (Schein, 1996), and that leaders need to be certain to make clear (a) why the change is necessary, (b) what the change is replacing, and (c) why the change is likely to be better than whatever it is replacing.

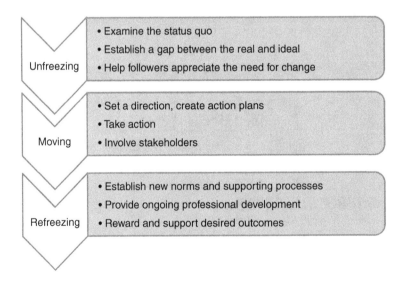

FIGURE 6.2 Lewin's Change as Three Steps

2. Change continues with *moving*. Schein (1996) points out that unfreezing is not a goal unto itself; it "creates motivation to learn but does not necessarily control or predict the direction" (p. 62). Moving involves planning and beginning to enact the change itself, what most of us think about as *action*. Higgs and Rowland (2005) note that during this phase, the leader identifies and applies resources needed to enact the change; Burnes and Bargal (2017) refer to it as "when the change actually occurs" (p. 93).

3. The final step is *refreezing*. During this final stage, leaders seek to institutionalize the change or "make it stick." Burnes (2004) observes that during this phase, leaders must make sure a new equilibrium is congruent with everything else that goes on in the organization. As new norms emerge that include the changed behaviors, beliefs, and practices, it is critical that existing practices do not serve as barriers. So, for example, if we add a new set of expectations into teachers' jobs (as may be the case in the opening vignette), we might need to examine whether professional development planned for the year supports the change, and/or whether performance evaluation schemes account for the new responsibilities. Leaders must also ensure that organizational members whose activities are critical to implementing the change feel competent and have the requisite knowledge and skills to sustain the change.

According to CATS, then, it is especially important for leaders to help followers understand the *need for change* from the beginning in order to help them *unfreeze* or disconnect from current beliefs and practices, and as a corollary, explain the vision of the future that the change will bring about. Having a sound action plan that serves to communicate the path forward and assure participants that needed resources are available is critical to *moving*; further, involving stakeholders in the change process adds to the likelihood that they will be motivated to embrace and support the change. Finally, reinforcing the new status quo by establishing policies and practices that are compatible with the change and supporting individual and group learning so that stakeholders can fully participate are crucial to *refreezing*.

CATS Reconsidered

In recent literature, Lewin's CATS has come under scrutiny as being too simplistic and linear in nature (Kanter, Stein, & Jick, 1992); in today's fast-changing organizations, it is unclear whether the concept of refreezing is even possible (Cummings, Bridgman, & Brown, 2016), much less preferable. By (2005) points to the reality that change is often unpredictable and unplanned, hence any model that focuses on planned change is limited in applicability. And yet, as Hendry (1996) states: "Scratch any account of creating and managing change and the idea that change is a three-stage process which necessarily begins with a process of unfreezing will not be far below the surface" (p. 624).

Bernard Burnes, in his various writings, explains and defends Lewin's theory, noting that Lewin did not think about change as necessarily linear, but rather as a part of an overall process of organizational learning (see, for example, Burnes 2004, 2007; Burnes & Bargal, 2017). He viewed change as a complex and iterative process, moving from one temporarily stable position to another. "Change and constancy are relative concepts," Lewin wrote. "Group life is never without change, merely differences in the amount and type of change exist" (Burnes, 2004, p. 996). *Refreezing* was not intended to suggest that change ends, but rather that leaders ought to be wary of stakeholders regressing to old ways of behaving and thinking if supports are not in place to prevent this.

Thought Partner Conversation

Can you recall a planned change that was introduced that produced immediate, but not lasting change? Reflect on the circumstances, and discuss how knowing the three stages of change we just discussed might have been helpful in this instance.

Weisbord (2012) is an admirer of Lewin, but he sees the change process slightly differently. Building from Lewin's and others' concepts, Weisbord sees individuals as residing in one of four rooms in an apartment. He claims that organization members resist being changed (just as Lewin did) if they have one of two perspectives, contentment or denial, which is how he labels the first two rooms of the apartment. Another factor that keeps people in those rooms is that in the third room is confusion, which is unsettling at best and frightening at worst. People would need to move into the confusion room (Lewin's equivalent of moving) before they could arrive at renewal, or an improved state appropriate for refreezing. Figure 6.3 demonstrates the sequential nature of the four-room apartment.

An important question for prospective school leaders is how one helps or persuades others to unfreeze or move through the four-room apartment. Lewin devised force field analysis to describe group dynamics that result in change initiatives and change resistance (Burnes, 2004) — may the stronger force win. Weisbord (2012) is not entirely happy with Lewin's implications of coerced change and claims that individuals must move from one room to the other of their own accord. Osterman and Kottkamp (2004) present something of a compromise with their claim that data analysis and discussions will help persuade teachers and administrators to make the necessary moves to improve student and school performance. Their position is consistent with organizational learning's examination of the gap between the outcomes we hope for and those we get. No matter the perspective, helping people to change—no matter how you might define "helping"—is dicey.

Regardless of various criticisms and/or defenses of CATS, we find the model to be extremely useful to leaders who intend to initiate and involve followers in school improvement in two ways. First, the model provides a heuristic device for understanding

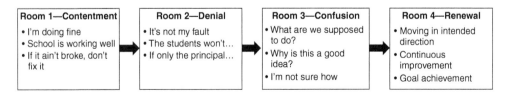

FIGURE 6.3 Weisbord's Four-Room Apartment

PREDICTING SUCCESS OF A PLANNED CHANGE

Beckhard and Harris (1987) suggest a "change formula" as a way of determining up-front whether a planned change seems likely to succeed. This formula embodies and extends Lewin's CATS model in some interesting ways. Briefly, they suggest:

$$(D \times V \times F) > R$$

Where

- D is dissatisfaction with the status quo
- V is a clear vision of the goal
- F is knowledge of the first steps needed to implement the change
- R is the psychological, emotional, and/or fiscal resistance to change.

Thus, a leader can expect that a change will be most successful when readiness for the change ($D \times V \times F$) is likely to overcome perceived costs to stakeholders and the organization.

Consider a change that you participated in or observed that was wildly successful—or one that failed miserably. How would using this thought exercise have helped predict the outcome? What might you have learned that could have led to useful modifications of the change process?

why a change may or may not have worked, and second, it may be used in planning change and analyzing the likelihood that a planned change will work. In particular, we have found over the years that leaders often undervalue the importance of unfreezing as a distinct stage in the change process, jumping to the enactment of change (moving) before stakeholders are convinced that a change is needed or preferable to existing practices.

This is the case in this chapter's vignette. Someone in the district office decided that the no-fail policy had to be implemented right away, just as the school year was about to begin. Teachers would obviously be "frozen" in grading practices they perceived to be serving them well. Principal Sipulski had the unenviable task of trying to unfreeze them immediately to move in a short period of time. Despite the mandate, it is not clear she would be able to unfreeze anyone in time for the start of school.

Similarly, we have observed that school leaders often disregard refreezing after a change is underway, assuming that stakeholders are onboard and able to support new ways of acting. This is most obvious when a new program is launched at the beginning of a school year after a few days of professional development, but needed training and reinforcement of new skills mid-year is neglected.

Thought Partner Conversation

Lewin is frequently quoted as observing that leaders never truly understand a system until they try to change it. In your experience, does this ring true? Discuss this idea with a critical friend, perhaps in the context of something important you learned about your school or school system as a result of being a change agent.

GETTING TO THE ROOT OF THE PROBLEM

There are a wide variety of process guides available to school staffs and leaders that recommend how to make evidence-based decisions to improve schools, including those that stress design thinking (e.g., Peurach et al., 2014; Mintrop, 2016), the application of improvement science (e.g., Bryk, Gomez, Grunow, & LeMahieu, 2015), and a range of inquiry processes (e.g., Militello, Rallis, & Goldring, 2009). All make valuable contributions to leaders' understanding of school change and provide guidance to teams engaged in school improvement planning. To varying degrees, most of these at least mention the necessity of change agents not only defining problems of practice that they plan to change, but exploring the root causes of these problems, that is, why the problems exist in their school at the precise time the change is contemplated. Duke, Carr, and Sterrett (2013) capture why this is such an important issue—the diagnostic work leaders and teams do to understand root causes allows them to pinpoint solutions that have the optimal chance of making a difference. In our experience, this step in planning is often omitted in texts and even more often skipped over in practice, to the detriment of change efforts. Hence, we take the opportunity to elaborate on our discussion from Chapter 4 and emphasize some process-oriented ideas that are critical to change leadership.

Elsewhere (Bauer & Brazer, 2012), we assert that all school improvement work is, at its heart, action research. That is, leaders and followers are engaged in a process of continuous improvement based in enacting changes that they believe will be productive; assessing the degree to which the "causal story" that guides these actions happens; thereby learning from experience and refining their beliefs and practices for future implementation. Our process model resembles the action research cycle typically associated with school improvement planning. It also differs in important ways, notably in the degree to which we stress root cause analysis as an explicit stage in planning. The four-stage process model builds on Osterman and Kottkamp's (2004) "cycle of experiential learning," connecting this school improvement process to what is known about effective techniques to promote reflective practice (see Figure 6.4).

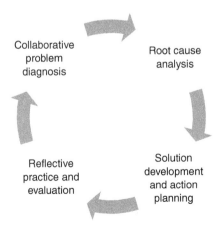

FIGURE 6.4 Continuous Improvement Process

Step 1: The process starts with collaborative problem identification. Putting Lewin's ideas to work, we note that for individuals to change and for the organization to improve, they must first become *unfrozen*. Unfreezing is most likely to come from an internal motivation to see the current situation differently (Weisbord, 2012). Once a sufficient number of people are unfrozen, it becomes possible to move the organization toward change before it adopts a new pattern of action. Central to this stage is assembling evidence to affirm the need for change, which is dependent on establishing agreement on "where we are" as well as "where we want to be," i.e., our aspirations as a school. We stress the importance of putting together a team to collect and analyze evidence (i.e., quantitative and qualitative data) to figure out where instructional challenges exist as a way of building support and motivation for the change.

Step 2: Once a problem or problems are selected, the process moves to root cause analysis, a stage that we believe must be made a central part of the change effort. As noted in Chapters 3 and 4, leaders and followers have a tendency to promote ready-made solutions in search of problems, and leaders are under a great deal of pressure to remedy any area perceived to be in need of improvement. This prompts, all too often, the adoption of solutions that treat the *symptoms* of the problem rather than its *causes*. You can be sure, for example, that someone at Principal Sipulski's district office perceived high failure rates as a problem and, without having any clue as to what was causing them, decreed that students could not be graded at less than 50 percent to mitigate the failure rate. This fictitious individual also probably didn't think about consequences that would follow from such a solution. Solutions that treat symptoms (single-loop learning from Chapter 4) are likely to provide brief mitigation but not lasting change. Too often, evidence of the problem (such as test scores) are mistaken for evidence of why a performance gap exists. Instead, if leaders and teams actually explore the root causes of a problem—building an understanding of why the problem exists in our school, at this time, with our students and teachers—the likelihood of selecting an appropriate solution skyrockets.

Step 3: The third stage of the process is identifying a solution and creating an action plan that spells out how this solution will be implemented, by whom, and so on. This blueprint frames Lewin's middle change stage, *moving*. Like problem identification, this stage is probably familiar to most teachers and leaders. What differs, however, is the connection to the previous stage, root cause analysis. Selection of research-informed actions to realize improvement is guided by the question: What solutions will help eliminate the root causes of the gap between the real and ideal? Solutions need to eliminate the causes of the problem, or change will be superficial. In this sense, we have endorsed a claim relating to cause and effect in schools: implementing solutions targeted to root causes will mitigate the cause of the problem, and consequently the problem will diminish. Action planning involves spelling out how the school will create the change, as well as how the implementation process itself is assessed for fidelity.

Step 4: This final step in the cycle involves taking time for learning through reflective practice and evaluation of the plan as enacted. This is critical to creating a new possibility, i.e., creating the potential for refreezing. Aside from the general lack of attention to root cause analysis, the second greatest weakness in school improvement efforts as they are practiced is failure to evaluate attempts to address the problem. Our experience suggests that school improvement efforts are seldom evaluated because of the time needed to do this, and because once a new program has been implemented it has already amassed a number of stakeholders who are devoted to it who resist critical examination. This is a huge mistake and a missed opportunity, one that serves to place a limit on the organizational learning that is possible as a result of the change effort. In Lewin's terms, it is possible that refreezing occurs too soon and because of unwarranted commitment to what was tried. It would be far better to demonstrate with evidence that a change generated actual improvement than to become invested in an idea or set of practices without knowing their effects. We advocate formative evaluation of action plan implementation, both to guide the implementation process and also to suggest modifications that may be suitable. Summative evaluation must also occur so that the school can determine whether the change as implemented is sustainable and, indeed, supportable based on the change it produces.

If all four stages of this process are helpful, why emphasize root cause analysis to the degree we have? First, as noted above, it tends to be glossed over in school improvement models and practices. Even more important, though, is the consequence of this omission; failure to analyze the causes of any gap between where you are and where you want to be is exceedingly detrimental to successful change because it precludes double-loop learning (see Chapter 4). What we suggest is similar to what City, Elmore, Fiarman and Teitel (2009) recommend in their work on instructional improvement, that is, developing a *causal story* or *theory of action* that explains your if-then propositions about how the problem came about; this becomes a testable proposition you use to build an action plan around a solution that is intended to eliminate the causes identified. As we wrote:

> The process of root cause analysis involves crafting a proposition that describes what you believe about the specific causes of the instructional problem you discovered in your school. We use the term "logic of action," rather than theory of action, to convey the idea that your propositions should try to explain the reasons the outcomes or processes you are trying to explain happen in your school and why. The "logic" you are proposing is a cause-and-effect rationale to explain the reality in your school. This serves as a bridge to discovering possible actions you might take to promote improvement.
>
> (Bauer & Brazer, 2012, p. 154)

To be clear, we advocate using a combination of published research and local inquiry to identify the most probable causes (and suggest a number of procedures for doing this; see Bauer & Brazer, 2012). Seeking applied research that explores why problems like yours exist in schools like yours (and how other sites tackled them), in combination with mining the craft knowledge of teachers and leaders in your own school, provides a powerful mechanism for discovering why particular problems exist, and provide the very best link to solutions that can make a real difference.

Thought Partner Conversation

Before we move on to read about vision, locate your school's vision or mission statement, and perhaps the vision or mission of one or two schools that are like yours. What can you learn about the schools based solely on these? Discuss with a critical friend how you believe these aspirational statements are (or might be) used by leaders to prompt or support change.

CHANGE BEGINS WITH CLEAR AND ELEVATING VISIONS

It is hard to dispute the prominence of vision as an important factor in leading change. The transformational leadership behaviors associated with *setting direction* attest to this, as do consistent findings in empirical work about the vital role school goals play in improvement efforts (Hallinger & Heck, 1996). If this is so well known and obvious, why isolate this as our final topic in this chapter?

There is a multitude of oft-confusing formulations for leading groups to create a vision and mission, and there is certainly a lot of ambiguity related to what we mean by vision and mission and how (if at all) they differ. In our experience, it is less important that leaders and followers get this "right" (whatever that means) than it is that they agree on a meaning they can live with and that will guide their efforts. It is extremely important that school staff and communities agree on and understand aspirations for the future; there is no one "best" process to get there or definition of the outcome (e.g., vision, mission, strategic objectives). Rather than endorse one process or another for establishing a vision, here we would like to touch on vision-related issues that seem to get lost in leaders' efforts at *setting direction*.

Extended Web Activities

With a critical friend, do an internet search to find different conceptualizations of the terms *vision, mission*, and *objectives*. Is there a scheme that resonates well and appeals to you as a leader?

We intentionally titled this section *"clear and elevating visions."* This deliberate use of language hints at two separate issues we believe significant for aspiring leaders of change. In much of the literature relating to setting direction, the emphasis on clarity is abundant—goal consensus is well established as an issue of importance to leaders (despite the difficulty of achieving such consensus noted in the first several chapters of this volume). Larson and LaFasto (1989), in their wonderful book on teamwork, extend this notion in an important way; they assert that team effectiveness is dependent not simply on goal clarity, but the degree to which the goal is "elevating," energizing, or worth pursuing. In their study, elevating implied a goal that was personally or organizationally challenging—a stretch. It can be elevating regarding the difference it would make in terms of organizational improvement or progress. A goal that makes a difference to leaders and followers—and those their organization impacts—provides a sense of urgency and focus. So compelling was this issue in their research that they emphasize that it was always present for teams that were deemed effective. Furthermore, in *every case* of a team that was failing, the team had replaced their clear and elevating goal with another, less important focus. Sometimes this was personal success of a leader or team member, and sometimes it was control or the ability to exert power. Whatever the reason, it seems worthwhile for leaders interested in transforming some aspect of their school to periodically reflect on whether the improvement goals being pursued, and the vision or mission to which they refer, are indeed elevating to followers and likely to result in good things for kids.

The second issue embedded in our section title is our use of the plural *"visions"* rather than the singular. School or district leaders are repeatedly admonished to lead followers in revisiting or creating "a vision of the future," as if one vision is sufficient. We agree that it is essential for a school staff and community to know and understand their aspirations and organizational direction. Yet, it may be equally important for subgroups within the school to think about their goals—aligned with the school's—in much the same fashion as a superintendent would expect each school to have a clear and elevating vision in sync with the district's. Similarly, we might ask whether it is helpful to have different visions in relation to different aspects of school operations. As an illustration, one exercise we believe to be quite helpful in any school is for teachers in a department or on a grade-level team to agree on their vision of effective teaching; a guidance department may likewise establish a coherent set of aspirations related to counselors' work. The point is that no complex organization relies on a single vision or set of objectives, and leaders who are interested in promoting change throughout the school might do well to raise the vision question periodically. Imagine the potential of each teaching team working to actualize their clear and elevating goals for powerful learning, aligned with the school's vision of effective teaching.

Although the importance of setting direction is present in virtually every discussion of leading school change, there seems to be considerably less dialogue on how leaders use a vision in their day-to-day practice. The Principal Sipulski vignette and Chapters 2 and 3 point to one reason why doing so is challenging: principals are constantly distracted by influences from outside the school and priorities can easily shift from day to day. It is obvious that a vision and/or improvement objectives should be monitored periodically, *at least* annually as a part of the process of beginning next year's plan. It is also helpful when various aspirational statements are used in school communications and/or marketing (if only on the banner in the atrium of the school). But if that's the extent to which vision is used, it is unlikely to motivate much change.

We encourage a much more active role for vision/mission: leaders need to view their aspirational statements as *decision criteria*, factors that are used day-in and day-out to weigh the viability of alternative courses of action and assess their preferences among decision choices. For commitment to the vision. Consider this example: What does it say to teachers when the principal espouses the value of teacher collaboration while eliminating planning time that served as the most obvious opportunity for grade-level teams to meet to plan together? What about when the administration emphasizes the need for teachers to differentiate instruction and meet students where they are, while admonishing teachers for veering even slightly from the pacing guide? This issue brings us back to the discussion in Chapter 4—any but the smallest and most routine decisions are indicators of the leader's beliefs about the difference between aspirations and outcomes and their role in organizational learning. When there is a wide chasm between what we espouse as a vision or goal and the policies and practices we endorse, followers rightly question commitment to vision, mission, and goals. For any decision option, actively questioning and discussing whether choices will promote movement toward the school or team vision brings the vision alive and ensures that progress is made continuously toward the outcome.

KNOWING WHAT VERSUS KNOWING HOW

One final reality associated with leading change that every leader must grapple with is this: describing an effective policy, practice, or program is not the same as knowing how to implement that policy, practice, or program. Ah, if it were only so easy. Consider this rather mundane example.

As we write this, baseball season is underway. In our lives, we may have pined for the pro ranks—even hallucinated about batting in Yankee Stadium in front of a sellout crowd. We can *describe* in vivid detail how stars hit for average and power; we know what they do to be so successful. We may have played competitively; some of us *coached*—meaning that at least someone thought we were knowledgeable enough to teach others how to play. The fact that we can describe and explain how to hit or throw or field is not sufficient to enable us to *become* successful professionals. Not even close.

This presents us with a conundrum as leaders. As we have discussed earlier in the book, leaders are under a lot of pressure to adopt practices associated with effective organizations as a source of legitimacy. When we are faced with a vexing problem, our go-to reaction is to seek examples of places that successfully navigated the path forward. We can describe sets of *best practices* for virtually any educational and organizational challenge based on *what worked* for other schools or universities. But *describing* an effective anything does not tell us how to *become* effective at that thing.

Reflect on a pressing problem of practice that your school or district faces, and how you would suggest engaging in a process of organizational learning that both enables you to understand what effective practices might make sense while acknowledging the need to make these practices "fit" your school or district structurally, culturally, and operationally.

CONCLUSION

As we said at the outset of this chapter, to lead schools today means that you are in the school improvement business. Change is demanded and expected from within the school and from powerful stakeholders in the environment. This chapter demonstrates that TL embodies a powerful set of concepts that provide a rationale for change. Knowing that TL makes a difference in school quality and student achievement means that successful schools transform themselves—they change. Our intent has been to breathe life into TL theory, research, and assertions by explaining specific change leadership practices, ideas that we find to be vital but often neglected in the voluminous work on leading school improvement.

Change is inevitable. Robinson (2018) reminds us that not all change leads to improvement, nor is all change desirable. To lead improvement—to be a truly transformational leader—is to accept an enormously complex role, a role that we know a great deal about but that requires agility, flexibility, and continuous attention to personal and organizational capacity building. Our review of TL models and the research available on them in school contexts reveals tremendous progress in recognizing the intricacies of school leadership. Indeed, the body of work shows a growing sophistication in theoretical development and accompanying empirical investigative work—and a healthy interest in ensuring that scholarly work contributes to improving practice.

IL played a supporting role in this chapter as a contrasting or competing set of concepts to which transformational leadership is often compared. As we have said more than once, our intent is not to set up one set of leadership theories against another. Rather, we would like you to see how different perspectives on leading schools complement one another. We turn our attention in the next chapter to IL, keeping in mind that school leaders who promote instructional improvement are seeking transformation.

EXERCISE 6.1 TRANSFORMATIONAL LEADERSHIP BEHAVIORS

Think about a large, pressing issue in your school. Such an issue might involve one particular group of students, such as English language learners. It could be school wide, possibly generating a sense of community. The issue is up to you. Pick one and write a sentence or two that describes it:

Use Worksheet F to think through approaches to this issue from the point of view of Leithwood's superordinate categories and transformational leadership behaviors. (You may wish to re-read The Meaning of Transformational Leadership in Schools section before proceeding.) Create a table of your own and answer the questions in the cells (and/or generate and answer your own questions).

Reflection: This exercise is intended to help you think through how you might apply the transformational leadership behaviors we emphasize in this chapter. How did that go?

1. Are some of the behaviors easier for you to imagine implementing than others?
2. Did you consider organizational influences from previous chapters that might facilitate or impede your use of TLBs?
3. What more do you need to learn to lead change that improves instruction?

WORKSHEET F

Setting Direction: Vision, Goals, Expectations	Developing People: Stimulation, Consideration, Values and Practices	Redesigning the Organization: Collaborative Cultures, Structures, Relationships	Improving the Instructional Program: Staffing, Instructional Support, Monitoring, Buffering
• What direction would you set for the school on this issue? • What specific goals would help you achieve this vision? • How might expectations for specific stakeholders change? • What values would you preserve and emphasize as you moved the school community forward in your direction?	• How might you work with potentially resistant individuals? • What kind of professional development will be required to help teachers (and staff) move in the desired direction? • What would you do to motivate teachers to address the issue in the manner you think best?	• How could you generate and/or support a collaborative culture to address this issue? • What new structures would need to be put in place to move in the direction you intend? • What old structures, policies, or procedures might stand in your way? • What relationships might need to be nurtured to support needed change?	• In what ways is staffing likely to need modification or augmentation? • Who will monitor progress toward addressing the issue and how will that be done? • What resources would be required to address this issue in the manner you imagine? • How would you protect the school against the kind of external shock experienced by Principal Sipulski?

EXERCISE 6.2 HELPING PRINCIPAL TERRY SIPULSKI UNFREEZE, MOVE, AND REFREEZE HER FACULTY

Terry's perception is that the teachers are frozen in their previous ways of thinking about grading students. She generally agrees with their point of view—students' should not receive credit for work they haven't done. Yet, she knows she has a professional responsibility to ensure that Madison High School implements the district mandate with reasonable fidelity. And Terry thinks it might be possible to use the mandate for the benefit of students without creating phony grades. She just needs to figure out how to thread this needle.

1. What are the most important cognitive and affective factors that are freezing teachers in their current perspective?
2. How might the requirement that no student receive below 50 percent on an assignment or test reveal gaps between aspirations and outcomes at Madison High School?

   • Thinking about your own teaching experiences, what are some likely root causes for these gaps?

3. What kinds of data or evidence could Terry provide that might help to unfreeze teachers?

    • Can you identify potential positive outcomes from the mandate that might mitigate the effect of its being a mandate delivered just before school starts?

4. What are some elements of an action plan to implement the mandate that would address the root causes you have identified?

5. How would you want to involve the faculty, if at all, in the process of conducting analysis and action planning?

6. If you were in Terry's shoes, how confident would you feel in your answers to these questions?

PRINCIPAL TERRY SIPULSKI'S FOCUS PUZZLE

Terry Sipulski faces a tricky puzzle. As principal, she works at the pleasure of the superintendent, meaning her 1-year contract as principal may not be renewed the following year if the superintendent becomes displeased. Yes, she has been around long enough that it would be difficult to remove her and there would be little cause to do so, but she is mindful that all the superintendents with whom she has worked expect principals to be loyal to their leadership and do what is asked of them.

Terry's faculty is angry about and distracted by the mandate for no grades below 50 percent. The mandate and teachers' reactions are threatening Terry's efforts to engage the faculty in leading teaching and learning improvements on the way to transforming her school into higher student performance. Finding a way to stay on a path of continuous improvement, to maintain her school's transformation, is of paramount importance to Terry Sipulski.

Working alone, with a partner, or in a small group, take on the role of leadership consultant to Principal Terry Sipulski. You may want to complete Exercise 6.2 first and reflect on your answers before beginning this puzzle. Answer the following question to help you develop a leadership plan for the coming year:

1. What is the minimum that Principal Sipulski must do to implement the district grading mandate?

    • What might the mandate reveal about strengths and weaknesses in teachers' current grading practices?
    • Are there ways in which the mandate can be authentically reframed for teachers so that it supports teaching and learning without undermining teacher professionalism?

2. Assuming success with question 1 above, how might Principal Sipulski re-energize efforts to improve instruction school wide?

    • What role would vision, mission, values, and/or goals play in this effort?
    • How would you suggest Principal Sipulski work with teachers to avoid cynicism that might have been engendered by the mandate? "Why should we do

anything when the district will just step in with reform of the year that will take us away from what we have been working on?"

- Would you recommend organizational learning processes? Why, or why not? If so, what might they look like?

3. Principal Sipulski has been principal of Madison High School for 12 years, a relatively long tenure for a high school principal. Assume the reasons for her longevity have a lot to do with her effective leadership.

    - How does the no-fail mandate affect her leadership in the eyes of teachers, students, and parents?
    - What, if anything, should Terry do to asset/reassert her leadership under these circumstances?

4. What would you recommend that Terry do:

    - Before students arrive?
    - By the end of the first quarter?
    - By the end of the year?

REFERENCES

Avolio, B. (1999). *Full leadership development: Building the vital forces in organizations.* Thousand Oaks, CA: Sage.

Bass, B. (1999). Two decades of research and development in transformational leadership. *European Journal of Work and Organizational Psychology, 8*(1), 9–32.

Bauer, S., & Brazer, S.D. (2012). *Using research to lead school improvement: Turning evidence into action.* Los Angeles: Sage.

Beckhard, R., & Harris, R. (1987). *Organizational transitions: Managing complex change.* Reading, MA: Addison-Wesley.

Berkovich, I. (2016). School leaders and transformational leadership theory: Time to part ways? *Journal of Educational Administration, 54*(5), 609–622.

Berkovich, I. (2017). Will it sink or will it float: Putting three common conceptions about principals' transformational leadership to the test. *Educational Management Administration & Leadership*, 1–20 (online first—Retrieved January 2, 18 from journals.sagepub.com/home/ema; DOI: 10.1177/1741143217714253).

Berkovich, I., & Eyal, O. (2017). The mediating role of principals' transformational leadership behaviors in promoting teachers' emotional wellness at work: A study in Israeli primary schools. *Educational Management Administration & Leadership, 45*(2), 316–335.

Bryk, A., Gomez, L., Grunow, A., & LeMahieu, P. (2015). *Learning to improve: How America's schools can get better at getting better.* Cambridge, MA: Harvard Education Press.

Burnes, B. (2004). Kurt Lewin and the planned approach to change: A re-appraisal. *Journal of Management Studies, 41*(6), 977–1002.

Burnes, B. (2007). Kurt Lewin and the Harwood studies. *Journal of Applied Behavioral Science, 43*(2), 213–231.

Burnes, B., & Bargal, D. (2017). Kurt Lewin: 70 years on. *Journal of Change Management, 17*(2), 91–100. DOI: 10.1080/14697017.2017.1299371.

Burns, J. (1978). *Leadership.* New York: Harper and Row.

Bush, T. (2011). *Theories of educational leadership and management* (4th ed.). Thousand Oaks, CA: Sage.

Bush, T. (2014). Instructional and transformational leadership: Alternative and complementary models? *Educational Management Administration & Leadership, 42*(4), 443–444.

Bush, T. (2017). The enduring power of transformational leadership. *Educational Management Administration & Leadership, 45*(4), 563–565.

Bush, T., & Glover, D. (2014). School leadership models: What do we know? *School Leadership & Management, 34*(5), 553–571, DOI: 10.1080/13632434,2014.928680.

By, R. (2005). Organisational change management: A critical review. *Journal of Change Management, 5*(4), 369–380.

Chin, J.P. (2007). Meta-analysis of transformational school leadership effects on school outcomes in Taiwan and the USA. *Asia Pacific Education, 8*(2), 166–177.

City, E., Elmore, R., Fiarman, S., & Teitel, L. (2009). *Instructional rounds in education: A network approach to improving teaching and learning.* Cambridge, MA: Harvard Education Press.

Cummings, S., Bridgman, T., & Brown, K. (2016). Unfreezing change as three steps: Kurt Lewin's legacy for change management. *Human Relations, 69*(1), 33–60.

Day, C., Gu, Q., & Sammons, P. (2016). The impact of leadership on student outcomes: How successful school leaders use transformational and instructional strategies to make a difference. *Educational Administration Quarterly, 52*(2), 221–258.

Duke, D., Carr, M., & Sterrett, W. (2013). *The school improvement planning handbook: Getting focused for turnaround and transition.* Lanham, MD: Rowman & Littlefield.

Geijsel, F., Sleegers, P., Leithwood, K., & Jantzi, D. (2003). Transformational leadership effects on teachers' commitment and effort toward school reform. *Journal of Educational Administration, 41*(3), 228–256.

Gumus, S., Bellibas, M., Esen, M., & Gumus, E. (2018). A systematic review of studies on leadership models in educational research from 1980 to 2014. *Educational Management Administration & Leadership, 46*(1), 25–48.

Hallinger, P. (2003). Leading educational change: Reflections on the practice of instructional and transformational leadership. *Cambridge Journal of Education, 33*(3), 329–352.

Hallinger, P., & Heck, R. (1996). Reassessing the principal's role in school effectiveness: A review of empirical research, 1980–1995. *Educational Administration Quarterly, 32*(1), 5–44.

Hallinger, P., & Heck, R. (1998). Exploring the principal's contribution to school effectiveness: 1980–1995. *School Effectiveness and School Improvement, 9*(2), 157–191.

Hendry, C. (1996). Understanding and creating whole organizational change through learning theory. *Human Relations, 48*(5), 621–641.

Higgs, M., & Rowland, D. (2005). All changes great and small: Exploring approaches to change and its leadership. *Journal of Change Management, 5*(2), 121–151.

Kanter, R., Stein, B., & Jick, T. (1992). *The challenge of organizational change.* New York: Free Press.

Larson, C., & LaFasto, F. (1989). *Teamwork: What must go right/what can go wrong.* Newbury Park, CA: Sage.

Leithwood, K. (1992). Transformational leadership: Where does it stand? *Education Digest, 58*(3), 17–21.

Leithwood, K. (1993). Contributions of transformational leadership to school restructuring. Paper presented at the Annual Meeting of the UCEA, Houston, TX.

Leithwood, K. (2005). *Emotional leadership.* Philadelphia: The Mid-Atlantic REL at Temple University Center for Research in Human Development and Education.

Leithwood, K. (2006). The 2005 Willower Family Lecture: Leadership according to the evidence. *Leadership and Policy in Schools, 5*(3), 177–202, DOI: 10.1080/15700760600646053.

Leithwood, K., & Duke, D. (1998). Mapping the conceptual terrain of leadership: A critical point of departure for cross-cultural studies. *Peabody Journal of Education, 73*(2), 31–50.

Leithwood, K., & Jantzi, J. (1997). Explaining variation in teachers' perceptions of principals' leadership: A replication. *Journal of Educational Administration, 35*(4), 312–331.

Leithwood, K., & Jantzi, J. (1999). Transformational school leadership effects: A replication. *School Effectiveness and School Improvement, 10*(4), 451–479.

Leithwood, K & Jantzi, D. (2000). The effects of transformational leadership on organizational conditions and student engagement with school. *Journal of Educational Administration, 38*(2), 112–129.

Leithwood, K., & Jantzi, D. (2005). A review of transformational school leadership research 1996–2005. *Leadership and Policy in Schools, 4*(3), 177–199.

Leithwood, K & Jantzi, D. (2006). Transformational school leadership for large-scale reform: Effects on students, teachers, and their classroom practices. *School Effectiveness & School Improvement, 17*(2), 201–227.

Leithwood, K., & Steinbach, R. (1995). *Expert problem solving: Evidence from school and district leaders*. Albany, NY: State University of New York Press.

Leithwood, K.A., & Sun, J. (2012). The nature and effects of transformational school leadership: A meta-analytic review of unpublished research. *Educational Administration Quarterly, 48*(3), 387–423.

Louis, K., Leithwood, K., Wahlstrom, K., & Anderson, S. (2010). *Investigating the links to improved student learning: Final report of research findings to the Wallace Foundation*. Minneapolis: University of Minnesota.

Marion, R., & Gonzales, L. (2014). *Leadership in education: Organizational theory for the practitioner* (2nd ed.). Long Grove, IL: Waveland Press.

Marks, M., & Printy, S. (2003). Principal leadership and school performance: An integration of transformational and instructional leadership. *Educational Administration Quarterly, 39*(3), 370–397.

Militello, M., Rallis, S., & Goldring, E. (2009). *Leading with inquiry and action: How principals improve teaching and learning*. Thousand Oaks, CA: Corwin.

Minckler, S. (2014). School leadership that builds teacher social capital. *Educational Management Administration and Leadership, 42*(5), 657–679.

Mintrop, R. (2016). *Design-based improvement: A practical guide for education leaders*. Cambridge, MA: Harvard Education Press.

Moolenaar, N., Daly, A., & Sleegers, P. (2010). Occupying the principal position: Examining relationships between transformational leadership, social network position, and schools' innovative climate. *Educational Administration Quarterly, 46*(5), 623–670.

Nasra, M., & Heilbrunn, S. (2016). Transformational leadership and organizational citizenship behavior in the Arab educational system in Israel: The impact of trust and job satisfaction. *Educational Management Administration & Leadership, 44*(3), 380–396.

National Commission on Excellence in Education (1983). *A nation at risk: The imperative for educational reform*. Washington, DC: US Department of Education.

Ninkovic, S., & Floric, O. (2018). Transformational school leadership and teacher self-efficacy as predictors of perceived collective teacher efficacy. *Educational Management Administration & Leadership, 46*(1), 49–64.

Osterman, K., & Kottkamp, R. (2004). *Reflective practice for educators* (2nd ed.). Thousand Oaks, CA: Corwin.

Peurach, D., Cohen, D., Glazer, J., Goldin, S. & Gates, K. (2014). *Improvement by design: The promise of better schools*. Chicago: University of Chicago Press.

Robinson, V. (2018). *Reduce change to increase improvement*. Thousand Oaks, CA: Corwin.

Robinson, V., Lloyd, C., & Rowe, K. (2008). The impact of leadership on student outcomes: An analysis of the differential effects of leadership types. *Educational Administration Quarterly, 44*(5), 635674.

Schein, E.H. (1996). Kurt Lewin's change theory in the field and in the classroom: Notes towards a model of management learning. *Systems Practice, 9*(1), 27–47.

Shatzer, R., Caldarella, P., Hallarm, P., & Brown, B. (2014). Comparing the effects of instructional and transformational leadership on student achievement: Implications for practice. *Educational Management Administration & Leadership, 42*(4), 445–459.

Stewart, J. (2006). Transformational leadership: An evolving concept examined through the works of Burns, Bass, Avolio, and Leithwood. *Canadian Journal of Educational Administration and Policy, 54*, 1–29.

Tesfaw, T. (2014). The relationship between transformational leadership and job satisfaction: The case of government secondary school teachers in Ethiopia. *Educational Management Administration & Leadership, 42*(6), 903–918.

Thoonen, E., Sleegers, P., Oort, F., Peetsma, T., & Geijsel, F. (2011). How to improve teaching practices: The role of teacher motivation, organizational factors, and leadership practices. *Educational Administration Quarterly, 47*(3), 496–536.

Urick, A., & Bowers, A. (2014). What are the different types of principals across the United States? A latent class analysis of principal perception of leadership. *Educational Administration Quarterly, 50*(1), 96–134.

US Department of Education, National Center for Education Statistics. (2017). The Condition of Education 2017 (NCES 2017–144), Public School Expenditures. Available online at: https://nces.ed.gov/fastfacts/display.asp?id=66.

Vermeulen, M., Van Acker, F., Kreijns, K., & van Buuren, H. (2015). Does transformational leadership encourage teachers' use of digital learning materials. *Educational Management Administration & Leadership, 43*(6), 1006–1025.

Weisbord, M. (2012). *Productive workplaces revisited: Dignity, meaning, and community in the 21st century* (25th anniversary edition). San Francisco: Jossey-Bass.

Yu, H., Leithwood, K., & Jantzi, D. (2002). The effects of transformational leadership on teachers' commitment to change in Hong Kong. *JEA, 40*(4), 368–389.

CHAPTER 7

Leading Instruction

On a summer afternoon, after the hoopla from the most recent graduation receded a bit in his memory, Miguel Suarez sat alone in his office to look at three sets of information for the just-graduated class: Smarter Balanced test results; student participation in Advanced Placement course separated by income, race, and English learner status; and self-reported college attendance patterns. These are three of the most important indicators of student success that Miguel, his administrative team, his teacher leaders, and his school district traditionally examined to produce a thumbnail of student success. He put this data into a quickly drafted spreadsheet and created a few charts for better visualization.

Working in a relatively well-resourced school district with a socio-economically, ethnically, and linguistically diverse student body was the right fit for Miguel, given his aspirations to create opportunities for adolescents through education. Devoted to high school students throughout his teaching and administrative career, Miguel felt as though he had arrived at his own professional mountaintop when he was named principal of Evergreen High School 4 years ago. Now, looking at the data he has organized and feeling wrung-out from the school year, he's not so certain. As the child of immigrants and someone who took advantage of educational opportunities to "make it" in the US, Miguel always believed that he had the knowledge and perspective to help students like himself raise themselves out of poverty and/or defy ethnic and linguistic stereotypes. Yet, the data show otherwise. Miguel understands that the process of closing achievement gaps is complicated and takes time, but in this moment he is feeling that efforts made thus far haven't really paid off for the majority of students on the wrong side of the gap. Why?

Thought Partner Conversation

The scenario you just read is an all-too-common one. Identifying, understanding, and remedying achievement gaps is the work of school leaders. Building on our discussion of root cause analysis from the previous chapter, discuss with a critical friend what you know and what you believe about why gaps persist and what role schools play in eliminating them.

LEADING INSTRUCTION: WHAT SHOULD THE PRINCIPAL BE DOING?

Leading instruction is challenging, complicated, and slow moving. Some would argue it's not really the job of the principal to do so (Horng & Loeb, 2010) and there is a consensus of sorts that principal effects on student learning are at best indirect (Hallinger, 2003; Leithwood, Harris, & Hopkins, 2008). Others claim that principals who become directly involved in efforts to improve teaching and learning have a large and meaningful effect on student achievement (Robinson, 2011; Robinson, Lloyd, & Rowe, 2008). All of the authors cited here would likely agree that identifying precise principal contributions to student achievement can be elusive, and all have made considerable efforts to understand and model these effects. Regardless of their take on the question, all agree that principals matter in the education of students, and that the primary impact principals make is through their ability to influence teacher learning and instruction. That last point is most important to us. We stress that principals must be directly involved in the process of trying to make teaching and learning better. This chapter explains the opportunities that abound within schools for leaders to create and participate in an environment focused on high-quality teaching, meaningful learning, and educational equity. We use the fictional Miguel as a foil in a manner that must by now seem familiar to the reader, and we extend our examples into elementary and middle schools.

Here is a question implied in Chapter 6: If transformation and change are important to school improvement, what should schools become? What should they transform into? Consistent with Chapter 4 about organizational learning, our answer is that in order to become schools that educate all students to the greatest extent of their potential, they need to foster teacher learning that improves instruction. The principal, along with other school leaders such as APs, department chairs, teacher coaches, and teacher peers, has a responsibility to shape and support that learning and its implementation in classrooms. In other words, principals lead teacher learning and, by extension, student learning in multiple ways (Robinson, 2011). Superintendents have a responsibility to keep equity issues front-and-center as they work with their communities and channel resources into efforts to give all students in their districts access to the best of what their schools offer, and they do this work through their leadership of and support for principals (Smith & Brazer, 2016). We must acknowledge from the start that making major, lasting changes that positively impact student learning is not entirely common in US education history because of teachers', schools', and districts' resistance to reform (Cuban, 1993; Tyack & Cuban, 1995). Nevertheless, as stated in Chapter 6, the work of the leader today is change and improvement, and we believe that if principals lead teacher learning focused on instruction, they can help teachers initiate change with high potential to narrow achievement gaps.

Returning to our leading change diagram from Chapter 5, we emphasize in this chapter the role of IL in the process of leading change.

FIGURE 7.1 Emphasizing Instructional Leadership for Leading Change

Essential Questions

1. Given that pedagogy has a personal "fit" element for different teachers in different settings, how can coaches, APs, and principals provide meaningful guidance and support regarding teaching methods?
2. How can schools be organized in a fashion that generates teacher collaboration focused on teaching and learning?
3. How can school leaders address multiple curricula in a school given that they have most likely been trained and taught in one, or possibly two, content areas?
4. Why emphasize instruction over sound school management?

STRENGTHS AND WEAKNESSES

We agree with those who claim that it is important to see the strengths that students, parents, and teachers bring to the educational process. But we also believe that it is important to be forthright about where a school may be falling short in its delivery of educational services. As was evident in Chapter 4, we think that schools cannot improve unless they understand the difference between what they aspire to achieve for students and their actual outcomes. This is the puzzle our fictional Principal Suarez is trying to figure out.

Gap analysis is vital to leading change and generating organizational learning and, as we learned in the previous chapter, to *unfreezing*. We do not dwell on individual or institutional deficits. Rather we use gap analysis as a jumping off point to solving problems in a manner that improves school and student performance and sustains the trend over time.

Thought Partner Conversation

In the introduction to this chapter, we assert that schools must be in the business of promoting teacher learning. With a critical friend, explore what this means—brainstorm a list of all of the ways teachers learn, what teachers most need to learn, and the various ways schools might promote this learning. Which of these, in your opinion, are most effective in promoting teacher growth and development?

Don't Expect a Simple Fix

You will notice that in this introductory section and throughout the chapter we have introduced teacher leaders as prominent players in IL. Doing so is quite deliberate because although we claim an important role for principals—and by extension APs—in the process of improving teaching and learning, we perceive teacher leaders of various kinds and teachers generally as critical partners in the process. Especially in large schools, administrators cannot be hands-on with all teachers simultaneously. What they can do instead is to ensure that robust webs of teacher collaboration characterized by important exchanges of ideas and experiences are present and nurtured in their schools to increase the frequency and depth of teacher learning. Teacher collaborative teams are powerful engines of change (Bauer, Brazer, Van Lare, & Smith, 2013).

Something else you may have noticed is that we have emphasized the challenge of achievement gaps in the vignette about Principal Miguel Suarez and the umbrella concept under which it falls, educational equity. Achievement gaps provide an important focus for IL efforts. Many schools similar to Miguel's do a fine job educating the majority student population. There is great value in doing so, of course, but it is insufficient for public education that purports to provide educational, social, and economic opportunities for *all students*. Acknowledging that there are many non-cognitive factors that contribute to achievement gaps—and that some of these are beyond the reach of any school—we argue that schools and districts have a responsibility to help the students in the bottom half of the achievement distribution to catch up to their higher-achieving peers. This is the portion of the population where teachers, teacher leaders, and principals such as Miguel can have the greatest impact with instructional improvement. Doing so may give them the greatest professional satisfaction as well.

We recognize that many education professionals have been striving to close achievement gaps for a very long time and that substantial resources have been poured into the effort for many years. The problem of achievement differences predictable along racial, linguistic, income, or disability lines easily frustrates many of us with good intentions. We are tempted to blame students, and by extension their families, for not trying hard enough: students not completing homework, students having weak English literacy skills, students unable to adapt their learning differences to the classroom, parents not reading to their children at home, parents not attending school events, etc. It is equally tempting to blame teachers: they don't differentiate instruction to meet students' needs, their content knowledge is poor, or they don't work hard enough.

Looking only to the student or only to the teacher in an effort to blame someone not meeting her or his responsibilities ignores the system that students and teachers find themselves in. There are forces at work that are not entirely within any individual's control. Schwab (1969) argued vigorously against identifying a single cause for weaknesses in educational outcomes and in favor of an eclectic approach to thinking about educational challenges. He urged employment of multiple theories and a focus on practice. For the purposes of this chapter, his most important claim for eclecticism is the need to think simultaneously about the critical influences in education.

> Schwab's argument was that every problem in education boils down to the inter-action of what he called four commonplaces—the teacher, the learner, the subject matter, and the context or the milieu. … If you're talking about education, you're always talking about somebody teaching something to somebody else in some setting.
>
> (Shulman, personal communication, April 18, 2010)

We envision Schwab's notion of eclectic approaches to educational challenges and Shulman's elucidation of the four commonplaces in Figure 7.2.

Students and teachers working together through an enacted curriculum within a specific classroom, school, and community context shape the individual and collective educational experiences of all students. The primary responsibility of IL is to work with the four commonplaces simultaneously to make the educational experience more meaningful for all students.

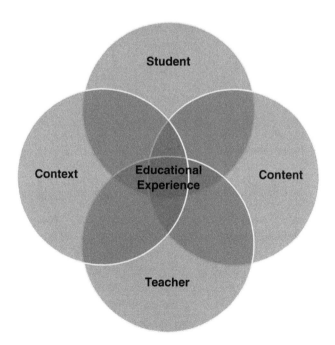

FIGURE 7.2 Schwab's Four Commonplaces that Shape Educational Experience

There is a rather large cognitive demand here: addressing instructional issues requires thinking about the challenging dynamics among teachers, students, intended and operationalized curricula, and context. Leading instruction means addressing the four commonplaces simultaneously from an expert perspective on pedagogy; curriculum; student needs, aspirations, and behaviors; and one's own school. We discuss the four commonplaces as they relate most directly to IL to inspire prospective school leaders to use specific leadership tools that address one of our most pressing contemporary educational challenges—narrowing achievement gaps. We focus on the teacher and content in our application of relevant theory and research and urge readers to combine these two with what is known about students and contexts through exercises in the chapter.

Thought Partner Conversation

To become familiar with Schwab's four commonplaces, explore with a critical friend a learning experience you shared (perhaps in a class in your leadership preparation program) using Schwab's scheme. How do the four commonplaces interact to affect your experience as a learner?

PEDAGOGY IS THE ART OF TEACHING

Similar to Principal Suarez, our expertise in pedagogy comes from our own teaching and observations of other teachers. Additionally, we have acquired some knowledge of contemporary pedagogy through our field-based research. Our understanding of multiple pedagogies is limited by our experience, and that might mirror your own situation. Nevertheless, when we put the question, *What is evidence of good teaching?* to our students and to ourselves, we often get answer such as these:

- student engagement;
- a caring attitude;
- thorough knowledge of content;
- dedication to student success.

All of the above and more are related to pedagogy, though some perhaps not directly. Each of the above characteristics could be exemplified by specific teacher practices, such as assigning group work, structuring problem-based learning, or using technology. Whatever the specifics may be, administrators have a responsibility to be knowledgeable about pedagogy because they are usually required by state law to evaluate teacher practice. They are limited in their ability to support and evaluate teaching practices by their knowledge of effective teaching strategies and techniques. Miguel and principals like him, consequently, have an obligation to continue learning about pedagogy so that they will know strong teaching when they see it and be able to nurture it through structuring teacher professional development (Resnick, 2010; Robinson, 2011).

In some ways, pedagogy is hard to capture because it is difficult to specify and fleeting in a series of moments in the classroom. One list that came from an effort to create a state-wide teacher evaluation system over 30 years ago included:

- lesson planning;
- assessment (of students);
- recognition of individual differences;
- cultural awareness;
- management

(Shulman, 1986)

This list seems remarkably current, yet important pieces are missing. What about students working in groups? Indicators of student initiative? According to Cuban (1988, 1993, 2018), educators and policymakers have been ambivalent for over a century about whether classrooms should be student-centered or teacher-centered. It seems surprising that consensus on good teaching appears to occur more readily when mechanics such as lesson planning and management are involved and less so regarding student engagement issues, particularly the larger ones such as the degree of student volition in the classroom. Ambivalence likely stems from teachers' need for control in the classroom while recognizing that students become more engaged when they have a greater hand in determining what and how they want to learn. Hence, classrooms tend to be a hybrid of teacher-centered and student-centered in an effort to achieve a reasonable compromise (Cuban, 1993, 2018). Assessing teaching quality is further complicated for administrators and coaches who may not know much about a particular subject area (about which we will have more to say later), and who operate in a policy context that often stresses alignment with an externally imposed pacing guide and standards of quality teaching that stress the easily observed mechanics of teaching. Administrators will most easily focus on commonly accepted mechanics of good teaching and leave the subtler parts, such as the nature of student discourse, alone. Doing so, however, may cause them to overlook some of the most powerful aspects of pedagogy.

To know good teaching—appropriate pedagogy—when in classrooms requires the use of basic principles that permit teachers to vary and adapt what they do with the particular students in their rooms, in a particular subject matter, on any given day. Shulman (1986) took a position consistent with a flexible, context-driven understanding of good teaching by acknowledging the importance of teacher judgment in the classroom:

> Knowledge guarantees only grounded unpredictability, the exercise of reasoned judgment rather than the display of correct behavior. If this vision constitutes a serious challenge to those who would evaluate teaching using fixed behavioral criteria ... so much the worse for those evaluators. The vision I hold of teaching and teacher education is a vision of professionals who are capable not only of acting, but of enacting—of acting in a manner that is self-conscious with respect to what their act is a case of, or to what their act entails.

(p. 13)

To know good teaching even more deeply requires a discerning eye; hence the deliberate reference in the title of this section to the "art" of teaching. We agree with

Eisner (1990) that recognizing good teaching requires the discernment of a connoisseur and the ability of an insightful critic to communicate what has been observed (Brazer & Bauer, 2013).

Thought Partner Conversation

Explore the question of what constitutes good teaching with a critical friend or two. On what attributes can you easily agree, and on what attributes do you differ? What kinds of factors might affect how you answer (for instance, content area, or level)?

Seeing What Happens in Classrooms

As a high school biology teacher, Miguel Suarez focused his teaching on laboratory work because of his fundamental belief in experiential learning. He also thought structure and inquiry were important, so he emphasized the Scientific Method with his students and careful write-up of lab reports. He often chuckled to himself when he thought of the stacks of laboratory notebooks he brought home many nights, reading himself blind trying to decipher adolescent scrawl. It didn't seem so funny at the time, but he believed the struggle was worthwhile so that students could learn to be scientists.

Engaging in instructional rounds (City, Elmore, Fiarman, & Teitel, 2009) observations this past year, Miguel was struck by what he saw in lower elementary grades. Second and third grade students he observed working in pairs for math lessons vigorously debated multiple pathways toward solving a specific problem. In large groups, their teachers presented student work without making a judgment and asked the whole group of 25 or so second or third graders (the method was similar at both levels) to determine the effectiveness and efficiency of the method presented. These whole group discussions were always animated. Miguel noticed that student participation varied in predictable ways, but what was more striking to him was the norm of engagement these teachers generated and the apparently genuine inquiry these lessons fueled. He was amazed. His high school biology classes rarely seemed to spawn such vigorous discussions or "aha moments" as students worked diligently on their labs.

Miguel wondered why high school classes seemed so much less inclusive and tolerant of divergent thinking that might arrive at a similar solution. Through this lens, high school teaching appeared stilted and flat to Miguel. At the same time, he knew that the adorable 8- and 9-year olds he'd observed were different people when they got to high school.

Thought Partner Conversation

With a critical friend, imagine a context in which you might observe teachers teaching (e.g., a particular school, department, level). Construct a walk-through instrument you might use to conduct brief observations of teachers teaching in that context, with one wrinkle: focus on what learners are doing in the classrooms, not teacher behavior. Now consider: would the attributes of quality teaching you outlined earlier engender such student behaviors?

Resnick (2010) identified a thinking curriculum similar to what Miguel valued as vital to obtaining the kinds of twenty-first century skills and dispositions that educators appear to appreciate for their students. Had she reflected with Principal Suarez on his instructional rounds, they would have agreed that pedagogy that encourages critical thinking, problem solving, and academic discourse is not currently in the playbook of many teachers. She would caution Miguel that if he wants his teachers to teach in a manner consistent with what he observed in elementary school, in an age-appropriate manner of course, they would need professional development. They would need opportunities to learn new methods. Elmore (2004) agrees, claiming that too often we impose new requirements on teachers without helping them develop the skills and knowledge needed to meet them. Harkening back to our discussion of motivation in Chapter 1, social psychologists like Herzberg would remind us that teachers need both *ability* to learn new ways of teaching and the *opportunity* to put these newfound skills to work in their classrooms.

Robinson (2011), were she to sit down with Resnick, Elmore, Herzberg, and Miguel, would also concur and promote the following ideas for teacher professional development. First, she places a strong emphasis on principals being directly involved in teachers' learning.

> The most powerful way that school leaders can make a difference to the learning of their students is by promoting and participating in the professional learning and development of their teachers. … [L]eadership practices go well beyond organizing and resourcing the professional development program. Much of the evidence that contributed to this finding [of a large effect from leader involvement] was about leaders themselves participating in the learning in the role of leader, learner, or both.
>
> (p. 104)

Miguel as principal is certainly one of those leaders Robinson had in mind, but she is also referencing teacher leaders such as grade-level or department chairs and coaches. Engaging in IL collaboratively is crucial, as Robinson notes, and we address collaboration in detail below. At this point, we want to emphasize that Principal Suarez learns about pedagogy by seeing what teachers are doing at different levels and in different schools. He can do the same within his own school through impromptu and planned classroom observations and discussions with his teacher leaders. This kind of on-the-job learning applies to pedagogy and content alike—two halves of a crucial whole.

Shulman (1986), in his influential American Education Research Association presidential speech, made the case for emphasizing content knowledge for teachers. What was new and different about his message is that he advocated for pedagogy and content to be considered together.

> Our work does not intend to denigrate the importance of pedagogical understanding or skill in the development of a teacher or in enhancing the effectiveness of instruction. Mere content knowledge is likely to be as useless pedagogically as

content-free skill. But to blend properly the two aspects of a teacher's capacities requires that we pay as much attention to the content aspects of teaching as we have recently devoted to the elements of teaching process.

(Shulman, 1986, p. 8)

We now add content and curriculum to pedagogy as we explain pedagogical content knowledge, one of the critical constructs that informs IL.

Thought Partner Conversation

Before reading on, discuss with a critical friend how you define *curriculum*. What elements make up the curriculum, and how does it affect what teachers and learners do?

CURRICULUM: ARTICULATION OF THE STUDENT EXPERIENCE

Everyone reading this book has experienced many curricula as a student and probably taught at least one curriculum to students of his or her own. At any given point in your career as a student or a teacher, you may not have been aware of the curriculum of the moment, but it existed simply because the curriculum determines the content that is engaged in the classroom. This may seem like a very short story about curriculum, but it isn't because curriculum is both designed (intentional) and enacted (Eisner, 1990). The designed and the enacted curricula have consequences and meaning for students and therefore ought to be considered in the context of IL.

The accountability movement in education that seems to have come to a head in the era of No Child Left Behind (2002–2015) and continues in somewhat modified form as the Every Student Succeeds Act (2016–present) has focused educators' attention on standards. And standards are themselves becoming more consistent across the US from the fact that 41 states have adopted the Common Core State Standards (CCSS). Intentions are good. With clear standards and a robust testing regime, who is succeeding and who is struggling in our school systems is better known, allowing educators to focus attention on helping students to improve their performance. At least, that is the hope. Among the many unintended consequences of elevating the importance of standards and outcomes may be a loss of focus on curriculum.

Curriculum, broadly defined, is the experience that students have in classrooms, schools, and school systems. Eisner (1990), writing early in the current standards movement, described curriculum planning as ranging from spontaneous to meticulous. Both of those descriptors of continuum endpoints have potentially positive and negative connotations. Focusing on spontaneous, it seems virtuous for teachers to be able to adjust what they are teaching at any given moment based on student needs and aspirations. On the other hand, when standards are the sole determinant of "what is taught" and the "how" of teaching standards is spontaneous, the sense of a coherent, planned curriculum may be lost as teachers focus on pacing themselves to hit their marks on the calendar for teaching specific standards in anticipation of state-mandated tests. Meticulous curriculum planning, especially when imposed from the central office, may feel stifling for teachers, but it also has the virtue of communicating to teachers sequence and content of students' learning based on rationales other than a pacing guide designed to "cover" standards prior to testing.

Recall from our discussion in Chapter 2 that organizational leaders, in the context of accountability pressures, tend to treat the system as closed and seek to reduce ambiguity and variability. In the example just described, stressing the common pacing guide and adherence to system-defined rules and procedures, leaders may feel more confident about their students' experiences in classrooms. But if teachers do not have the capability and operating space to make spontaneous adaptations to students' needs, then Shulman would argue that teaching and learning are compromised. Balancing predictability with appropriate variability is a difficult, but critical, leadership act. Miguel and others working in IL positions should look at curriculum planning as a tool for shaping the student experience, particularly in light of persistent achievement gaps that emerge in state testing data. Teachers shape the enacted curriculum every day in their classrooms. Doing so deliberately and flexibly, with specific learning goals in mind, is an opportunity to improve the quality of instruction.

> ### Thought Partner Conversation
>
> Discuss your answer to this question with a critical friend—who is responsible for the generation of achievement gaps? What policies and practices (intended or not) contribute to such outcomes? What role might curriculum be playing?

Curriculum, whether intended or not, is a powerful force in school. The concept of schools as sorting mechanisms is certainly well known. Schools deliberately sorted students into various curricula and, by extension, different kinds of work or higher education through much of the twentieth century. This role for schools was rhetorically rejected by civil rights efforts of the 1950s–1970s intended to generate more equitable educational outcomes (Tyack, 1974). Now sorting is less deliberate, but still evident. Eisner (1990) uses the metaphor of a sieve—as students progress through school some are unable to achieve at a level that gives them access to more advanced learning and they drop through the holes in the educational sieve, generally away from opportunities in higher education. This is not necessarily intentional. It just happens as students take classes and make too little progress toward proficiency in one or more content areas. An important and difficult question is *who is responsible for this outcome, for the generation of achievement gaps?*

Curriculum organizes student and teacher behavior in the classroom, thus tying together three of the four commonplaces in obvious ways. The classroom, the school in which it is found, and the community surrounding the school create the fourth commonplace—the *context* in which students and teachers live and work. One source of achievement gaps may be that students feel alienated from the classroom experience because there are contextual tensions or contradictions among the community, the school, and the classroom, especially for students in some type of minority status.

Educators have named an antidote to such alienation, at least for ethnic, racial, and language minorities, *culturally relevant pedagogy* (Ladson-Billings, 1995). A specific strategy, among many, is to include in the curriculum references to, celebrations of, and perspectives from non-white, non-English speaking, or non-European people, events, and sources. What culturally responsive pedagogy and other efforts to reach students who are not presently committed to the education system in which they find themselves have in common is a recognition that values are embedded in curriculum (Eisner, 1990). When values promoted in the classroom are in conflict with those brought from family or embedded in a particular identity, conflict may ensue and students may feel that they are in a place that doesn't value them. Reduced motivation and participation seem likely to cause a downward spiral in achievement and therefore contribute to achievement gaps experienced by ethnic, racial, and language minority children.

Eisner (1990) wrote from a somewhat different perspective about the power of curriculum to support or alienate students. He highlights the negative potential of curriculum when writing about "miseducational" experiences that produce undesired outcomes, such as math phobia from poor math instruction.

> Miseducational experiences are those that thwart or hamper our ability to have further experiences or to cope intelligently with problems in a particular arena of activity. In schooling, many students develop disinclinations to encounter certain fields of study. Their experience, say in mathematics, has been so unfortunate and uncomfortable that they avoid that field of study whenever it is their option to do so.
>
> (Eisner, 1990, p. 37)

Thought Partner Conversation

What ways have you experienced that schools attempt to construct and deliver instruction that mitigates or eliminates the kind of miseducational experience or alienation discussed above? How have these worked, and what barriers might exist that limit the effectiveness of these strategies?

Teachers and instructional leaders are positioned to create more accessible curricula that respond to student, teacher, and contextual needs. The daily experiences students have in school as embodied in the operationalized curriculum present an opportunity for school leaders to shape students' lives in classrooms and schools. First, they must see opportunities to build curriculum, for if principals and others view the teaching and learning process as merely addressing and achieving standards, the opportunity is lost. How to *create* more accessible and challenging curricula is a topic for readers in education leadership programs to address in their curriculum courses. How to work toward *enacting* such empowering curricula is an important focus of IL.

Managing curricula is an agreed-upon instructional role for principals and others, but how that work is done is a matter of some dispute (Hallinger, 2003; Leithwood,

Harris, & Hopkins, 2008; Louis, Leithwood, Wahlstrom, & Anderson, 2010; Robinson, 2011; Robinson, Lloyd, & Rowe, 2008). Before we advocate for a particular strategy to improve pedagogy and curriculum, we want to bring the two areas together as Shulman did over 30 years ago.

PEDAGOGICAL CONTENT KNOWLEDGE

Pedagogical content knowledge (PCK) begins with understanding content deeply, beyond the facts into the theories that organize information and the reasons why a particular content perspective arrives at certain conclusions (Shulman, 1986). Understanding and teaching the "why" of content is crucial to instruction so that students will understand how ideas fit together and lead to more complex notions of how the world works. Shulman referred to this, obviously enough, as content knowledge, which consists of knowing the field or the subject (chemistry, for example) and knowing the curriculum. In the absence of a clear or well-constructed curriculum, a teacher with content expertise may be well positioned to create or improve a curriculum, but understanding pedagogy is a necessary component of that ability. Deep knowledge of content is only the beginning of the chain Shulman (2010) described that makes up PCK, the "knowing something" more than those to whom it will be taught.

KNOWING WHY: NOT THE SAME AS KNOWING HOW

Early in my high school teaching career, I taught principles of economics to high school students. Economics is replete with arcane terms, diagrams, and relationships that students struggle to memorize, with most falling short of their aspirations when they rely on memorization. My approach was to teach students how to construct a diagram that depicts profit maximization under conditions of imperfect competition from basic concepts they already understood. This method improved most students' understanding of why profits would be maximized when marginal revenue equals marginal cost. But one day I hit the bottom of the well of my knowledge of economic principles when a student asked a particular "why" question that required calculus for an answer.

Content knowledge can never be too deep, but neither can the ability to communicate effectively. After consulting with a friend earning his PhD in economics at the time, I returned triumphantly to the classroom the next day to provide the calculus pathway to the answer. None of the students understood it or seemed to care very much.

—Brazer

Pedagogy is, of course, the other side of PCK, the "knowing how." Knowing how means knowing effective means of teaching content to particular students in a given context. For example, a teacher expert in US history aspiring to teach a non-dominant, critical perspective would use different approaches with third graders, middle schoolers, or students in an Advanced Placement US History class. Likewise, she would consider many other dimensions such as students' literacy levels, life experiences, and circumstances, and the multiple curricula they encounter.

Pedagogical content knowledge defines what any given teacher knows and is able to do. Thus, PCK is the basic asset that comprises the quality of teaching and learning in a classroom, grade level, subject area, and school. Conceptually, PCK provides a central focus for IL. By definition, if content knowledge and/or pedagogical knowledge can be improved to strengthen PCK, teaching and learning will improve. Simple to say, harder to do. Teacher motivation interacts with PCK to complicate the situation further.

Adopting the perspective of Principal Suarez, Evergreen High School has some work to do on equity. But it also has much to be proud of in terms of student achievement. Miguel would not want to trade off excellence against equity. Improving PCK in a manner that improves instructional quality *and* equity in the classroom simultaneously is a substantial challenge, both conceptually and practically. Literacy and mathematics present two of the biggest academic hurdles in the *equity with excellence* challenge because both comprise gatekeeper sets of skills and knowledge. Those students who read well are better able to supplement classroom experiences with print and online sources. Those students adept at basic operations with whole numbers, fractions, and decimals are better equipped to understand and manipulate more abstract mathematical operations in algebra, statistics, and calculus. Furthermore, literacy and math combine to support student learning in science, particularly chemistry and physics. Principal Suarez understands these interactions as a teacher and administrator pondering student achievement data.

As Miguel dug deeper into the assessment and participation data stored in his laptop computer, he was able to identify three important trends:

- *Students who enter Evergreen High School testing more than one grade below grade-level in reading are at much higher risk for earning multiple D's and F's in ninth grade.*
- *A majority of ninth grade students in Algebra 1 are ethnic or language minority students and/or low income. A majority of white and Asian ninth grade students are in Geometry, a level above. D and F rates in Algebra 1 are typically 30–40 percent.*
- *Students who take Algebra 1 in ninth grade or later typically graduate with only one or two college-preparatory laboratory science classes. Three is considered the minimum necessary for admission to a selective 4-year college.*

TEACHER LEARNING

Accepting that pedagogical content knowledge, by combining pedagogy with content, is the conceptual building block for effective teaching, it stands to reason that *enhancement of PCK should be the primary focus of IL*. We recommend that instructional leaders assess their teachers' PCK to learn where the strengths and weaknesses are. Pedagogical content knowledge variability within a school points to opportunities and needs that exist within the faculty. Teacher learning is an important means to exploit opportunities to meet needs.

Clearly implied at this point is that teachers can learn through collaboration. Evidence that this is a common belief is the ubiquity of various forms for teacher collaborations, often referred to as professional learning communities (PLCs). Our preferred terms are teacher collaborative teams or teacher collaboratives because PLCs have become tightly linked to a specific model and a specific method of collaboration (see Van Lare, Brazer, Bauer, & Smith, 2013). We favor a more fluid concept of teacher collaboration that allows for adaptation to a range of contexts and needs. Bringing teachers together for collaboration makes sense from many perspectives, not the least of which is the idea of bounded rationality (March & Simon, 1993). The knowledge that any one teacher has at any given point in time is limited, but it can be augmented through collaboration. Teacher collaboratives create opportunities for teacher leadership, progressing naturally to the notion of principals distributing leadership across their schools to help generate change and improvement. Distributed leadership is the topic of Chapter 8 where we discuss how principals might harness organizational dynamics and teacher initiative to generate synergistic action for school improvement. Here we stay focused on describing the nature and purpose of teacher collaboration as a tool for teacher learning and improvement of instruction.

Thought Partner Conversation

With a critical friend, reflect on your most recent experiences as a team leader or member—what were the team's goals or purposes, how did you operate as a team, what were your products or outcomes, did you reach your goals? Why or why not?

Merely putting teachers together in groups does not necessarily lead to teacher learning. The structural perspective from Chapter 1 helps to explain why. Research that we conducted in a large suburban school district revealed that the ways in which teacher collaborative teams were structured and supported made a difference in terms of the learning groups of teachers experienced (Bauer et al., 2013). This work first employed and then validated four important components of organizational design that facilitate teacher collaboration (Bauer, 1996, 1998, 2001; Shedd, 1987; Shedd & Bacharach, 1991). Administrators and teachers who wish to lead, participate with and/or organize effective teams will have better results if they are thoughtful about each of the components described.

1. *Scope* refers to the content of the team's work and its ultimate purpose. From a design perspective, uncertainty or ambiguity are resolved, for the most part, contingent on articulation of *focus*, an important component of scope. How often have you found yourself on a committee or in a work group when someone asks, "What are we supposed to be doing?" When communication about purpose is ambiguous, teachers get confused about the decision-making boundaries and

authority their team is operating within. It is incumbent upon leadership to articulate objectives (and often deliverables—what a team is expected to produce and by when this is expected to be done), boundaries, and authority for a team's work. For many teams, this is pre-defined based on the challenge named when the team is convened. In some cases, the team is instrumental in defining focus for itself (again within specified boundaries), as in the case with teams that are convened to explore the possible causes of an achievement gap. Regardless, leaders can hardly expect a team to contribute meaningfully to progress on any puzzle or challenge without some understanding about why the team was convened and what it is accountable for deciding or doing.

2. Who participates on a team and the roles they play can have a big impact on team effectiveness. Well-functioning teams have complementary expertise (an idea we elaborate in Chapter 8). Being deliberate about which individuals and what roles are brought into a team creates its *formal structure*. Should a high school team be made up of members of a department, or should it be by grade-level and across content? Should elementary teams be vertically or horizontally constructed? Answering these questions should be considered in terms of team focus. If improving PCK within a specific subject area is the focus, then a team comprised of US history teachers and a special education teacher might make the most sense.

3. *Decision-making process* appears to be the most neglected of the four critical design factors (Bauer, Van Lare, Brazer, & Smith, 2015). Teams often do not know where their decision-making discretion begins and ends, or if they even have any. We observed collaborative teams that followed agendas very carefully and had active principal participation where decisions about teacher practices were made and carried out. Other teams talked about issues on their own, but showed no evidence that any decision was made, resulting in changes in teacher practice being sporadic or non-existent. These two categories of examples demonstrate a wide range in teams' knowledge of how decisions are to be made and the influence or authority the team had to do its work. Principals should be thoughtful and clear about what decisions teams are empowered to make, how decisions should be made, and how they should be communicated. In particular, it is important to be clear about when a team is empowered to decide versus when the team is asked to make a recommendation to a decision maker who will subsequently decide.

4. Resources provided to teams constitute their *support*. A remarkably scarce resource is time because of the highly structured school day that is often constrained by a collective bargaining agreement. Teams need time to meet, and our research demonstrates that this resource varied greatly from school to school (Bauer et al., 2013). To some degree use of time is impacted by structure—who serves on the team (and how many people serve) constrains when the team can meet (Bauer, 1998). Principals have some discretion over how teacher time is used, but they do not always take full advantage of this organizational lever. District leaders and principals can buy time by paying for teachers and other staff to work collaboratively outside of the school day and/or paying for substitutes. Other support issues that may prove important include the training or

professional development needed to augment team members' skills and knowledge, depending on the puzzle being addressed; access to accurate and timely information; tools for data management and analysis; and books, and other materials. Accountability is our final support factor that catalogues the team's progress and impact. Though this might not seem at first blush to be "support," we believe that principals can be supportive of teams when they help them define success.

We have described these four factors for organizational design so that you can consider how to use them collectively to create an environment in which teams can function at their peak. There may be struggles in addressing one or more of these critical factors, particularly support, but awareness of these opportunities is the beginning of being able to take advantage of them. Schools that better support collaborative teacher work are likely to see added benefits in terms of motivation as professionals have better opportunities to self-actualize and to achieve meaning in their work by contributing to something beyond their own classrooms.

All of the scholarly perspectives on IL presented early in this chapter would agree that each of the four design components just presented are well within the principal's reach, thus creating an important opportunity to shape teacher learning. If scope, structure, decision making, and support are adequately stipulated and provided, then teacher collaboratives have a better likelihood of enhancing individual and collective PCK.

Think about an Algebra 1 team (*formal structure*): if teacher attention *focuses* on evidence (both qualitative and quantitative) of student learning, if the team has *decision-making* discretion to modify curriculum and pedagogy, and if Principal Suarez provides *support* in the form of time and resources such as assistance from a math coach, then Evergreen High School has an improved prospect for creating academic opportunity for students while lowering the D and F rate. The key is combining knowledge with action that is then evaluated, leading to modified and improved action—in other words teacher learning. But, what does teacher learning look like in practice?

Empirical research focused on what happens in teacher collaborative teams is scant. Earlier, in-depth studies tended to focus on the interpersonal relationships among teachers engaged in long-term collaboration and how they developed a PLC (in a general sense) without presenting a great deal of evidence about what teachers learned in the process and how they used this learning in their classrooms (Grossman, Wineburg, & Woolworth, 2001; McLaughlin & Talbert, 2001). Later, Little (2003), Horn (2010) and Horn and Little (2010) specified what teacher learning looks like in practice. We then applied these concepts in field-based research that revealed wide variation among teacher teams in terms of the degree of learning we were able to detect (Van Lare et al., 2013).

Evidence of teacher learning comes in at least three forms: (1) the ways in which they speak about their classroom experiences, (2) anticipation of future moves in the classroom, and (3) interpretations of real and anticipated outcomes. Horn (2010) applies the term *replay* to describe a teacher's recollection of a particular teaching practice and how students responded. For example, in research we are conducting as of this writing, teachers observed in a second grade collaborative team were striving to have their students discuss different methods of solving arithmetic problems. They typically made the following kind of statement: "When I asked the students to talk in pairs about their preferred methods for approaching the subtraction problem, discussions were lively except in two or three pairs." This kind of statement reports back to colleagues one teacher's experience with a method called teaching through problem solving. Anticipation of future classroom moves Horn classifies as a *rehearsal*. Carrying our example forward, a rehearsal might be: "Next time, I will approach the more silent students and prompt them with the sentence stems we have been using to spur academic conversations." Replays and rehearsals help teachers to *revision* or extend their learning into more sophisticated PCK development (Horn, 2010). In the hypothetical case we have built with two quotations of replays and rehearsals, a teacher team might find new ways to draw out the thinking of students who thus far have not responded consistently to tactics such as paired discussions and sentence stems intended to engage students in considering multiple problem-solving strategies.

Thought Partner Conversation

Observe a teacher team, or reflect on a team meeting you may have attended, to observe how replays, rehearsals, and revisioning may be used to facilitate teacher learning. What factors might help or hinder discussions from reaching revisioning—making a commitment to trying something new?

How school leaders foster the kind of learning briefly described above can be seen by using the four structural factors described above to define the organizational design work leaders need to do when establishing teams. Principals can begin by establishing what teams are intended to do (*focus*) or their boundaries within which they determine their own direction. In our previous study of teacher collaborative teams, there was a heavy emphasis on following prescribed procedures and little direction about teaching and learning. Results tended to look bureaucratic in the sense that we observed consistent meeting procedures and surprisingly few discussions focused on instruction. In contrast, our current investigation into teacher collaboration in a different district reveals heavy emphasis on curriculum and pedagogy through adoption of Lesson Study method, and teacher teams have discretion about the subject area on which they will focus. The teacher learning method (Lesson Study) supports a collaborative team-determined focus, e.g., math. Results appear very different in the later setting, with most observed meetings addressing teaching and learning issues teachers face daily.

As noted above, a second critical organizational design task is forming teams (*structure*). Elementary schools we have observed were often organized into grade-level teams, middle schools by subject and/or cross-disciplinary teams, and high schools by course (Van Lare et al., 2013). Though typical, these may not be the "right" configurations. More recently, we have observed cross-grade-level elementary teams that report great benefit from fifth grade teachers learning how their students behaved in third grade and third grade teachers learning how their method of teaching may have impacted fifth grade outcomes. Additionally, the presence of coaches or special education teachers changes and enriches the dynamics of teams. Beyond the mix of expertise, however, are the individual motivations and group dynamics generated in teams (think about the human relations theorists' emphases from Chapter 1). Individual expertise and motivation combine in a team matrix as an important factor for team effectiveness (Bauer & Brazer, 2012), and we are observing wide variation in teacher collaborative team effectiveness based on the apparent motivations of team members. Some enjoy working together and others do not, creating noticeable influences on team outcomes.

Principals and teacher leaders have an opportunity to help make collaborative teams productive by stipulating the *decision-making process*. In our older study, how decisions would be made and who would make them was unclear to us, and we believe this led to teacher teams filling the void by following procedures for creating and running through agendas (Bauer et al., 2013). We observe much less of that in the current study in which teachers understand that they are to decide collectively how to teach specific portions of a curriculum, evaluate the results, and determine what teaching practices for the team will look like in the future. Principals who foster teacher collaboration can stipulate decision-making processes that focus PCK development where they determine it is most needed while maintaining teacher discretion of what is learned, how it is learned, and how the learning is applied. The principal could guide teams toward more cognitive areas such as English or math, or more affective learning that is often categorized as social–emotional.

As noted above, we have observed teacher teams without adequate *support* in terms of the time afforded to teams to engage in their work. Of course, the support needed is highly related to the purpose of the team and the timeline involved for their work. For departmental or grade-level teams, generally, we estimated that approximately 60–90 minutes per week most weeks of the month was necessary, or teamwork fizzled (Van Lare et al., 2013). Our current investigation reveals that teacher teams that meet consistently for at least 60 minutes a week demonstrate remarkable progress in terms of planning; meaningful discussions that include replays, rehearsals, and revisioning; and execution of revised methods with follow-up evaluation and reflection. It is important to emphasize that in the current research context, lead teachers receive an annual stipend they report as a meaningful incentive and teachers on their teams receive workshop pay for collaborative time that occurs outside the school day. Teams are also able to obtain materials they need to support their classrooms. Their instructional improvement process includes multiple opportunities to assess outcomes of their efforts and discuss these publicly in forums that include outside experts and other teacher teams—i.e., accountability is part of the support provided. An important implication here is that the kind of support most likely to fuel effective collaboration requires principals to work with their central offices to provide adequate resources for teacher learning.

Well-supported teamwork opens the door to enhancing pedagogical content knowledge. Teacher collaborative teams that function effectively engage in learning about content, curriculum, and pedagogy. We have observed teams consulting curriculum documents while planning specific lessons on a commonly accessed Google document. As they imagine new content they debate the pedagogical moves they believe necessary to make it come alive. Teams observe each other's teaching, provide specific feedback based on pre-determined criteria, and imagine how to take the next steps toward instructional improvement. These observations validate our belief that teacher collaborative teams are potentially powerful engines of teacher learning, instructional change, and improvement.

PRINCIPAL IDENTITY AND ROLE

With growing evidence that IL is associated with improved student achievement (Hallinger, 2003; Louis et al., 2010; Robinson et al., 2008) it seems obvious to us that principals can no longer focus only on the management side of their schools. They have an obligation to understand teaching and learning, to set the direction for instruction (Leithwood, Harris, & Hopkins, 2008), and to foster IL capacity in others, such as their APs, department and grade-level leaders, and teacher collaborative team leaders (Robinson, 2011). Thus, the identity of the contemporary principal who will impact student achievement in her or his school is both transformational and instructional. The instructional portion of principal identity is enacted through three primary roles: (1) leader of learning, (2) instructional thought partner and critical friend, and (3) team coordinator.

> **Thought Partner Conversation**
>
> With a critical friend, discuss what you believe may be involved in each of these roles for principals. Assume for the moment that similar roles may be relevant for other school leaders as well—how might these be extended, for example, for the role of teacher leader?

Leader of Learning

> **Thought Partner Conversation**
>
> We acknowledged at the outset of this chapter that principals cannot hope to be everywhere in the school or to participate in all teacher team meetings. Brainstorm ways you, as a principal, might engage with teacher teams and/or keep abreast of teacher learning, perhaps using various technologies and/or formal and informal communication methods.

We emphasized the importance of leading learning within the school in Chapter 4, with most of our focus on organizational learning as a means to changing the status quo and fostering improvement. We mentioned also that learning in the sense of individual and collective growth within schools and districts was important to figuring out how to make instruction better. We return to this latter point here.

Principals are in a unique position—both structurally and symbolically—to emphasize the importance of their faculties' growth and development so that they can improve professional practice. We see teacher collaborative teams as the most effective structures to engage teachers in learning, but they can easily go awry and devolve into organizational task completion mechanisms and gripe sessions. We agree with Robinson et al. (2008) and Robinson (2011) that principals learning alongside teachers has potential to keep teacher learning on track and moving forward because when they join with collaborative teams and engage teachers in discussions of classroom practice, principals signal the importance of teacher and student learning. Additionally, when principals engage in at least some of the learning teachers are experiencing, they keep themselves up to date about the latest thinking and results from tools such as learning through problem solving and educational technology.

School leadership researchers agree that an important principal role is to shape and provide professional development for the teacher corps (Hallinger, 2003; Leithwood, Harris, & Hopkins, 2008; Robinson, 2011). It is important to recall, however, common professional development experiences in which teachers convene in an auditorium prior to students' arrival for a new school year. They are often lectured to by a speaker promoting some form of student-centered learning, apparently oblivious to the irony of doing so. There may be appropriate times for all teachers to receive a certain kind of professional education at the same time, but we believe that professional development through the kind of teacher collaboration we have described in this chapter has much greater promise because of teachers' co-creation of professional development experiences and immediate applications to classroom instruction. Principals' and district officials' time and energy would be far better spent shaping learning experiences in these ongoing meetings rather than focusing on beginning or end-of-year extravaganzas in large venues. By encouraging teacher collaboration through high-functioning teams, principals seize the potential to generate professional learning within the school that will drive change and improvement.

When principals are aware of, involved in, and supportive of what their teachers are learning, they are better positioned to understand how the school as an organization needs to grow and develop to support continuous improvement of classroom instruction. They can provide professional development and necessary resources in a more thoughtful and targeted manner when they have first-hand understanding of teachers' developmental and practical needs. As leaders who learn, with teachers, they are better able to lead learning.

Extended Web Activities

To become more conversant with ways to promote teacher learning, explore what is known about attributes of effective educator professional development (see, for example, *learningforward.org*).

Instructional Thought Partner and Critical Friend

Principal Miguel Suarez is disturbed by the achievement gaps evident in student outcomes and participation data. He may also be inhibited about speaking with teachers outside of science about this issue. At the secondary level in particular, teachers can be quite siloed into subject areas—they are experts within and have little to say across content. This perspective carries over into school administrators as well. But as the most visible school leader with the greatest symbolic and political power, Principal Suarez cannot afford to take himself out of discussions in the non-science content areas.

LEARNING PHYSICS ON THE FLY

I never took a physics course—ever. Eighth grade Introductory Physical Science is as far as I got. Early in my career, I had the great good fortune to be assigned to evaluate a master physics teacher who loved his subject and was eager to teach it to anyone who would engage with him. I needed his help to understand physics PCK more than he needed my suggestions about good teaching. My evaluation of him was a learning experience that ultimately enhanced my leadership content knowledge.

I remembered enough trigonometry and calculus to engage the physics teacher in an explanation of why he taught one level of physics conceptually, one using trigonometry, and the third using calculus. I learned how a teacher can differentiate physics instruction to bring students with different math abilities to their highest potential for understanding physical properties and outcomes.

In later years, I was able to use this knowledge in my role as principal to engage physics and math teachers in discussions about curriculum that helped reshape course offerings and sequences to meet a range of student needs and interests.

—Brazer

City et al. (2009) and Robinson et al. (2008) argue that principals such as Miguel have a responsibility to be knowledgeable across a wide range of teaching and learning in their schools. Stein and Nelson (2003) tackled the problem of limited content expertise among leaders by encouraging principals and others to grow their knowledge of content and pedagogy from the foundation of their own teaching and what they have learned from others. They coined the term *leadership content knowledge* to draw a distinction between the knowledge required for teaching (PCK) and knowledge needed to lead instruction. The term is helpful in differentiating leader attributes from teacher attributes, but somewhat unfortunate in that it leaves out pedagogy. We encourage leaders to think of leadership content knowledge as encompassing both content and pedagogy. The physics illustration in the text box helps explain what we mean.

Growing leadership content knowledge from one's own PCK means going deep into selected additional grade levels (elementary) or content areas (secondary and possibly elementary) to be able to engage with teachers outside of one's area of teaching expertise to lead instruction and shape teacher learning in meaningful ways (Stein & Nelson,

2003). This can happen through formal study, but more likely in the lives of busy administrators it will occur though classroom observations and discussion as described in the text box and through learning alongside teachers. We call this becoming *conversant* in a wider range of content and pedagogy (Brazer & Bauer, 2013). Exercise 7.1 demonstrates how leaders might grow their expertise along these dimensions.

> **Thought Partner Conversation**
>
> Discuss with a critical friend what it means to be a critical friend. In your experiences, who has served in this role and how has this been beneficial to you? What kinds of structures and processes make it possible to maintain such a relationship and what can leaders do to foster thought partner relationships?

The goal of expanding one's leadership content knowledge is to take on the roles of thought partner and critical friend in discussions focused on improving teaching and learning. These might take place with teachers one-on-one, in the context of teacher collaborative team meetings, and when addressing an entire faculty regarding school-wide instructional challenges. The principal as thought partner draws out ideas and questions from teachers to understand their perspectives and to help them think through inevitable instructional puzzles. Leadership content knowledge is vital to give the principal meaningful things to say in such a conversation. But not all ideas are born as good ideas. Consequently, principals also need a critical perspective, one that can discern what makes sense for student learning and what might better serve teacher convenience instead of student needs. As a *critic* in the neutral sense of being able to see value and problems and as a supportive professional *friend*, principals can exercise great influence over the educational experiences of the students entrusted to them in their schools.

Team Coordinator

Beyond designing the structure that supports collaborative teams, principals have a responsibility to ensure organizational coherence. To avoid having multiple teams running in different directions and creating diffuse or contradictory experiences for students, the principal should ensure teams are pulling in the same direction. The starting point is establishing a clear mission for teacher teamwork over one or more years. Principal Suarez might adopt the mission of narrowing achievement gaps. Another might focus on instilling a growth mindset within students. A common problem is that principals and other members of the school community feel the need to address many major problems simultaneously. Creating multiple initiatives that are not coordinated often leads to confusion, energy dissipation, and meager progress toward goals. Although we understand the urgency generated by difficult student circumstances and sometimes many years of educational neglect within a certain school, we believe that organizational coherence and focus are important for maintaining a direction and achieving improvement when schools are buffeted by outside influences (Chapter 2) and coping with chronic ambiguity and uncertainty (Chapter 3).

An important issue within coordination—and one that may greatly facilitate or inhibit trust building—is being clear about team power and accountability. Specifically, teams often, and for very good reason, have constraints on their ability to enact a change. To the extent this is true, it is vital to be as clear as possible about what these limits might be and about how the team should seek authority to finalize and implement a decision. Often what is most important to teams isn't having free rein; it is knowing how their recommendation will be considered, by whom, and in what form and how quickly feedback on a decision will occur. Principal Suarez, for example, would not likely empower a teacher team to eliminate a program in favor of another (especially if the other required resources to purchase), but might specify that the team could make such a proposal and would receive feedback within 7 days (which might include asking for further consideration, dialogue, or a change in the proposal). The same team, by the way, might be empowered to make significant adjustments to the order and pace of instruction in their content area. It is important to stress that principals have the broad view and are accountable for teaching and learning across all grade levels and content areas. The school leadership team has a unique responsibility to weigh a recommendation or decision from one team against the good of the school.

Teams can be coordinated if focused on a core mission with one or two major goals and a limited set of objectives. Yet, concern about ongoing coordination will leave the principal in a quandary about how much to let teams go and how much authority they should exercise. We address, but do not resolve, this tension in Chapter 8's deep dive into distributed leadership. For now, we suggest a coordinating team that checks in regularly with collaborative teams to stay abreast of their progress, understand their needs, and keep them focused on the mission. We have seen a few administrative teams coordinate teacher collaboratives in this fashion (Van Lare et al., 2013), but such coordinating teams may also consist of teachers who lead collaborative efforts within or across grade levels, in departments, or in specific courses.

CONCLUSION

IL requires a deep commitment to working directly with teachers to understand and improve teaching and learning. IL is an important mindset and toolkit for generating progress on learning outcomes, narrowing achievement gaps, and creating more equitable educational outcomes. It requires courage to step outside of one's deepest pedagogical content knowledge and presumption to think that we might be able to help those more expert than we, but an inquiry stance embedded in the role of a leader of learning helps to provide fortitude and mitigate images of unwarranted interference in the name of helping students to survive and thrive in school.

An undercurrent of much of this chapter is the idea of stepping away from traditional authority to foster learning throughout the school. That takes courage too. Chapter 8 addresses the difficult choices, potential benefits, and disparate theories and research embedded in distributing leadership as a means of transforming schools into learning organizations focused on classroom instruction and capable of organizational learning.

EXERCISE 7.1 ARTICULATING ATTRIBUTES OF GOOD TEACHING

Pair up with someone whose teaching experience is different from yours—either from a different grade level, a different content area, or a substantially different educational setting. Reflect individually on questions 1 and 2, then discuss 3 and 4 together.

1. List two to four teaching methods you have found to be most effective.

   - For each, write a brief explanation for *why* you believe it to be effective.
   - How do you know what is effective?

2. List one to three areas in which you believe your teaching to be weak. These could be related to content, a particular grouping of students, or a technique you have tried with disappointing results.

   - What strategies might you use to shore up these weaker areas in your own teaching?

3. How do your lists compare with each other?

   - Do different teaching settings seem to surface different strengths and weaknesses?

4. What would be helpful ways for each of you to learn from the other's perceived strengths and weaknesses?

   - What would you need to learn to help one another more effectively?
   - How might you learn those things?

EXERCISE 7.2 MOTIVATION AS A CRITICAL FACTOR

Recall from Chapter 1 our emphasis on motivation as an important explanation for worker behavior in organizations. Teachers, like everyone else, have multiple and sometimes conflicting motivations that cause them to engage with good ideas in various ways. It would be naïve to assume that exposing them to more content and/or new techniques for teaching it would be sufficient for all to teach differently and more effectively. Consider a specific teacher or group of teachers in your own school as you answer the following questions:

1. Why are these teachers teaching in this school at this particular time in their careers?

   - How many years have they been teaching?
   - Did they aspire to come to this school, or were they placed here?

2. How do these teachers feel about their current placements in grade level or subject area?

   - Are they teaching content they enjoy with students whom they understand?
   - Are they part of a collective of other teachers, or do they keep to themselves?

3. How would you describe these teachers' habits of mind?

    - Are they more inquisitive, authoritative, or defensive?
    - Do they listen well?
    - Are they inclined to help other teachers?

4. How would you describe the overall professional climate in your school?
5. Thinking about your answers to the first four questions, what would it take to get the group of teachers (or a single teacher) you have in mind to work on improving their PCK?

    - What motivations would help you to lead PCK improvement?
    - What motivations would have to be mitigated or altered to allow for PCK improvement?

EXERCISE 7.3 BREAKING PATTERNS

Work with one or two partners to explain and elaborate the systemic patterns evident in the vignette featured throughout this chapter, then address the following questions keeping in mind the students represented in the pattern descriptions:

1. What specific student needs can you identify in Miguel's school?
2. What do the patterns suggest about curricula these students need?
3. How might pedagogy need to change for these students?
4. What do you imagine to be contextual challenges for students represented in the vignette extension?
5. What kinds of actions should Miguel take at the high school?

    - What might Miguel want to discuss with principals from feeder elementary and middle schools?

LEADING TO SOLVE INSTRUCTIONAL PUZZLES

Miguel decides that, if he is to get any traction on achievement gaps manifest at Evergreen High School, he needs to get as many teachers as possible focused on the issue and using creative problem solving to address it. He is unsure about what teachers need to know and be able to do specifically to improve the learning of his underserved students, but he believes that he has some outstanding teachers in various departments who are effective at reaching socio-economic, racial, and linguistic minority students. One or two district office experts might be helpful too.

Work in a group of three or four and assume the role of IL consultants for Miguel Suarez. (Alternatively, you can work on this puzzle with one of your own schools in mind.) Think through his whole situation as presented and answer the following questions in as much detail as you can:

1. In what ways should teaching and learning look different at Evergreen High School by the next summer? Three years in the future?
2. What should Miguel be doing this summer to get started?
3. What should happen starting in the fall?
4. How should Miguel redesign Evergreen High School to take on the mission of narrowing achievement gaps?

REFERENCES

Bauer, S. (1996). *Site based management: A design perspective.* Unpublished doctoral dissertation. Ithaca, NY: Cornell University.

Bauer, S. (1998). Designing site based systems, deriving a theory of practice. *International Journal of Educational Reform, 7*(2), 108–121.

Bauer, S.C. (2001). An initial investigation into the effect of decision-making and communication practices on the perceived outcomes of site-based management. *Research in the Schools, 8*(1), 13–27.

Bauer, S., & Brazer, S.D. (2012). *Using research to lead school improvement: Turning evidence into action.* Thousand Oaks, CA: Sage.

Bauer, S.C., Brazer, S.D., Van Lare, M., & Smith, R.G. (2013). Organizational design in support of professional learning communities in one district. In S. Conley & B. Cooper (Eds.), *Moving from teacher isolation to teacher collaboration: Enhancing professionalism and school quality* (pp. 49–80). New York: Rowman and Littlefield.

Bauer, S., Van Lare, M., Brazer, S., & Smith, R. (2015). Teacher leadership in collaborative teams: The importance of process. In P. Tenuto (Ed.), *Renewed accountability for access and excellence: Applying a model for democratic professional practice in Education* (pp. 131–146). Lanham, MD: Lexington,

Brazer, S.D., & Bauer, S.C. (2013). Preparing instructional leaders: A model. *Educational Administration Quarterly, 49*(4), 645–684.

City, E., Elmore, R., Fiarman, S., & Teitel, L. (2009). *Instructional rounds in education: A network approach to improving teaching and learning.* Cambridge, MA: Harvard Education Press.

Cuban, L. (1988). *The managerial imperative and the practice of leadership in schools.* Albany, NY: State University of New York Press.

Cuban, L. (1993). *How teachers taught: Constancy and change in American classrooms, 1880–1990* (2nd ed.). New York: Teachers College Press.

Cuban, L. (2018). *The flight of a butterfly or the path of a bullet? Using technology to transform teaching and learning.* Cambridge, MA: Harvard Education Press.

Eisner, E. (1990). *The educational imagination: On the design and evaluation of school programs* (3rd ed.). Upper Saddle River, NJ: Pearson Education.

Elmore, R. (2004). *School reform from the inside out: Policy, practice, and performance.* Cambridge, MA: Harvard Education Press.

Grossman, P., Wineberg, S., & Woolworth, S. (2001). Toward a theory of teacher community. *Teachers College Record, 103*(6), 942–1012.

Hallinger, P. (2003). Leading educational change: Reflections on the practice of instructional and transformational leadership. *Cambridge Journal of Education, 33*(3), 329–351.

Horn, I. (2010). Teaching replays, teaching rehearsals, and re-visions of practice: Learning from colleagues in a mathematics teacher community. *Teachers College Record, 112*(1), 225–259.

Horn, I., & Little, J. (2010). Attending to problems of practice: Routines and resources for professional learning in teachers' workplace interactions. *American Educational Research Journal, 47*(1), 181–217.

Horng, E., & Loeb, S. (2010). New thinking about instructional leadership. *Phi Delta Kappan, 92*(3), 66–69.

Ladson-Billings, G. (1995). But that's just good teaching! The case for culturally relevant pedagogy. *Theory Into Practice, 34*(3), 159–165.

Leithwood, K., Harris, A., & Hopkins, D. (2008). Seven strong claims about successful school leadership. *School Leadership and Management, 28*(1), 27–42.

Little, J. (2003). Locating learning in teachers' communities of practice: Opening up problems of analysis in records of everyday work. *Teaching and Teacher Education, 18*(8), 917–946.

Louis, K., Leithwood, K., Wahlstrom, K., & Anderson, S. (2010). Learning from leadership: Investigating the links to improved student learning. Final report of research to the Wallace Foundation. The University of Minnesota.

March, J., & Simon, H. (1993). *Organizations* (2nd ed.). New. York: John Wiley and Sons.

McLaughlin, M.W., & Talbert, J.E. (2001). *Professional communities and the work of high school teaching*. Chicago: University of Chicago Press.

Resnick, L. (2010). 2009 Wallace Foundation distinguished lecture: Nested learning systems for the thinking curriculum. *Educational Researcher, 39*(3), 183–197.

Robinson, V. (2011). *Student-centered leadership*. San Francisco: Jossey-Bass.

Robinson, V., Lloyd, C., & Rowe, K. (2008). The impact of leadership on student outcomes: An analysis of the differential effects of leadership types. *Educational Administration Quarterly, 44*(5), 635–674.

Schwab, J. (1969). The practical: A language for curriculum. *The School Review, 78*(1), 1–23.

Shedd, J. (1987). *Involving teachers in school and district decision making*. Ithaca, NY: Organizational Analysis and Practice.

Shedd, J., & Bacharach, S. (1991). *Tangled hierarchies: Teachers as professionals and the management of schools*. San Francisco: Jossey-Bass.

Shulman, L. (1986). Those who understand: Knowledge growth in teaching. *Educational Researcher, 15*(2), 4–14.

Shulman, L. (2010). Interview conducted with author, April 18, 2010.

Smith, R.G., & Brazer, S.D. (2016). *Striving for equity: District leadership for narrowing opportunity and achievement gaps*. Cambridge, MA: Harvard Education Press.

Stein, M.K., & Nelson, B.S. (2003). Leadership content knowledge. *Educational Evaluation and Policy Analysis, 25*(4), 423–448.

Tyack, D. (1974). *The one best system: A history of American urban education*. Cambridge, MA: Harvard University Press.

Tyack, D., & Cuban, L. (1995). *Tinkering toward utopia: A century of public school reform*. Cambridge, MA: Harvard University Press.

Van Lare, M., Brazer, S., Bauer, S., & Smith, R. (2013). Professional learning communities using evidence: Examining teacher learning and organizational learning. In S. Conley and B. Cooper (Eds.), *Moving from teacher isolation to teacher collaboration: Enhancing professionalism and school quality* (pp. 157–182). Lanham, MD: Rowman and Littlefield.

CHAPTER 8

Leading With Others: Distributed Leadership and its Conceptual Ancestors

Principal Brian Washington, in his third year at the helm of Highland High School, is beside himself. He created this team of math and special education teachers to lead the school in their efforts to meet CCSS in mathematics. Brian assumed addressing math achievement would be a priority for everyone because the school—and Principal Washington in particular—has been put on notice by the superintendent that the achievement gaps related to student performance in math, especially in terms of the difference between white and Asian students on the one hand and second-language learners on the other. Soon after discussion got started—and maybe even before—the teachers started lobbying for the school to adopt the Atlas program, a computer-aided math instruction tool that could provide supplementary opportunities for students to learn. This makes no sense to Brian because he has read negative reports about the program, especially in relation to its accessibility for English learner students, those most in need in his school.

"Look, Brian, why did you bother to invite us to talk about this topic?" asked Joe, a more than 20-year veteran of the math department. "You don't seem to value our input. We believe the Atlas program is exactly what we need, and you already told us that the district is willing to make funds available to implement whatever we need, within reason. This isn't an expensive option, either." Joe seemed to express the frustration of the entire team present at the meeting. "Why ask for our input if you don't plan on taking it?"

"It's not that," Brian responded. "I value your opinion and rely on your expertise. I just don't think your answer is likely to help much, and my understanding is that this program is less than optimal for English learners, the group we most need to help." Brian believed that he had an ethical responsibility to oppose adoption of the Atlas program. To add to his stress, it was his job on the line here. If the school doesn't show improvement, he is likely to get a notice that his principal days in the district are over. If that happens, he will be blamed for the flat growth and persistent gaps in student math performance.

Thought Partner Conversation

If you were a teacher on Brian's team, would you consider his efforts to involve teachers manipulative or insincere? If you were Brian, what would you do in this circumstance?

INTRODUCTION

Much of organizational theory in the past century dwelt on hierarchy and the various configurations of organizational structure (Harris, 2009). Leadership theory was dominated by a focus on the person of the leader even as theorists acknowledged leadership's relational nature (Bush & Glover, 2014; Harris, 2013). In the face of growing complexity in organizational forms and environments, changes in technology that often feature networked structures, increasing demands in terms of the pace and nature of change (Feng, Hao, Iles, & Bown, 2017), and growing awareness of the inadequacies of the solo-leader perspective (Bennett, Wise, Woods & Harvey, 2003; Harris, 2013; Lynch, 2012), questions were raised about whether leadership is best characterized as a specialized role or a shared influence process (Bolden, 2011; Fitzsimmons, James, & Denyer, 2011). Bolden (2011) recognized that many management theorists have explored the notions of shared leadership, informal groups, organizational learning, and other practices that involve formal leaders leading with others. It was not until fairly recently, however, that the notion of distributed leadership came to the fore, particularly in the study of education leadership.

Awareness of the expanding complexity in the role of principal and the reality that principals are overloaded with leadership, administrative, and compliance demands has fueled interest in how some of these responsibilities might be shared (Bush, 2013; Lynch, 2012). As Bennett et al. (2003) note, schools operate in a data-rich environment epitomized by increasing complexity and pressure; the "intensification of administrators' work" (p. 17) increases interdependence and the need for new forms of coordination and control. "In a shifting school context fraught with the pressure of accountability, the tasks and challenges of leadership become increasingly complex and beyond the knowledge, skill and capacity of any single individual leader" (Bellibas & Lu, 2016, p. 4). Furthermore, even the casual observer would find it hard to ignore the reality that in schools, many people lead informally, particularly when the school embarks on a significant change agenda. Leithwood, Mascall, and Strauss (2009) note that the concept of distributed leadership (DL) might also be thought of as a response to the "decidedly unheroic leadership experienced by many within schools" (p. xvii) in addition to the growing complexity of schools as organizations.

"The field of school leadership," Harris (2009) writes, "is currently preoccupied with the idea of distributed leadership" (p. 3). DL distinguishes itself as a concept by moving away from the notion of leadership as an attribute of the single, heroic, or positional leader. It is characterized by three core ideas: leadership is an emergent property rather than positional; leadership can and is performed by many and varied actors; and expertise required to lead can and is found in many individuals (and groups) rather than a select few (Crawford, 2012). DL has become the "normatively preferred leadership model for the twenty-first century" (Bush & Glover, 2014, p. 566); similar to charismatic and transformational leadership, it has a "strong, rhetorical pull" (Crawford, 2012, p. 616). "Few ideas, it seems, have provoked as much attention, debate and controversy, in the school leadership field, than this particular concept" (Harris, 2010, p. 55). "Whatever your position on distributed leadership, and you cannot fail to have one," Harris (2009) writes, "it is irrefutable that distributed leadership has become the leadership idea of the moment" (p. 3). As Harris (2013) summarizes:

> While the concept of shared, collaborative or participative leadership is far from new, distributed leadership theory has provided an alternative and powerful empirical lens on a familiar theme. The seminal work of Spillane et al. (2001) has provoked renewed interest in *leadership practice* focusing essentially on the interactions between leaders, followers and their situation. Distributed leadership theory reinforces that there are multiple sources of influence within any organisation and has focused particular attention on the "leader plus" aspect of the leadership work (Spillane 2006, p. 6).
>
> (p. 545)

Gronn (2000) also concludes that DL appears to be a concept whose time has arrived, and scholarship on educational leadership has embraced it, as have policy makers.

Lumby (2013) notes that DL was offered first "as a heuristic tool, not a type of or prescription for practice. Such detachment swiftly gave way to explicit or implicit assertions by others that distributed leadership was a form of practice and, moreover, a recommended one" (p. 582). Some scholars, such as Lynch (2012), express concern that "the policy on distributed leadership is ahead of the evidence" (p. 37), that the concept has adopted a taken-for-granted status that may be unwarranted based purely on the evidence. As of the writing of his volume, he located fewer than 30 empirical studies attempting to link DL and student outcomes. However, just a few years later, we observe a burgeoning knowledge base on DL (Tian, Risku, & Collin, 2016) and growing optimism about the worth of the concept, though we also note that this research base expands in the context of "competing and sometimes conflicting interpretations of what distributed leadership actually means" (Leithwood et al., 2007, p. 38).

Thought Partner Conversation

With a critical friend, discuss the reasons why you believe DL has become so popular, so fast, in education. In your view, is this a new idea, or an established one whose time has come?

In the opening vignette, we eavesdrop on an all-too-typical example of a leader seeking to distribute influence for an important school decision. Whether ad hoc or ongoing, teams are a popular vehicle for teacher and staff input. And yet, as we have come to understand, sharing decision making and distributing leadership are not as simple as creating a forum for dialogue. What happens when the formal leader seeks to broaden input and problem solving, but the input resulting is problematic from the perspective of the person with legitimate authority and responsibility? Is this really an instance of distributing leadership, or is it faux collaboration—a device the formal leader uses to provide the appearance of distribution? And what, exactly, is being distributed in this circumstance anyway?

In this chapter, we take on the question of what it means to distribute leadership, i.e., what theorists mean by DL and how it is similar to and different from other leadership models. We then review the research on DL, concluding with a discussion of the question of how leaders might construct opportunities for DL in the context of leading planned change. See Figure 8.1 for DL as the third of our three theoretical and research-based approaches to education leadership. After introducing this chapter's essential questions, we begin with a brief digression to situate our discussion in historical and theoretical contexts.

Essential Questions

1. What is being distributed, by whom, and to whom?
2. What should be distributed and why?
3. What happens to principal authority and responsibility when leadership is distributed?
4. Does distributed leadership generate better outcomes?

IN A REFORM MOVEMENT NOT SO LONG AGO OR FAR AWAY ...

It is important to locate distributed leadership in its historic context since it is connected firmly to a rich lineage in management thought, which both strengthens our current interest and, likely, explains a degree of the confusion over what DL is and what it isn't. DL is based, in part, on decades of work on the effects of participatory management and collegial leadership styles (Harris, 2010) and research that indicates

FIGURE 8.1 Emphasizing Distributed Leadership for Leading Change

that this type of leadership engenders greater satisfaction and commitment among followers (Bellibas & Liu, 2016; Bush, 2011; Lawler, 1992; Weisbord, 2012). The shift from other manifestations of participative management and leadership to DL can be viewed in part as an acknowledgment of a general pivot in management cultures in all types of organizations as we adapt to the realities of a post-bureaucratic world (Lynch, 2012).

In industry and general management studies, the notion of involving employees in decisions that are consequential at work can be traced back decades, at least to the writings of Barnard (1938) and the seminal work of Lewin on the benefits of participation in the context of organizational change and development in the 1930s and 1940s (Weisbord, 2012). In the 1950s, leadership theorists focused squarely on the question of whether leaders who involve followers in decision making are more effective (see Chapter 5 for a discussion), and the seminal work of McGregor (1960/2006) likewise explored this conceptual ground. The total quality movement first enacted in post-war Japan by W. Edwards Deming and his colleagues (Garvin, 1988) and later popularized in the United States in the 1970s (especially in the auto industry, but later in education) included a prominent role for employees to engage in problem solving in the context of quality circles (Garvin, 1988; Ishikawa, 1985). The benefits of involving workers in decisions about the conduct of work may be one of the most questioned and studied topics in business.

Thought Partner Conversation

Discuss with a critical friend the kinds of decisions you feel are most important for school leaders to share with teachers. In your experience, are teachers typically involved in these decisions? Why or why not?

Motivation for Sharing Decision Making

Shifting our gaze to the education sector, the beginning of the reform movement that followed publication of *A Nation at Risk* in 1983 (National Commission on Excellence in Education, 1983) featured a multitude of state-mandated changes to policy that sought, predictably, to tighten the system through top-down change (Fuhrman, Elmore, & Massell, 1993). Teachers, leaders, and administrators were to blame for the alleged failure of schools and the resulting economic peril, so the reasoning went, and players in the various statehouses had to act and act quickly (which they did). As these reforms proved less than helpful, calls to restructure educational systems emerged (Conley, 1993; Reavis & Griffith, 1992). A number of laudable goals were included, including treating teachers and other educators as professionals and endorsing the notion of the school as the center of change and reform (Sirotnik, 1989). After decades of centralization in education, the concept of decentralizing the management of schools and promoting teacher (and other stakeholder) involvement in decision-making took hold (Bauer, 1996).

Sometimes Brian Washington just felt confused about how to involve teachers and others in decision making at Highland High School. He was taught in his leadership preparation program that teachers would be more committed to decisions they had a hand in making. He has found that to be true, generally, both in his AP roles and now as principal, but it didn't consistently work out well. As an administrator, he was always the one who had to answer to higher-ups when a decision turned out to be a bad idea—teachers who had a hand in the decision were nowhere to be seen in that scenario. The problem, as Brian saw it, was to make teacher participation genuine and meaningful while guiding them in a direction he could live with. He was in the awkward position of giving up authority while retaining responsibility. His effort to improve math instruction was starting out wrong with teachers resenting the little bit of authority he exercised to define the boundaries of what was acceptable while pressuring him into what he believes will be a poor choice. Striving to be an effective change agent, Brian sometimes wondered if he shouldn't just take the reins and lead, regardless of common wisdom about sharing leadership.

Although there had been calls to broaden stakeholder involvement in decision making before (Malen, Ogawa, & Kranz, 1990), from the 1990s forward teacher involvement in decision making was a centerpiece of the restructuring movement and often envisioned as something of a magic bullet. It was quickly enshrined in policy and adopted by more than a few state and local jurisdictions as the core idea of how to improve schools (Bauer, 1996, 1998). In various iterations, it was called teacher participation, shared decision making, site-based management, or school-based management. Schools, districts, whole states, and several prominent comprehensive school reform models (e.g., Accelerated Schools) included the idea of greater teacher, staff, and sometimes community involvement in decision making. Educators' adoption of this policy existed in the context of the enormous and growing popularity of employee involvement and total quality management in industry.

Thought Partner Conversation

With a critical friend, outline all of the reasons it makes sense to involve teachers and others—perhaps including students and parents—in consequential decisions relating to teaching and learning. Given the energy and time needed to collaborate, why bother?

Even with great enthusiasm for participative management and leadership, though, there was substantial confusion over what was meant by terms such as site-based management and what they looked like in practice. Policy moved far faster than the research base available to support it, with study after study casting doubt on the efficacy of school-based management and the complexity of making it work in school settings (e.g., Kirby, 1992; Murphy, 1989, 1991; Weiss, 1993; Weiss, Cambone, & Wyeth, 1992). In hindsight, we might add, we cannot recall many practitioners or scholars associating school-based management with leadership, per se, despite the fact that a rationale for sharing decision making is achieving organizational goals. The reform raised questions about power and accountability, especially whether decision-making teams including various stakeholders would have the power to make decisions school leaders may not agree with and whether they would be held accountable for these decisions. But just as Lumby (2013) noted about DL, school-based management was "depicted both as more inclusive and more effective, indeed more effective because more inclusive" (p. 583). Inconsistency and ambiguity about what it meant and how it could be implemented in practice limited the capacity of the reform to realize its promise. And similarly, the lack of a vocabulary for describing and modeling the variables that comprised this change limited the usefulness of research (Bauer, 1996, 1998).

Why Does Sharing Authority and Initiative Persist?

Despite conceptual and rhetorical ambiguity and their attendant weak research base, it is worthwhile to step back a bit and review why the idea of stakeholder involvement was so popular in the last century and currently, regardless of flawed implementation. Why pursue this reform in the first place? Does the rationale still hold? Shedd and Bacharach (1991) provide an outstanding review, drawing on what was known from the business/organization literature, and then relating this to the context of schools. First, they summarize that there are four traditional arguments made for employee involvement in decision making:

1. Involvement is an ethical issue. It is right to involve individuals in decisions that affect their work and well-being.
2. Involvement enhances morale and increases job satisfaction.
3. Involvement enhances motivation, commitment, and acceptance of change.
4. Involvement promotes cooperation and reduces conflict.

Evidence suggests that involvement can have each of these benefits, but "There is equally strong evidence that involving employees in decision making does not, in and of itself, guarantee any of those benefits" (Shedd & Bacharach, 1991, p. 9). Research is strongest in relation to the notion that involvement enhances job satisfaction and morale, which also reduces absenteeism and attrition. However, there are contextual and intervening factors that mitigate any effects involvement might have. Shedd and Bacharach (1991) observe, further:

> Implicit in the traditional arguments for involving employees in decision making, then, is the assumption that it is employees who want involvement in decision making and that involvement is something management *gives* to its employees— perhaps out of good will, perhaps to buy something else, but certainly not because it needs their advice.
>
> (p. 10)

Limited utility to the positional leader results in an exceedingly shallow commitment to involvement and what Hargreaves (1994) later termed *contrived collegiality*. "Indeed, such strategies often backfire and generate more dissatisfaction, less commitment, and higher levels of organizational conflict" (p. 11).

The primary point Shedd and Bacharach (1991) make in their work is that in professional organizations like schools, where teachers must make consequential judgments constantly about what to teach, how to teach, classroom management, and so on, involvement is not something administrators *give to* certain people some of the time. It is something administrators *get from* professional staff and others, and it is a necessity for change and improvement to happen. It is a requirement in order to lead and manage. Involvement has to do with having quality and timely information with which to make decisions. Unless principals find a way to be in all classrooms at all times gathering data on what is going on, they need input, feedback, and participation of teachers and other school staff. Without it, administrative decision making will be based largely on after-the-fact information or worse, on conjecture and guesswork.

If leadership involves exercising influence over important decisions and/or the actions of others, it is a short leap from this discerning observation about the involvement of front-line staff to the notion that school leaders need others to lead and that leadership may be best conceptualized as a *quality of the many, not the few*. The possibility of promoting a learning organization as discussed in Chapters 4 and 7 depends on the active leadership participation of many, and the sharing of evidence about what works for our students, in our school, at any given time. Among the reasons for this are the limitations of relying on the single, omniscient leader and a recognition that tapping into the ideas, creativity, skills, and initiative of many in a group or organization unleashes a greater capacity for organizational change, responsiveness and improvement (Woods, 2010).

Thought Partner Conversation

Discuss with a critical friend: What is the meaning of the term distributed leadership? How (if at all) does it differ from shared decision-making or participative management?

DISTRIBUTED LEADERSHIP

Somewhat like school-based management years ago (Bauer, 1998), there is definitional confusion about what we mean by distributed leadership. In some cases, it is clearer what DL is not than what it is. For instance, Harris (2005) states clearly that DL is not the antithesis of hierarchical leadership since it involves both vertical and lateral dimensions of leading; likewise, DL might involve formal and informal leadership roles and practices, so it is not one or the other. Spillane (2006) specifically notes that there is nothing in DL theory that negates the role of the principal. Some insist that DL is not the same as school-based management, participative leadership or shared decision making; however, it is not clear that scholars, practitioners or policy makers draw a hard line between these phenomena (Bolden, 2011). A review of literature on DL published in 2003 by Bennett et al. found that there was no clear definition of DL, or as Lynch (2012) concluded nearly a decade later: "Despite the craze, distributed leadership has not yet eliminated confusion due to its perceived conceptual elasticity" (p. 36). A subsequent review conducted by Tian, Risku, and Collin (2016) concluded that this conceptual confusion persists, although they identified over 80 articles devoted to either modeling DL practice, comparing DL to other models, or questioning DL as a theoretical construct.

The concept of distributed leadership is sometimes confused as or considered overlapping with shared leadership, collaborative leadership, and participative leadership (Leithwood et al., 2007; Spillane, 2005). This is hardly surprising in the sense that each denotes that leadership is an attribute of more than a single individual and that leadership is an inherently social process (Bolden, 2011). Leithwood et al. (2006) observe that there is an overlap between DL and shared, collaborative, democratic, and participative leadership, though this does not render the concepts one and the same. Fitzsimmons et al. (2011) share this observation, but observe that shared leadership tends to retain the notion of leadership as an attribute of individual actors, albeit ones that are working in a team or group. Timperly (2005) points out also that the distinction between DL and transformational leadership can be confusing in the sense that one of the features of TL theory deals with engaging and involving followers in change and improvement, a decidedly DL-like attribute. She notes also, though, that there is nothing inherent in DL theory about change.

Crawford (2012) acknowledges that DL moves us away from the idea of leadership as an attribute of the solo leader, but points out that the concept is nonetheless tied to notions of power and influence. DL is sometimes used to describe any devolution of decision-making influence from formal leaders to followers, resulting in the mistaken notion that DL means that everyone leads (Bennett et al., 2003; Bolden, 2011; Harris, 2008). Gronn (2008) also worries, "In the sphere of school education, now that distributed leadership is well entrenched in the linguistic furniture, there is a somewhat promiscuous inclination to think of virtually every initiative on the part of teachers and administrators as leadership" (p. 144). Adding to the confusion is the fact that DL is presented as a normative, descriptive, predictive, and discursive concept by various proponents (Harris, 2009). While Spillane (2006) concludes, "The appeal of distributed leadership lies in the ease with which it can become all things to all people" (p. 102), Harris (2009) concurs:

> The chameleon like quality of distributed leadership invites both misinterpretation and misunderstanding. One common misunderstanding is that distributed leadership is a convenient "catch all" descriptor for any form of shared, collaborative or extended leadership practice. This view is certainly quite prevalent, blurring further the meaning of the term.
>
> (p. 5)

Yet, Harris (2009) also claims that unlike many other perspectives, DL brings a strong theoretical base and growing empirical support, reviewed below.

Thought Partner Conversation

Lost in our discussion of DL is the question: do teachers and other school staff want to be leaders in their schools or districts? Discuss this based on your own perspective and experiences.

Where Does Leadership Reside?

Conceptual clarity might be more than we can ask for related to any image of leadership; a loose consensus is probably the best we can do. But the somewhat murky image of DL and its frequent uses/misuses does raise some provocative questions. For example, scholars that have advanced DL models argue that leadership itself ought to be conceptualized as something other than the person of the leader, that "leadership practice refers to the outcome of the interaction between the leaders, the followers and their situations" (Liljenberg, 2015, p. 153). Leadership, then, is used as a more fluid descriptor that may involve varied actors and situations. As a theoretical construct, however, using this conceptualization of leadership as "stretched over" individuals and situations (Spillane, 2006) prompts us to ask: *Exactly who is distributing what when distributed leadership is occurring?* These seem to be important questions for schools in which the core technologies are inherently distributed over a wide variety of tasks, people, and locations. To simply say that DL is happening when someone other than a formal administrator is doing important work in an authentic context with the authority to make consequential decisions related to teaching and learning would seem to imply that all work done in classrooms the vast majority of the time qualifies as DL. Instead, it might be better to think in terms of leadership spheres. Cuban (1988) claimed long ago that teachers behave as leaders in their classrooms along several dimensions, but conceptualizations of DL suggest that the leadership in question goes beyond individual classrooms.

Before moving on to explore the conceptualizations offered in the literature for DL, it is worth reminding ourselves that especially in schools there are many ways leaders involve others and there are many others to be involved. Different conceptions and names are associated with various structures and processes that include someone other than the formal leader in leading—shared decision making, school-based management, collaborative teams, cross-functional teams, participative leadership, and PLCs among them. While we agree that DL is not merely meant to refer to collaboration among formal leaders, informal leaders, and followers (Spillane & Diamond, 2007), it seems equally valid to contend that any of the above-mentioned collaborative processes *may be* instances of DL, depending on features of their enactment. Our discussion of IL in Chapter 7 and elsewhere (Van Lare, Brazer, Bauer, & Smith, 2013) assumed that teachers working collaboratively on improving instructional practices had *opportunities* to lead but whether they do is uncertain. As Spillane (2005) observed, a distributed perspective allows for the notion of shared or democratic leadership, but in any given instance such leadership may or may not be present.

Thought Partner Conversation

Have you experienced being given responsibility, even partially so, for a decision that affected your school beyond your own classroom? How much autonomy did you have in that situation? How much choice? Did your judgment matter?

Distributed Leadership Defined

Bush (2013) suggests that a starting point for understanding distributed leadership is to distinguish it from positional authority and posit that leadership is not necessarily confined to formal leaders. DL is inherently a relational notion (Lynch, 2012) involving the co-performance of leadership practice and the interactions of the actors engaged in this co-performance (Harris, 2005). It represents an alternative to traditional power-over notions of hierarchy, accentuating the potential for actors to exercise power with one another in an effort to increase the capacity to take action and accomplish organizational tasks. Similarly, however, DL does not replace the hierarchy or formal leadership (Spillane, 2006). Often, opportunities for DL are initiated by formal leaders who distribute influence and agency to other members of the organization—in schools that generally means teachers—who then lead alongside formal leaders.

Gibb is widely attributed as the first scholar to use the term *distributed leadership* when he observed that leadership may well be best conceptualized as an attribute of the group and may be dispersed, shared, or distributed (Feng et al., 2017; Gronn, 2000; Harris, 2010). While a clear definition of DL may be elusive, as we noted above, Bennett et al. (2003) identified a number of elements of the concept that they believe to be distinctive and widely shared. From a distributed perspective,

- leadership is an emergent property of a group rather than belonging to a single leader;
- leadership is open to many rather than restricted to a select few;
- leadership may be open to members of the community or actors formally outside the boundaries of the organization; and
- expertise may be found and applied to leadership tasks from many sources.

DL, Bennett et al. (2003) write, is not something done by or to individual actors, nor is it a set of particular interactions; it is group activity that works within and through relationships. DL, then, is not simply the aggregation of individual acts or the division of labor, but an interaction between leaders and followers in which tasks are distributed across roles (Timperly, 2005). It is dynamic in the sense that DL may emerge involving quite different actors doing different tasks depending on the instance (Bolden, 2011).

Thought Partner Conversation

Looking over the attributes of DL just outlined, can you think of ways teachers as leaders with formal authority seek to distribute leadership within their classrooms? What about as members of teacher teams? Why might teachers lead this way in these contexts?

Leithwood et al. (2009) suggest that for many authors, DL incorporates shared, democratic, dispersed, or other forms of leadership, and from this angle might be considered a normative concept, i.e., a preferred means for enhancing the effectiveness of an organization or group. For other theorists, including the two highlighted below, it is a descriptive theory, best characterized as an analytic framework. Spillane and Diamond (2007), in fact, suggest that DL may occur even when two or more leaders seek different ends or work quite separately from each other; these factors are merely separate dimensions of the leadership phenomenon that need to be accounted for in an analysis.

WHAT IS DISTRIBUTED TO WHOM AND WHY?

Brian Washington has a problem. He wanted to distribute some decision-making authority—leadership—to a group of math and special education teachers, but then he didn't like the direction they took. Brian and the teachers differed perhaps because they had different sensitivities to the context. Principal Washington was focused on the achievement gap issue, whereas it is possible his teachers were focused on searching for a convenient program that would help remediate students whose math skills are weak without disrupting the pace or methods of instruction.

The result is that Brian is construed to give the teachers a decision to make, then take back that authority when he didn't like the solution they adopted with, in his mind, too little analysis. From afar, we might see the following flaws in Principal Washington's process:

- The authority relationship between the principal and his group of teachers was unclear.
- Process criteria for making a decision—deliberative versus expedient—were understood differently.
- Outcome criteria for the decision—adopting a program versus addressing root causes—may have been misunderstood.

One way to interpret what happened is that Principal Washington delegated a task to the group of teachers, even though he and the teachers alike may have believed in the beginning that he was granting them agency to make a decision. The resulting mixed message creates substantial ill will between the principal and his teachers.

Robinson (2008) contends that depictions of DL tend to involve viewing leadership either as task distribution or the distribution of influence, with most work on DL adopting the former focus. As a prime example, Spillane, Diamond and Jita (2003) write: "We define school leadership as the identification, acquisition, allocation, coordination, and use of the social, material, and cultural resources necessary to establish the conditions for the possibility of innovation in teaching and learning" (p. 535). This perspective situates leadership as the performance of tasks and the interactions among actors who are completing or enacting these tasks. From this perspective, DL encompasses the leader, the follower, and the task (Lynch, 2012; Spillane, 2006).

Two scholars are largely responsible for the emergence of DL as a theory in education contexts: Peter Gronn and James Spillane (Devos, Tutyens, & Hulpia, 2014;

Harris, 2009, 2010). Both incorporate elements of activity theory as underpinnings of their perspectives (Harris, 2008). For example, Gronn (2002) incorporates elements of Engestrom's activity theory into his model, including the idea that activity is jointly performed and involves the division of labor elements of context that both affect and are affected by activity during enactment. The interdependency of context and leadership activity, Gronn (2002) believes, has been a missing element in leadership theory, as has the reality that except for the most trivial of actions, multiple leaders interact with one another in the enactment of any activity. "This interdependency," Ho and Ng (2017, p. 224) write, "between the context and the activity in focus is reflected in Spillane's argument that the situation in which distributed leadership is practiced 'both defines leadership practice and is defined through leadership practice'" (Spillane, 2006, p. 4). Activity theory treats the unit of analysis as the collectively enacted activity system, taking account of the contextual factors that affect practice (Gronn, 2002; Spillane, Halverson, & Diamond, 2001).

In addition to activity theory, Gronn and Spillane's DL perspectives build on the notion of distributed cognition (Harris, 2008), and the concept that "mind and mindfulness are not solely features of the interior mental life of individuals, but are manifest in jointly performed activities and social relations" (Gronn, 2000, p. 323). Distributed cognition, Harris (2009) writes, "suggests that capacities are distributed throughout the social and material conditions of the organization and that they are fluid rather than fixed" (p. 4). Distributed cognition relates to sources and patterns of influence in the organization (Harris, 2009). Additionally, learning is socially constructed (see Chapters 4 and 7) as an outcome of the interactions among elements of the activity system.

Distributed cognition implies that learning takes place through interactions within and across various teams. DL similarly implies that the practice of leadership is one that is shared and realized within extended groupings and networks, some of these groupings will be formal while others will be informal and in some cases, randomly formed (Harris, 2008, p. 175).

Hence, social context plays a major role in interaction and learning; the interaction between actors, artifacts, and the environment is of utmost importance. Furthermore, "distributed mind and distributed learning are especially evident in working environments in which decision making is heavily dependent upon the rapid processing of large amounts of information as part of networked, computer-mediated work practices and similarly complex technological artefacts" (Gronn, 2000, p. 323).

Thought Partner Conversation

Think of a time in your education career when you were called upon to help make an urgent and important decision. Why were *you* involved? Did you work with others, and if so do you recall whether collaboration helped or impeded the process? Was the decision in which you were involved ultimately implemented? Why or why not?

Gronn (2000) asserts that the two dominant depictions of leadership in the literature involve either agency or structure. His perspective emphasizes *conjoint agency*—the idea that the completion of leadership tasks involves the concertive efforts of organizational members. Consequently, "The properties displayed by leadership are more likely to take a distributed, rather than a concentrated, form…" (p. 318). Leadership theory therefore has to account for a new division of work that moves beyond the leader–follower depiction. Conjoint agency, for Gronn (2002), represents the unit of analysis in leadership studies, with activity (or the flow of activities) representing the focus of leadership study.

Gronn (2002) writes about two different kinds of distributed leadership: numeric/additive and concertive. Numeric or additive DL is defined as the sum of its parts—it is DL in which individuals exercise leadership over a problem or puzzle contributing to the leadership activity disparately.

> If focused leadership means that only one individual is attributed with the status of leader, an additive or numerical view of distributed leadership means the aggregated leadership of an organization is dispersed among some, many, or maybe all of the members.
>
> (Gronn, 2002, p. 429)

Concertive DL suggests participants leading together in a fashion that promotes more of a synergy or value-added through collective action, suggesting agency beyond taking on tasks delegated by others. Rather than aggregated individual acts, concertive DL is conceived as a more holistic phenomenon, more than the sum of its parts. Gronn (2000) describes three types of concertive actions: *spontaneous collaboration* refers to concertive activity that emerges naturally or to address an unanticipated problem or puzzle, which is temporary in nature; *intuitive working relations* include partnerships or alliances that emerge as close working relationships among actors; and *institutionalized practices* include structures developed to establish and maintain collective action. Actors engaged in concertive activity, Gronn (2002) states, represent units that act conjointly—they coordinate their actions and create a synergy in which each player contributes to enactment of the activities involved and influence and are influenced by each other. In other words, there is reciprocity in organization members' actions and contributions to leading. Their work is both interdependent and coordinated.

Gronn (2000) also takes up the question of the role of power in conceptualizing leadership, asserting that influence may be overt or covert (i.e., expressed indirectly), is often reciprocal rather than unidirectional, and is best conceived as being emergent rather than fixed. Influence over any organizational activity might thus be expressed by more than the person with legitimate authority and involves much more than giving directions or orders. A purely role-bound perspective, he writes, presents a limited view of who influences the enactment of an activity and its outcomes. As an example, who is exercising influence (and leading) when a formal leader mandates the implementation of a specific reading program and during enactment teachers make adjustments in practice to meet the needs of a diverse student body? A distributed perspective would suggest that the formal leader, teachers, and perhaps students exercise consequential influence over enactment of activities associated with the program as they respond to the reading program in the context of their classrooms.

Spillane, Halverson, and Diamond (2001, 2004) argue for a distributed perspective as a way of better understanding not only what leaders do, but also how and why they act. A focus on individual agency, they assert, is inadequate or insufficient because focusing on the actions of formal leaders alone leaves out the contributions and actions of many who are involved in enactment of organizational activities. They argue that DL is a process of thinking and acting in a given context, a process of sensemaking involving the situation, actors, and actions. Cognition is *stretched over* actors and artifacts and may be thought of as co-enacted by leaders and followers. Spillane (2005) explains, further, "Distributed leadership is first and foremost about leadership practice rather than leaders or their roles, functions, routines, and structures" (p. 144). Spillane and Diamond (2007) note that DL may involve the *leader-plus aspect* which acknowledges the number of actors who play a role in leadership, and the *practice aspect*, which focuses on the practice of leading and managing. These perspectives, they assert, provide a framework for examining the enactment of leadership as day-to-day practice.

Distributed leadership is a process perspective (Spillane, 2006). Leadership practice, Spillane (2005) writes, is "...a product of the interactions of school leaders, followers, and their situation. Rather than viewing leadership practice as a product of a leader's knowledge and skill, the distributed perspective defines it as the interactions between people" (p. 144). Spillane (2006) describes three forms of DL—collaborated, collective, and coordinated. *Collaborated distribution* involves leadership activity stretched over two or more individuals working in the same space and time, for instance a team of leaders tackling a leadership puzzle. *Collective distribution* involves individuals working separately but interdependently, for instance, a cross-functional team working on the same puzzle within their own functions. An example might be Principal Washington's math and special education teachers working with students (possibly with the assistance of the Atlas program) separately for the interdependent hoped-for outcome of improved achievement. *Coordinated distribution* is leadership practice that is performed in a temporal sequence, for instance leaders working to enact a common action plan over the course of a semester or year.

From a research perspective, then, to study DL requires investigating the interaction of actors, the situation or context, and the tools and structures employed during execution of important organizational activities in order to understand who and in what ways actors contribute to this enactment. Harris (2008) notes, for example, where teachers are working together to solve pedagogical puzzles they occupy a particular space characterized by the actors, contact, and artifacts present, potentially engaging in leadership practice. Artifacts may include such things as language, tools, structures, equipment, etc. (Spillane, Halverson, & Diamond, 2004). Leadership is "stretched over the work of a number of individuals and the task is accomplished through the interaction of multiple leaders" (Spillane, Halverson, & Diamond, 2001, p. 20).

Spillane, Halverson, and Diamond (2004) assert that the unit of analysis in DL must be leadership activity, which is defined as the interaction of leaders, followers, and elements of the situation in which they are acting.

In other words, a distributed perspective on human activity presses us to move beyond individual activity to consider how the material, cultural, and social situation enables, informs, and constrains human activity. In this view, activity is a product of what the actor knows, believes, and does in and through particular social, cultural, and material contexts.

(Spillane, Halverson, & Diamond, 2004, p. 10)

The situation, therefore, is not merely a backdrop to be explained away or controlled in an examination of leadership activity; it is a part of leadership. "We consider sociocultural context as a constitutive element of leadership practice, an integral defining element of that activity" (Spillane, Halverson, & Diamond, 2004, p. 15). "Human activity," Spillane, Halverson, and Diamond (2001) assert, "is best understood by considering both artifacts and actors together through cycles of task completion because the artifacts and actors are essentially intertwined in action contexts" (p. 23). Distribution, from this definition, is inherently situational—who is involved, how they are involved, with what tools they are involved, etc., are all dependent on the puzzle. Leadership is emergent in the execution of tasks through which collections of individuals have influence and exercise agency.

To summarize, in Spillane's model elements of the situation both define and are defined by distributed practice. Drawing on the notions embedded in distributed cognition and activity theory, the context is presented as an important constitutive part of leadership activity. DL thus emphasizes how cognition is held among individuals and aspects of the situation; cognitive activity is "stretched over" positional leaders, other organization members, and aspects of the context in which leadership is enacted. Context is elevated beyond a setting external to the leadership act; instead, it is part of that act. As Fitzsimmons, James, and Denyer, (2011) point out, this implies that sensemaking is thus enabled by both the leaders' cognition and elements of the situation itself. Aspects of the situation are then seen to be "actively constituting and shaping leadership practice in a reciprocal relationship" (Fitzsimmons, James, & Denyer, 2011, p. 318).

Thought Partner Conversation

With a critical friend, outline the case against DL—from a leader's or follower's perspective, what's wrong with the notion? Why not buy into it as a productive model of leading schools?

CRITICISMS OF DISTRIBUTED LEADERSHIP

Before moving on to our review of the effects of DL and the conditions that either support or hinder it in schools, it is important to acknowledge that not everyone is wildly enthusiastic about the notion of distributed leadership, even ignoring the voices that believe that DL is simply a repackaged version of shared or collaborative leadership. Some commentators (e.g., Bolden, 2011) point out that despite the interest in DL, the heroic leader is still very much with us. Many people find the notion of everyone leading as counterintuitive; from their perspective, leadership is essentially an individual trait or characteristic.

Lumby (2013) notes that the theory of DL has morphed from a tool that could help us understand leadership practice to a prescribed practice that is widely advocated; "The theory is no longer the new kid on the block, but almost the only child in sight" (p. 583). DL entices followers to believe that they, too, can lead. "The assertion that everyone could lead is not generally accompanied by deep reflection on the implications of this stance and what inclusion of more in leadership might imply" (p. 583). The implication of an apolitical workplace emerges, ignoring issues of power and privilege and, Lumby concludes, the realities of organizational life. Bolden (2011) notes that most conceptualizations of DL give short shrift to issues of power and politics, and that while tasks may be distributed to informal leaders, whether power is distributed as well is less clear. Bush and Glover (2014) similarly note that DL inevitably implies the redistribution of power, requiring the formal leader to relinquish something, which they may be quite reluctant to do (possibly for good reason in Principal Washington's case), constraining the potential for DL.

> **Thought Partner Conversation**
>
> In cases familiar to you in which DL was evident, were you aware of power differentials among those whom leadership was "stretched over"? How was power associated with interpersonal relationships with positional leaders such as principals and APs? What does this experience teach you about your own future leadership?

Lynch (2012) notes that distributing leadership may be seen as risky business—some people will not have the talent, skill, or disposition to accept the responsibility of leading. To the degree that formal leadership is associated with competence, why encourage others to lead? Crawford (2012) points out that to the degree that formal leaders remain responsible and accountable for mandates or performance targets (generally the case for school principals), the likelihood of the distribution of influence is reduced (perhaps necessitating a constrained opportunity for DL) at best. Harris (2008) observes that DL may be associated with increased levels of ambiguity and confusion over who does what and who is responsible, an increase in conflicting goals and agendas, and competition related to goals and roles. Ho and Ng (2017) comment that activity theory predicts that tensions are likely to emerge due to overlapping or conflicting needs and demands over goals, roles, boundaries related to influence and responsibility, and so on. Harris (2009) states that leadership dispersion can contribute to team inefficiencies and that in some circumstances, fewer leaders may be far better than more. In short, more cooks in the kitchen may indeed spoil the broth. This may be one reason Gronn (2009) has argued for a hybrid notion of leadership, recognizing that sources of leadership and influence may at some instances be highly concentrated and at other times quite dispersed or distributed.

Tian, Risku, and Collin (2016) and Harris (2010), among others, mention that some commentators have concluded that DL is merely a new form of managerialism, a mechanism to induce greater effort from teachers and other school staff. "More critical voices have pointed out distributed leadership's political use in providing a mechanism by which staff members willingly commit to a new world order of ever-increasing workload and surveillance" (Lumby, 2013, p. 591).

We conclude from our own reading of the literature that, quite often, descriptions of DL as a theoretical construct are less than clear about what is being distributed. To rely solely on the notion of DL as a process of distributing tasks or activities that might have otherwise been completed by the solo leader seems to come close to equating DL with delegation. From our perspective, we question whether DL must be conceived as involving the distribution of influence and agency. Absent the sharing of power—the ability to make consequential decisions involving the enactment of important tasks—we are not sure what is being actually *distributed*.

Shortly after the unpleasant meeting with his teachers, Brian Washington invited Professor Hiura who taught the course that included collaborative leadership practices to lunch. This gave Brian time for an extended, reflective conversation. Together they analyzed the makeup of the team. Brian realized that he chose teachers on the basis of their teaching assignment, not according to their capacity to lead on the important question of adjusting math instruction to narrow achievement gaps. Professor Hiura helped Brian to realize that it was his organizational responsibility to be thoughtful about what kind of decisions should be distributed and to whom.

Brian realizes he cannot uninvite the teachers who are giving him a hard time about Atlas. He can, however, try a reset with this group in which he does a better job of explaining what he wants them to do, the area in which they have influence and agency—initiative to decide—and the non-negotiable boundaries he will place around their decision-making sphere. It doesn't feel as collaborative as what Professor Hiura seemed to advocate in class, but it might be a position from which Brian can move ahead with his somewhat unruly group of teachers.

Thought Partner Conversation

Based on your experiences in schools, what would you expect to be the most critical factors necessary to make DL possible and productive? When you have experienced barriers to DL, what have these been and how might they have been avoided?

RESEARCH ON DISTRIBUTED LEADERSHIP IN SCHOOLS

Whatever the purported benefits and potential liabilities of DL, emergence of the construct has prompted renewed investigation of the interdependence of various actors in school organizations and the potential impact of leading with others. Gronn's and Spillane's conceptual work has served to accentuate the notion that leadership distribution is a process involving the interaction of individuals with expertise to work together to solve puzzles of practice and thus—potentially—promote school improvement (Bellibas & Liu, 2016). In terms of supporting the distributed perspective itself, Spillane et al.'s (2001, 2004) longitudinal study looking at leadership as distributed practice suggests that focusing on the school rather than the individual leader was more appropriate to understand the development of leadership expertise. It is far harder to document the effects of DL than it is heroic leadership because of its dispersed nature and the fact that co-leaders may flow into and out of leadership instances (Harris, 2010). Nevertheless, there is a growing empirical knowledge base on the topic.

Harris (2008) reminds us that the literature on school improvement consistently highlights the importance of teacher involvement and the benefits of collegial relationships to school improvement and change.

> Distributed leadership also is assumed to enhance opportunities for the organisation to benefit from the capacities of more of its members, to permit members to capitalise on the range of their individual strengths, and to develop among organisational members a fuller appreciation of interdependence and how one's behaviour affects the organisation as a whole.
>
> (p. 177)

Notions related to DL feature prominently, as well, in the literature on PLCs, which is associated with positive outcomes for staff and students. Strongly implied in Chapter 7's emphasis on teacher collaborative teams is that principals would distribute decision-making volition to their teams so they could act in the best interest of students. Although some commentators, as we have said, draw a firm line between concepts such as shared decision making or professional community and DL, it is worth remembering that each concept encompasses some element of formal leaders leading with others.

Moving to the research on distributed leadership, Tian, Risku, and Collin (2016) observed that the research can be divided into a number of categories, including research on the effects of distributed leadership on various outcomes, and research that attempts to illuminate ways to strengthen or foster DL in schools. The research on the effects of DL can be separated into two broad categories: research on the impact of DL on student outcomes, and research on the impact of DL on teachers. In terms of the research on the impact of DL on student performance and achievement, relatively few studies address this directly. Silins and Mulford (2002) found that student outcomes are likely to be enhanced when leadership is distributed throughout the school community. Harris and Muijs (2004) found that teacher involvement in decision making promotes student motivation and self-efficacy. Day et al. (2009) concluded that leadership distribution was important to improving student outcomes although this was a mediated rather than a direct relationship with DL affecting staff morale, which in turn impacted outcomes. Heck and Hallinger (2009) test the effect of DL on math achievement over time in a sample of US elementary schools using a growth model. Their research shows that DL has an effect on math achievement, and that growth in DL would result in a modest but significant increase in math achievement as well. They also found that the initial degree of DL in schools influences change in academic capacity (i.e., conditions that support effective instruction), which in turn has a significant positive impact on math achievement growth. As Harris (2009, 2010) and others have concluded, the evidence is growing and tends to lean in the direction of DL boosting student performance, but it is hardly conclusive, nor do we fully understand the mechanisms through which DL might promote student learning.

As a part of their massive, multi-year study, Wahlstrom, Louis, Leithwood, and Anderson (2010) examined collective leadership, shared leadership, and distributed leadership as separate constructs. Collective leadership is defined as "the sum of influence exercised on school decisions by those educators, parents and students associated with the school" (p. 8). Their findings suggest that this type of leadership has the strongest effect on student learning, and that all leaders in high-performing schools seem to have greater influence on school decisions than leaders in low-performing schools. The impact of collective leadership on student achievement was mediated by teacher capacity for improvement, teacher motivation, and elements of the school setting. Shared leadership in their work is defined "as teachers' influence over, and participation in, school-wide decisions with principals" (p. 10), which they found to influence teachers' professional community, which in turn influences improvements in instruction and, consequently, student achievement. Strong professional relationships, they concluded, encourage professional community, which encourages teachers to act as leaders. In terms of distributed leadership, this study focused on patterns of distribution and practices that impact DL. Notably, they found that few teachers attribute leadership to a single actor:

> The array of individuals or groups identified as providing leadership included a mix of principals, assistant principals, teachers in formal leadership roles, teachers informally recognized by peers as influential, parents, district administrators and professional staff, and external consultants linked to curriculum, program, and teacher development initiatives at the school level. Overall, principals stood out because they were more likely than any other group to be simultaneously involved in multiple leadership responsibilities.
>
> (Wahlstrom et al., p. 11)

Thought Partner Conversation

In your experience, how would you expect DL to most affect teachers? How has being involved as a leader affected you? Jot down your thoughts based on conversations with one or more thought partners.

They conclude, among other things, that while many people lead in schools, the principal is still the central leadership actor. "Principals are involved in many leadership activities; others who act as leaders in the school ordinarily do so in respect to one or a few initiatives" (p. 12).

The majority of the work on the effects of distributed leadership focuses on the impact of DL on a variety of teacher outcomes. For example, using the Distributed Leadership Inventory (Hulpia, Devos, & Rosseell, 2009), Hulpia and colleagues studied the impact of DL on teachers' organizational commitment (Devos, Tutyens, & Hulpia, 2014; Hulpia, Devos, & Van Keer, 2011; Hulpia, Devos, Rosseell, & Vlerick, 2012); they found that school staff appeared to welcome support from both formal and informal leaders, but teachers' commitment seemed to drop if multiple leaders supervised them. Interestingly, Devos, Tutyens, and Hulpia (2014) concluded that the largest effects were associated with the leadership of the principal, suggesting perhaps that DL enhances rather than detracts from the principals' impact. Ross, Lufti, and Hope (2016) also demonstrated a relationship between DL and teachers' affective commitment, and Torres (2018) found that DL significantly predicts teacher satisfaction.

In terms of the research focusing on organizational conditions necessary for creating opportunities for DL, Tian, Risku, and Collin (2016) identified four elements that appear key to making DL work: formal leaders' support, a climate of trust, strategic staff policy, and utilization of artifacts in leadership. The most consistent research in this category, though, seems to be about patterns of DL when implemented. In addition to those presented earlier from Spillane and Gronn, a number of schemes describing the forms of DL have been suggested (Bolden, 2011); these are summarized in Table 8.1.

Three of these models are conceptual in orientation. Leithwood and colleagues (2007, 2009) present a scheme derived from empirical investigation. They suggest that whether leadership is distributed appears to be less important than how it is distributed. From this perspective, DL is not intrinsically beneficial; it can be helpful or productive, however, if done purposefully. The four types of DL they observe in their work are as follows (see Table 8.1):

- *Planful alignment* occurs when resources and responsibilities are deliberately distributed to those best able to contribute to an activity or function (Think about Brian Washington's rethinking of his distributed leadership effort.)
- *Spontaneous alignment* occurs when resources and responsibilities are distributed in an ad hoc fashion yet results in a useful alignment of leadership sources.
- *Spontaneous misalignment* occurs when resources and responsibilities are distributed in an ad hoc fashion resulting in a misalignment of leadership resources.
- *Anarchic misalignment* occurs when actors pursue their own goals independently, reject organizational or common goals, and work at cross-purposes with others.

Their research indicated that certain patterns of leadership distribution are most likely to produce positive outcomes:

- planful and spontaneous alignment are likely to contribute to short-term organizational productivity;
- planful alignment is most likely to produce long-term productivity; and
- spontaneous misalignment and anarchic misalignment are likely to have a negative effect on short and long-term organizational productivity.

TABLE 8.1 Configurations of Distributed Leadership

Gronn (2002)	Spillane (2006)	Leithwood et al. (2007)	Feng et al. (2017)
Spontaneous collaboration refers to concertive activity by actors with differing skills or knowledge that emerge naturally or to address an unanticipated problem or puzzle, which are temporary in nature	*Collaborated distribution* involves leadership activity stretched over two or more individuals working in the same space and time	*Planful alignment* occurs when resources and responsibilities are deliberately distributed to those best able to contribute to an activity or function	*Shared DL* exists when team members engage in concertive action with others who share their basic role space or function in the organization as might be the case on a collaborative grade-level team
Intuitive working relations occur when actors with close working relationships partner or form an alliance	*Collective distribution* involves individuals working separately but interdependently	*Spontaneous alignment* occurs when resources and responsibilities are distributed in an ad hoc fashion yet results in a useful alignment of leadership sources	*Conjoint DL* exists when people from different roles engage in concretive action as might be the case in a cross-functional team
Institutionalized practices are enduring or lasting structures developed to establish and maintain collective action and foster collaboration	*Coordinated distribution* is leadership practice that is performed in a temporal sequence	*Spontaneous misalignment* occurs when resources and responsibilities are distributed in an ad hoc fashion resulting in a misalignment of leadership resources	*Fragmented DL* occurs when people from the same basic role space engage in numerical action, i.e., they operate relatively independently on the same problem or puzzle
		Anarchic misalignment occurs when actors pursue their own goals independently, reject organizational or common goals, and work at cross-purposes with others	*Dispersed DL* exists when individuals from different role spaces engage in numerical action

Mascall, Leithwood, Straus, and Sacks (2008) showed that high levels of academic optimism were positively and significantly associated with planned approaches to leadership distribution, and conversely, low levels of academic optimism were negatively and significantly associated with unplanned and unaligned approaches to leadership distribution. This work suggests, overall, that formal leaders can have a strong impact on both the form and efficacy of DL; when they purposefully restructure or redesign leadership practice and/or distribute leadership to actors who either have or can develop expertise, more positive outcomes result.

Somewhat paradoxically, the success with which leadership is distributed to teachers depends quite crucially on administrative initiative. Principals encourage distributed forms of leadership when they create problem-solving teams to substitute for administrative leadership. Leadership distribution is influenced either positively or negatively by teachers' and principals' willingness to view their jobs differently. Leithwood et al. (2007) conclude that their work shows that DL does not reduce the need for formal leadership; it demands however that leaders act to coordinate DL, monitor its enactment, and provide feedback to those involved.

Feng et al. (2017) attempt to create a typology of DL built on two important dimensions that include what they call dependency of action (Gronn's concertive or numerical) and role space allocation (i.e., whether actors are in the same or different roles/functions). This scheme results in four types of DL, as shown in Table 8.2:

- shared DL exists when team members engage in concertive action with others who share their basic role space or function in the organization as might be the case on a collaborative grade-level team;
- conjoint DL exists when people from different roles engage in concretive action as might be the case in a cross-functional team such as the APs and principal of a high school;
- fragmented DL occurs when people from the same basic role space engage in numerical action, i.e., they operate relatively independently on the same problem or puzzle; and
- dispersed DL exists when individuals from different role spaces engage in numerical action.

Feng et al. (2017) hypothesize that none of these are ideal in every circumstance, but may be contingent on a number of factors—characteristic of the leaders involved (e.g., participatory style), the task at hand (e.g., task complexity), and the context (e.g., technologies involved). They recommend future research on a number of propositions they derive from this conjecture.

TABLE 8.2 Typology of Distributed Leadership

		Role Space (Job Function)	
		Same	Different
Dependency of Actions	Concertive	Shared DL	Conjoint DL
	Numerical/additive	Fragmented DL	Dispersed DL

Source: Adapted from Feng et al., 2017, p. 288.

Summary

Harris (2008, 2009, 2010) notes that the research on distributed leadership supports the following conclusions:

- Studies show a clear and positive relationship between DL and outcomes for teachers (e.g., self-efficacy, motivation).
- Investigations of DL as a form of work or organizational design show that some configurations lead to more positive outcomes than others (e.g., planful distribution).
- Distributed leadership research shows that schools that are successful appear to have redesigned themselves to spread leadership across more people and/or decision opportunities.
- Studies that have taken on, directly, the link between DL and student outcomes (e.g., student engagement) tend to reveal promising patterns of results.

It is fair to say that while the research still has considerable gaps and there is much work to be done, it is equally valid to conclude that the research base is no longer in its infancy, and the prognosis tends to support the validity of the claim that DL is indeed a promising practice for school leaders.

DISTRIBUTING LEADERSHIP FOR PLANNED CHANGE

Although DL is not the same as collaboration or shared decision making, they are often mechanisms used to distribute leadership, and an argument can be made that sharing decision making is a frequent, if not necessary, part of DL. Leithwood, Harris, and Strauss (2013) stress the importance of promoting a collaborative culture as a critical element in reaching high performance in schools, which they say is "at the heart of a positive organization culture" (p. 265). This may involve the redesign of organizational structures to disperse authority to make or influence critical decisions, removing structural barriers, and providing resources necessary to support a new way of working. "The main task of leaders therefore is to create the organizational conditions through redefinition and redesign, where a different way of working is not only possible but absolutely required because of the new organizational arrangements and associated set of expectations" (Leithwood, Harris, & Strauss, 2013, p. 265).

   Much of the literature reviewed in this chapter accentuates the view that DL is grounded in practice. Hence, the form it takes and who might be involved depends on the actors, the activity or challenge, and the context. You might wonder, *what guidance is there for aspiring and practicing school leaders to know how to engage in DL?* From our perspective, some of the most promising aspects of the research on DL reviewed above reveal the form and practice of DL, not just the outcomes associated with it. Research on earlier phenomena such as site-based management suffered greatly because the process itself was treated as a "black box" that was generally unexamined (Bauer, 1998; Sharpe, 1996) either descriptively or critically. And the same might be said about the current literature on learning communities and teacher collaborative teams (Bauer, Brazer, Van Lare, & Smith, 2013; Bauer, Van Lare, Brazer, & Smith 2015; Brazer, Van Lare, Bauer, & Smith, 2014), though there is certainly plenty of advocacy for particular models, often from the originators of the models themselves. The DL research presented earlier that conceptualizes and investigates various forms and their consequences on implementation and outcomes provides a terrific starting point for practicing leaders to understand how DL might work in practice.

Our discussion of the framework for considering the organizational design of teacher teams presented in the last chapter is a tool for understanding some of the critical decisions leaders make to distribute leadership in a *planful* fashion. We encourage you as a leader to consider each design dimension carefully as you construct opportunities for leading with others.

In this section, we briefly add to this discussion by drawing on research we have conducted related to earlier and other manifestations of teamwork in schools (site-based management and PLCs) to suggest a framework for understanding additional decisions that leaders need to make to engage others in planned change. While we recognize that not all change is planned, and not all DL occurs in contexts such as formal teams or the implementation of defined action plans, the fact is that quite a lot of activity does take place in schools with intentionally designed collaborative structures intended to improve student and school performance. For those instances in which you, as an administrative or teacher leader, plan to engage a team in improvement work, this material may be helpful.

Thought Partner Conversation

We have noted in Chapter 7 and here that not all change is *planned change*, but we assert that much of what we do to improve schools falls into this category. With a thought partner, brainstorm opportunities to lead planned change in schools. See if you can imagine ways you might, as a leader, involve others in such efforts. Who might you involve, how would you involve them, and what would you hope to accomplish through this distribution of leadership?

Distributing Leadership to Teams

Group work permeates much of what we do in education, and many of us endure a love–hate relationship with working in teams for a wide range of reasons. Although we may recognize the potential synergy in working with others, we often recall vivid tales of endless meetings, irresponsible group members, and group work outcomes that never saw the light of day. Despite these weaknesses, as this chapter emphasizes, no one working in administration can accomplish his or her goals alone. Working with others expands our own knowledge, involves others in decision making important to their work lives, and creates a coalition with a common understanding of a particular problem and how to approach it. Collaborative work done well provides opportunities to generate a sense of belonging, esteem, and self-actualization among co-workers, and may lead to individual and collective self-transcendence.

At the risk of splitting hairs, we think it is valuable to differentiate between a work group and a team. Work groups tend to exist in perpetuity, possibly with a general mission and likely with the responsibility to discuss and solve ongoing management problems. Principals and their APs often function as a work group in this way, as superintendents and their cabinets are likely to do. These groups certainly have value and are necessary to the function of any organization. In contrast, teams are more focused and temporary than work groups. They come together for a specific, explicit purpose. When that purpose has been accomplished, they disband. Language is often fuzzy, but we might refer to this kind of team as a task force, which connotes its temporary and important nature. Although a work group may be determined by roles (e.g., the collection of all department heads), a team is made up of individuals who bring distinct and complementary skills and knowledge. In the vernacular of DL, the team is emergent. Well-constructed teams can be very effective for moving the organization forward in specific areas (Hackman & Walton, 1986; Katzenbach & Smith, 2003; Larson & LaFasto, 1989).

Extended Web Activities

Use web resources at your disposal to explore what is known about the differences between groups and teams, and as a corollary, what is known about effective teams. From this search, what ideas might you apply as a leader interested in effectively leading with others?

PLCs, teacher collaborative teams, and collaborative learning teams are currently popular terms for collections of educators who work together to solve problems. Most do not conform to the characteristics of teams described in relevant research, mainly because of their perpetual nature and because members are selected based on their roles and not their expertise. As a school or district leader, you may want to think about restructuring such groups into teams—both the positive and negative consequences of doing so. If you can get these teams focused on teaching and learning as described in Chapter 7, then they will likely receive your distributed leadership messages productively and help you improve school performance.

As we emphasized in Chapter 7 and in this chapter, when principals establish teacher collaborative teams and the decision-making process for their work, it is vital for the teams to know their role in a specific decision process. Contingency theory (Chapter 5) suggests that a team's contribution to a particular decision depends on their competence, where responsibility resides, and the general context. One of the most important decisions a principal can make is how a decision will be made. We perceive the possibility of four types of team involvement in decisions with respect to the principal. These are listed below with examples for how each one would work for Principal Washington in parentheses.

1. The principal decides and informs the team of her or his decision. The team participates by implementing the decision. (Washington tells his team that he has decided *not* to use the Atlas program and he explains why.)
2. The principal decides, but before doing so takes feedback from the team. The principal informs the team how their feedback was used. (Washington tells the

team that he wants them to recommend two alternative programs to Atlas with a report on the strengths and weaknesses of all three. He will select one of the three and inform the team about how he made his choice.)

3. The principal works with the team as a peer. The principal essentially expands the team by one and is as active as any other member. Decisions are made on a consensus basis. (In a reset, Washington joins the team in renewed deliberations regarding how to address achievement gaps in math.)

4. The principal delegates the decision to the team. Goals and standards for assessing the quality of the decision are established in advance. The principal monitors decision progress while allowing the team to proceed unimpeded. (Washington seems to have started here by letting the team come up with their own decision. He would need to reset in these circumstances too, letting the team know the criteria he has in mind for an appropriate program or approach to the math achievement gap and the standards for assessing an ultimate plan.)

For a more detailed discussion of these four types of decision making, see Bauer and Brazer (2012), Chapter 3.

CONCLUSION

One of our former students commented recently that *leadership is collaboration*, that when he or she started to involve others, communicate more, and listen more, a network of support emerged that allowed for more rapid and more significant improvements. Broadly speaking, leading with others—and DL in particular—stresses an appreciation for the importance of multiple voices and the fact that many people without formal leadership roles and responsibilities impact what goes on in schools (Harris, 2010). As Bush and Glover (2014) mention, the perspective starts with a separation of leadership and formal positional authority and the idea that leadership effort and expertise might come from many different parts of the enterprise. Position or hierarchy, consequently, does not define leadership capacity; it is a resource to be developed and nurtured so that over time more and different individuals can and will lead (and follow) to help meet the goals of the school and people who work and learn within it. Distributed leadership is characterized by interdependence and emergence, according to Harris (2010); the joint performance of leadership unfolds through the influences of multiple actors and is situationally negotiated and renegotiated. "Together, the dynamic interactions form the basis for developing knowledge creating systems and the ability to secure organizational change" (Harris, 2010, p. 66).

If our extended discussion of relationships among leaders and followers in this chapter and throughout Part II of this book is leaving you a little uncertain about the roles principals and other leaders play in their schools, you are probably not alone. For now, we can say that their primary role is to design the school as an organization in which individuals can flourish as members of a collective focused on a common purpose—the education of children to their fullest potential. We will have more to say about the specifics of what school leaders do in the next chapter, but first this chapter's puzzle.

EXERCISE 8.1 REFLECTION ON DISTRIBUTED LEADERSHIP

A strong undercurrent of this chapter is ambiguity regarding DL. Definitions are varied, often vague, and sometimes conflicting. Effects look promising, but the influence on students is largely mediated through other, sometimes multiple, factors. It is difficult to know *why* the effects of DL occur, which may plant seeds of doubt about whether DL is worth the effort and inherent risk. All of these factors may lead you into a sense of ambivalence about whether you wish to pursue distributed leadership when you find yourself in a position of authority. Hence, this seems to be an appropriate moment to reflect.

1. To what degree have you seen DL practiced in schools where you have worked?

    *   How well does DL *theory* as presented in this chapter *explain* what you have seen?
    *   What were the most prominent features of the DL practice you experienced?
    *   Based on what you have learned from this chapter, what might have been missing or modified that affected your experience of DL?

2. What about DL seems promising to you as you imagine yourself in an administrative leadership role in the future?

    *   How might DL help you to support and enhance effective teaching and learning?
    *   What would DL do for you in terms of building relationships among various stakeholders in your school?
    *   What risks do you perceive if you were to pursue a DL path? How might you mitigate those risks?

3. If you were to land in a position within a traditionally hierarchical system, would you pursue DL strategies? Why, or why not?

EXERCISE 8.2 TRANSFORMATIONAL, INSTRUCTIONAL, AND DISTRIBUTED LEADERSHIP

Consider Figure 5.1 from Chapter 5.

Our intent in Part II of this book is for you to think about the ways in which three important streams in education leadership theory and practice offer insights into how to lead change focused on school improvement. Now that you are familiar with all three we would like you to reflect on how they fit together (or not) in your thinking.

1. In what ways do transformational leadership, IL, and distributed leadership cause you to focus on *different* aspects of leading schools?
2. In what ways do the three perspectives on leadership *complement* or *reinforce* one another?

3. How would you describe the mix of these three leadership perspectives you would like to employ as a school leader focused on improving instruction?

BRIAN WASHINGTON'S DISTRIBUTED LEADERSHIP PUZZLE

A major theme of this book is that individuals and groups operate within larger systems we refer to as organizations. Understanding the dynamics among individuals, groups, and the organizations in which they are embedded is critical to unlocking the puzzles of how schools and districts work and reveals opportunities for leadership. One powerful lever school and district leaders have is the design of their various spheres of influence. Too often, leaders accept the status quo for how work is organized, which can lead to organizational contradictions that stymie innovation and improvement. Our hope for you is that you will see opportunity in organizational design, and this puzzle gives you a chance to practice design work in schools, at least in a limited way.

We take a somewhat different approach to this chapter's puzzle in two ways: (1) we encourage you to apply learning from this and the previous chapters in Part II, and (2) we provide a framework to support your thinking about the puzzle. We encourage you to refer back to the research in earlier chapters to provide tools and ideas for addressing the puzzle.

Put yourself in Principal Brian Washington's shoes. You've made a false start with the math/special education team, but you still feel committed to DL as a means to unlocking, talent, wisdom, and energy latent in Highland High School. Assume you want to try to work with another team on the issue of the achievement gap experienced by the English learner population in your school. The math work will continue, but you think you can make progress by simultaneously working in another curricular area. Using what you know about this group of students, teachers in general, the challenges of second language acquisition, and typical high school contexts, apply what you have learned from this book and your class to address the following prompts.

1. What subject area(s) do you wish to address for English learner (EL) students at Highland?

    - How would you frame the problem, challenge, or gap you would like the team to address?

2. Think about the structure needed to support teachers' collaborative work. Write a description of what you would do in each of the following categories:

    - *Scope*: Determine the teams' goal (focus), what the team should work on, and what they should not work on.
    - *Formal structure*: Which personnel would you want to recruit for the collaborative team that will address improving EL instruction in the area(s) you have chosen? What knowledge, skills, personal attributes, and/or dispositions would you seek?
    - *Decision-making process*: How will the team make decisions? What should your role be, if any, in decision making? Can you differentiate between what you would take as a recommendation from the team and what you would accept as a decision? Are you willing to live with whatever the team decides within the scope you have set? Consider the following leadership dimensions for this team and write brief descriptions of what each might look like:

        - autonomy
        - choice
        - influence
        - agency.

    - *Support*: What time, material, and/or monetary resources will this team need to function well? Do you anticipate any external source of expertise they may need? How will you hold the team accountable, and accountable for what?

3. Plan for speedbumps, potholes, and dead ends. What will you do to keep this team moving forward toward a tangible goal and set of objectives?

REFERENCES

Barnard, C. (1938). *The functions of the executive*. Cambridge, MA: Harvard University Press.

Bauer, S. (1996). *Site based management: A design perspective*. Unpublished doctoral dissertation. Ithaca, NY: Cornell University.

Bauer, S. (1998). Designing site based systems, deriving a theory of practice. *International Journal of Educational Reform, 7*(2), 108–121.

Bauer, S., & Brazer, S. (2012). *Using research to lead school improvement: Turning evidence into action*. Thousand Oaks, CA: Sage.

Bauer, S., Brazer, S., Van Lare, M., & Smith, R. (2013). Organizational design in support of professional learning communities in one district. In S. Conley & B. Cooper (Eds.), *Teacher collaboration: Advancing professionalism & school quality* (pp. 49–80). New York: Rowman and Littlefield.

Bauer, S., Van Lare, M., Brazer, S., & Smith, R. (2015). Teacher leadership in collaborative teams: The importance of process. In P. Tenuto (Ed.), *Renewed accountability for access and excellence: Applying a model for democratic professional practice in Education* (chapter 9). Lanham, MD: Lexington.

Bellibas, M., & Liu, Y. (2016). The effects of principals' perceived instructional and distributed leadership practices on their perceptions of school climate. *International Journal of Leadership in Education (online)*, DOI: 10.1080/13603124.2016.1147608.

Bennett, N., Wise, C., Woods, P., & Harvey, J. (2003). *Distributed leadership.* London: National College for School Leadership.

Bolden, R. (2011). Distributed leadership in organizations: A review of theory and research. *International Journal of Management Reviews, 13*(3), 251–269.

Brazer, S., Van Lare, M., Bauer, S., & Smith, R. (2014). Decision making for and by teacher collaborative teams. Paper presented at the Annual Meeting of the University Council on Education Administration, Washington, DC.

Bush, T. (2011). *Theories of educational leadership and management* (4th ed.). Thousand Oaks, CA: Sage.

Bush, T. (2013). Distributed leadership: The model of choice in the 21st century. *EMAL, 41*(5), 543–544.

Bush, T., & Glover, D. (2014). School leadership models: What do we know? *School Leadership & Management, 34*(5), 553–571.

Conley, D. (1993). *Roadmap to restructuring: Policies, practices and the emerging visions of schooling.* Eugene, OR: ERIC Clearinghouse on Educational Management.

Crawford, M. (2012). Solo and distributed leadership: Definitions and dilemmas. *EMAL, 40*(5), 610–620.

Cuban, L. (1988). *The managerial imperative and the practice of leadership in schools.* Albany, NY: State University of New York Press.

Day, C., Sammons, P., Hopkins, D., Harris, A., Leithwood, K., Gu, Q., Brown, E., Ahtaridou, E., & Kington, A. (2009). *The impact of school leadership on pupil outcomes: Final report.* Nottingham: Department for Children, Schools and Families.

Devos, G., Tutyens, M., & Hulpia, H. (2014). Teachers' organizational commitment: Examining the mediating effects of distributed leadership. *American Journal of Education, 120*(2), 205–231.

Feng, Y., Hao, B., Iles, P., & Bown, N. (2017). Rethinking distributed leadership: Dimensions, antecedents and team effectiveness. *Leadership & Organization Development Journal, 38*(2), 284–302.

Fitzsimons, D., James, K., & Denyer, D. (2011). Alternative approaches for studying shared and distributed leadership. *International Journal of Management Reviews, 13*(3), 313–328.

Fuhrman, S., Elmore, R., & Massell, D. (1993). School reform in the United States: Putting it into context. In S. Jacobson & R. Berne (Eds.), *Reforming education: The emerging systemic approach* (pp. 3–27). Thousand Oaks, CA: Corwin Press.

Garvin, D. (1988). *Managing quality: The strategic and competitive advantage.* New York: Free Press.

Gronn, P. (2000). Distributed properties: A new architecture for leadership. *Educational Management & Administration, 28*(3), 317–338.

Gronn, P. (2002). Distributed leadership as a unit of analysis. *Leadership Quarterly, 13*(4), 423–451.

Gronn, P. (2008). The future of distributed leadership. *Journal of Educational Administration, 46*(2), 141–158.

Gronn, P. (2009). Hybridized. In K. Leithwood, B. Mascall, & T. Strauss (Eds.), *Distributed leadership according to the evidence* (pp. 17–40). New York: Taylor & Francis.

Hackman, J., & Walton, R. (1986). Leading groups in organizations. In P. Goodman & Associates (Eds.), *Designing effective work groups* (pp. 72–119). San Francisco: Jossey-Bass.

Hargreaves, A. (1994). *Changing teachers, changing times: Teachers' work and culture in the postmodern age.* New York: Teachers College Press.

Harris, A. (2005). Distributed leadership. In B. Davies (Ed.), *The essentials of school leadership* (pp. 133–190). London: Paul Chapman Press.

Harris, A. (2008). Distributed leadership: According to the evidence. *Journal of Educational Administration, 46*(2), 172–188.

Harris, A. (Ed.) (2009). *Distributed leadership: Different perspectives*. London: Springer.

Harris, A. (2010). Distributed leadership: Evidence and implications. In T. Bush, L. Bell, & D. Middlewood (Eds.), *The principles of educational leadership & management* (2nd ed., pp. 55–69). Thousand Oaks, CA: Sage.

Harris, A. (2013). Distributed leadership: Friend or foe. *EMAL, 41*(5), 545–554.

Harris, A., & Muijs, D. (2004). *Improving schools through teacher leadership*. London: Open University Press.

Heck, R., & Hallinger, P. (2009). Assessing the contribution of distributed leadership to school improvement and growth in math achievement. *American Educational Research Journal, 46*(3), 659–689.

Ho, J., & Ng, D. (2017). Tensions in distributed leadership. *Educational Administration Quarterly, 53*(2), 223–254.

Hulpia, H., Devos, G., & Van Keer, H. (2011). The relation between school leadership from a distributed perspective and teachers' organizational commitment: Examining the source of the leadership function. *Educational Administration Quarterly, 47*(5), 728–771.

Hulpia, H., Devos, G., & Rosseell, Y. (2009). Development and validation of scores on the distributed leadership inventory. *Educational and Psychological Measurement, 69*(6), 1013–1034.

Hulpia, H., Devos, G., Rosseell, Y., & Vlerick, P. (2012). Dimensions of distributed leadership and the impact on teachers' organizational commitment: A study in secondary schools. *Journal of Applied Social Psychology, 42*(7), 1745–1784.

Ishikawa, K. (1985). *What is total quality control? The Japanese way*. Englewood Cliffs, NJ: Prentice Hall.

Katzenbach, J., & Smith, D. (2003). *The wisdom of teams: Creating the high-performance organization*. New York: HarperCollins.

Kirby, P. (1992). Shared decision making: Moving from concerns about restrooms to concerns about classrooms. *Journal of School Leadership, 2*(3), 330–344.

Larson, C., & LaFasto, F. (1989). *TeamWork: What must go right/what can go wrong*. Newbury Park, CA: Sage.

Lawler, E. (1992). *The ultimate advantage: Creating the high-involvement organization*. San Francisco: Jossey-Bass.

Leithwood, K., Day, C., Sammons, P., Harris, A., & Hopkins, D. (2006). *Successful school leadership: What it is and how it influences pupil learning*. Nottingham: DfES Publications.

Leithwood, K., Harris, A., & Strauss, T. (2013). How to reach high performance. In M. Grogan (Ed.), *The Jossey-Bass reader on educational leadership* (3rd ed., pp. 255–273). San Francisco: Jossey-Bass.

Leithwood, K., Mascall, B., & Strauss, T. (2009). *Distributed leadership according to the evidence*. London: Routledge.

Leithwood, K., Mascall, B., Strauss, T., Sacks, R., Memon, N., & Yashkina, A. (2007). Distributing leadership to make schools smarter: Taking the ego out of the system. *Leadership and Policy in Schools, 6*(1), 37–67.

Liljenberg, M. (2015). Distributing leadership to establish developing and learning school organisations in the Swedish context. *Education Management and Leadership, 43*(1), 152–170.

Lumby, J. (2013). Distributed leadership: The uses and abuses of power. *Education Management and Leadership, 41*(5), 581–597.

Lynch, M. (2012). *A guide to effective school leadership theories*. New York: Routledge.

Malen, B., Ogawa, R., & Kranz, J. (1990). Unfulfilled promises: Evidence says site-based management hindered by many factors. *The School Administrator, 47*(2), 30–32, 53–56, 59.

Mascall, B., Leithwood, K., Straus, T., & Sacks, R. (2008). The relationship between distributed leadership and teachers' academic optimism. *Journal of Educational Administration, 46(2)*, 214–228.

McGregor, D. (1960/2006). *The human side of enterprise: Annotated edition* (J. Cutcher-Gershenfeld, ed.). New York: McGraw-Hill.

Murphy, J. (1989). The paradox of decentralizing schools: Lessons from business, government, and the Catholic church. *Phi Delta Kappan, 70*(10), 808–812.

Murphy, J. (1991). *Restructuring schools: Capturing and assessing the phenomena.* New York: Teachers' College Press.

National Commission on Excellence in Education (1983). *A nation at risk: The imperative for educational reform.* Washington, DC: US Department of Education.

Reavis, C., & Griffith, H. (1992). *School restructuring: Theory and practice.* Lancaster, PA: Technomic Publishing Co.

Robinson, V. (2008). Forging the links between distributed leadership and educational outcomes. *Journal of Educational Administration, 46(2)*, 241–256.

Ross, L., Lufti, G., & Hope, W. (2016). Distributed leadership and teachers' affective commitment. *NASSP Bulletin, 100*(3), 159–169.

Sharpe, F. (1996). Towards a research paradigm on devolution. *Journal of Educational Administration, 34*(1), 4–23.

Shedd, J., & Bacharach, S. (1991). *Tangled hierarchies: Teachers as professionals and the management of schools.* San Francisco: Jossey-Bass.

Silins, H., & Mulford, W. (2002). Leadership and school results. In K. Leithwood & P. Hallinger (Eds.), *Second international handbook of educational leadership and administration* (pp. 561–612). Dordecht: Kluwer Academic Publishers.

Sirotnik, K. (1989). The school as the center of change. In T. Sergiovanni & J. Moore (Eds.), *Schooling for tomorrow: Directing reforms to issues that count* (pp. 89–113). Boston: Allyn and Bacon.

Spillane, J. (2005). Distributed leadership. *The Educational Forum, 69*(2), 143–150.

Spillane, J. (2006). *Distributed leadership.* San Francisco: Jossey-Bass.

Spillane, J., & Diamond, J. (2007). A distributed perspective on and in practice. In J. Spillane & J. Diamond (Eds.), *Distributed leadership in practice* (pp. 146–166). New York: Teachers College Press.

Spillane, J., Diamond, J., & Jita, L. (2003). Leading instruction: The distribution of leadership for instruction. *Journal of Curriculum Studies, 35*(5), 533–543.

Spillane, J., Halverson, R., & Diamond, J. (2001). Investigating school leadership practice: A distributed perspective. *Educational Researcher, 30*(3), 23–28.

Spillane, J., Halverson, R., & Diamond, J. (2004). Towards a theory of leadership practice: A distributed perspective, *Journal of Curriculum Studies, 36*(1), 3–34.

Tian, M., Risku, M., & Collin, K. (2016). A meta-analysis of distributed leadership from 2002 to 2013: Theory development, empirical evidence and future research focus. *Education Management and Leadership, 44*(1), 146–164.

Timperly, H. (2005). Distributed leadership: Developing theory from practice. *Journal of Curriculum Studies, 37*(4), 395–420.

Torres, D. (2018). Distributed leadership and teacher job satisfaction in Singapore. *Journal of Educational Administration, 56*(1), 127–142.

Van Lare, M., Brazer, S., Bauer, S., & Smith, R. (2013). Professional learning communities using evidence: Examining teacher learning and organizational learning. In S. Conley & B. Cooper (Eds.), *Teacher collaboration: Advancing professionalism & school quality* (pp. 157–181). New York: Rowman and Littlefield.

Wahlstrom, K., Louis, K., Leithwood, K., & Anderson, S. (2010). *Investigating the links to improved student learning: Executive summary of research findings.* New York: Wallace Foundation.

Weisbord, M. (2012). *Productive workplaces: Dignity, meaning and community in the 21st century.* San Francisco: Jossey-Bass.

Weiss, C. (1993). Shared decision making about what? A comparison of schools with and without teacher participation. *Teachers College Record, 95*(1), 69–92.

Weiss, C., Cambone, J., & Wyeth, A. (1992). Trouble in paradise: Teacher conflicts in shared decision making. *Educational Administration Quarterly, 28*(3), 350–367.

Woods, P. (2010). Democratic leadership: Drawing distinctions with distributed leadership. *International Journal of Leadership in Education, 7*(1), 3–26.

CHAPTER 9

Epilogue: Where We Stand at This Moment

Our intent with this volume has been to provide a broad overview of school leadership—its essence, goals, defining contours, and perennial challenges—while demonstrating the practical uses of organization and leadership theory and research. In the process, we have covered a great deal of conceptual and theoretical ground. Much like walking through a forest, we've stopped here and there to examine *this* plant or *that* tree, observe this topographical feature or the wildlife around us. In doing so, we've shifted back and forth between the proverbial forest and trees, the parts and the whole. This strategy has been directed toward developing your leadership knowledge and expanding your understanding of the conditions needed to help schools learn, grow, and thrive. We see the content of this book as fundamental to becoming a skilled and effective school leader.

Leadership has long interested and excited people. As a concept it connotes images of powerful, dynamic individuals who command armies, direct corporate empires, and shape the course of nations. Much recorded history is focused on leadership, more specifically as the story of military, political, and religious leaders credited or blamed for important events. While such descriptions tend to emphasize the melodramatic and charismatic qualities of leaders, leadership is, *more often than not*, more pedestrian and distributed than many would assume. Our fascination with dramatic images of leadership arises from its elusive, ineffable nature and the impact it has on our lives.

As we have discussed throughout this volume, although questions about leadership have long been a subject of speculation, systematic theorizing on leadership is of recent origin. The scholarly work has traveled a long and winding road, from its early focus on the *traits* of effective leaders to more recent conceptualizations that include leader behaviors and the variables that define the context of leadership. While much is known about leaders and leadership dynamics, our collective understanding of leadership remains somewhat *elusive*. Like effective teaching, effective leadership is difficult to nail down or distill with precision. Yet we all seem to know it when seen or experienced. Stated differently: we know more about leadership *experientially* than has been written about it *systematically* and *formally*. Our experiences outdistance our theorizing.

Combining theory with experience means that leadership cannot be examined apart from the organizational context in which it occurs, and vice versa. Leadership and organizations go together like hand-in-glove. Leaders influence organizations for good or ill. They are two sides of the same coin; the former is the context for the latter. Whereas the general focus of the first part of this book was on leadership in formal organizations and the conceptualization of organization itself, with examples drawn from education, our specific focus in Part II has been on understanding leadership in *educational* organizations—specifically schools. More precisely, our explorations have been bounded by a discussion of the three primary theoretical depictions of effective school leaders evident in scholarly writing: transformational, instructional, and distributed leadership. As with all theory, each perspective has a valuable set of messages for prospective and in-service school leaders, and each is limited in some important ways. We argued at the outset of Part II that the three perspectives are important—in combination—to understanding the school leaders' role in change and improvement. The destination of Part II is your understanding the central message of all three perspectives so that they may contribute to your development as an effective leader capable of leading change and improving schools.

Our series of vignettes, thought partner conversations, extended web activities, exercises, and puzzles are intended to help you to "feel the weight" of a concept or set of ideas—both in terms of their importance *and* how theories might be used as analytic tools to move back and forth between the world of theory and practice, between thinking and doing. Note our deliberate use of the singular "world" here. The world of thought and action are not two separate worlds. Rather they are two aspects of the same world that find expression as *praxis* or *reflective/reflexive action*.

While knowledge of leadership, organizations, people, and teaching and learning is an important component of effective leadership, as noted in Chapter 5 *knowing about* is distinct from and yet related to *knowing how*. Knowing about leadership begins by reflecting on one's own experiences in organizations. It continues as one examines and considers the leadership literature, identifies its dominant theories and compares these with one's lived experiences. It progresses further as one enters into conversations with others about this literature, seeks to identify and refine emergent themes, articulate working assumptions, and reconcile competing theories with our collective experience.

The interactive approach used in this book is intended to assist you in developing your own leadership knowledge, skills, and dispositions. Knowing *how* to combine this knowledge in strategic ways to promote a learning, growing, and thriving school is equally important as *knowing about*. It is not an issue of either/or—knowing *about* versus knowing *how*—but both/and. The former is a critical input to the latter. Hence, leadership is about: (1) the *thinking* provoked, and (2) *action* informed by this knowledge. Regardless of the breadth and depth of one's knowledge, effective leadership is a function of *how* this knowledge is used to inform a leader's *theorizing* or *problem solving*—how adroitly this knowledge is synthesized to make sense of the situation at hand and address uncertainties that prevent the realization of organizational goals.

This *thinking* is reflected in the exercise of informed discretionary judgment "on the ground," in a specific context, in real time, and in the face of uncertainties. In short, *thinking about leadership informs leadership action*. This *doing* consists of an array of skills informed by knowledge and craft wisdom (Drucker, 1997; Johnson, forthcoming; Schon, 1987; Shulman, 2004). A certain quality of thinking is needed to transform one's working knowledge of leadership (*knowing about*) into effective leadership behavior (*knowing how*). Theorizing lies at the heart of this process.

Thus, what distinguishes effective from ineffective school leaders is not necessarily *how much* they know in terms of raw information, but *how adept* they are at using this knowledge to address problems and issues that prevent the school from increasing and maintaining acceptable levels of instructional capacity. The key to becoming an effective leader is not merely knowing *about* leadership and motivation, but knowing *how* to translate these and other potent concepts and theories addressed in this volume into a viable set of action strategies that promote school success on an ongoing basis. We are convinced that it is easier to master the knowledge base of education leadership than it is to *strategically combine* and *consistently apply* this knowledge to create an effective school (Johnson, forthcoming). For many aspiring leaders, something gets "lost in the translation." Yet as we have suggested throughout, successful translation from theory and research into practice is a defining mark of competent leadership.

As practitioners, we are apt to utter (often under our breath) the sentiment that research and theory "just don't work in practice," and bemoan the fact that in the real world, things are just a lot more complicated than in research. True. Among other things, this is evident in the fact that there are many and varied ways to approach the exercises and puzzles we have included in the preceding chapters, each designed to give you an opportunity to try out the "big ideas" evident in the theories we have explored and decide for yourself the degree to which these big ideas resonate with your leadership.

As scholars, though, we remind you that this is a valuable function of theory. As Hall and Lindzey (1957, p. 9) remind us, "The function of a theory is that of preventing the observer from being dazzled by the full-blown complexity of natural or concrete events." Theory focuses us on particular elements of the social world so that we can develop an appreciation and understanding of them, while excluding other elements from our view. For example, distributed leadership theory may focus us on the leaders' role in involving others and developing leadership capacity in schools while dimming our view of other aspects of the context and leadership practice. As we have explored transformational, instructional, and distributed leadership we have seen that although there are common behaviors that define effective leadership and some that cut across the various theories (and hence seem generalizable at a broad level), the specific constellation these behaviors assume will differ across school contexts. It is up to you to combine the three traditions in a manner that works for you and appears most effective at a given point in time in a specific context.

These various combinations of leadership strategies are a function of at least two factors: (1) personal differences between individual leaders, and (2) differences in organizational context. In the "real world," you might be thinking, leader behavior depends on an array of factors that define a given organization, and leaders must adapt their behavior accordingly. That which proved effective in one school may be less so in another. Both adaptation and adaptability are required (Weick, 1976, 1982; Weick & Quinn, 1999). Effective leaders develop a repertoire of behaviors that enable them to adapt as circumstances dictate. They remain *protean* in their disposition and thinking. Hence, no single way to skin the same proverbial cat is applicable or valid to all contexts.

As we conclude the volume, we depart from the structure of previous chapters. The thoughts that follow bring you back to the complexities of leadership in the "real world" of schools. They rely on no one theory or body of research, but rather represent a set of generalities we invite you to ponder that we believe cut across the various theories and provide a means of situating the varied array of "big ideas" offered throughout the text in a fashion that enables each of you to situate these in your own leadership practice. By this point you may agree with us that there is no answer, no formula, no "secret sauce" we can reveal that defines "best practice" (a concept we don't really believe in anyway), but rather a set of ideas intended to further provoke your thoughts and opportunities to grow as a leader.

INTO THE FUTURE: THE *FOREST* OF TREES

This book, and the course for which you may have read it, can be both a scaffold and foil to the thoughts and experiences you bring to the text. Both images serve generative functions. As *scaffold*, it is our hope that readers will use the ideas present here to build and refine their thinking. Scaffolds are emergent, temporary structures that are arranged and periodically rearranged. Individual sections are linked in tandem with others to create a superstructure. They are used to construct and reconstruct. As *foil*, we offer these concepts, theories, and exercises as challenges intended to stimulate and provoke thought as you encounter leadership challenges in the years ahead. We urge you to refresh your thinking on a regular basis and in the company of others. It is healthy to try a new perspective on previous thinking, to view your work world through a different frame. In so doing, you will give yourself the opportunity to reconcile what you know and think with the puzzles you face.

The *Trees* of the Forest

With our "forest view" observations as context, themes from individual chapters (specific trees in the forest) may be summarized as follows. Each theme has chapter numbers in parentheses to help you refresh your memory for ideas that may have slipped your mind. Italicized text provides brief thoughts about how school leaders might apply each them.

Theme 1 (1) The twin pillars of organization theory are structure and human relations. Effective leaders design organizations to work effectively, mindful of human needs. The probability of developing productive relationships increases as leaders understand those factors that motivate people to invest in the organization of which they are a part. *Principals have considerable discretion to design their schools in a manner that meets the affective and cognitive needs of students and teachers.*

Theme 2 (2) Schools and districts exist as *systems* open to influences originating outside of their physical boundaries. Environmental influences present educational leaders with uncertainties that must be addressed in functional ways. At the same time, schools and districts act on and influence this environment. *Leaders throughout the school, and principals in particular, may seek opportunities and resources from beyond school and district boundaries and should be mindful of buffering the school from unwanted or unwise influences.*

Theme 3 (3) Like other types of educational organization, schools exhibit a distinct configuration of features that simultaneously promote predictability and unpredictability, order and chaos. The moniker *organized anarchy* captures this paradox. *Accepting organized anarchy as part of reality means mitigating or resolving what is uncertain, negotiating ambiguity, and studying the effects of choices made under conditions of equivocality. Reflective practice allows leaders to "ride the wave" of organized anarchy.*

Theme 4 (4, 6, 7, 8) Positive working relationships can be engendered through a combination of transformational, instructional, and distributed leadership that simultaneously takes care of human needs while offering opportunities for leadership beyond the standard hierarchical structure. *Principals and teachers can find opportunities to be more collaborative and inclusive in their decision making in a manner that takes advantage of collective understanding of teaching and learning challenges and good ideas to address them.*

Theme 5 (4, 7) As formal organizations, schools and districts pursue goals and objectives. Organizational uncertainties and a lack of total control prevent the full realization of school aspirations. For this reason, leaders initiate changes intended to improve organizational performance. Beginning with gap analysis, they pursue organizational learning as a means to improving teaching and learning. *Principals can structure their schools to encourage teacher learning while keeping an eye on important ways of changing the status quo—the school as system—to enable continuous improvement.*

Theme 6 (4, 5, 6, 7, 8) Regardless of title, a primary responsibility of all education leaders is to initiate and manage change directed at increasing the school's instructional capacity so as to improve the learning experience of *all* students. Helpful concepts and practices for doing so are embedded in transformational, instructional, and distributed leadership. *Managing change is an inevitable task in education leadership; better to lead change through inspiration, a focus on instruction, and involving as much talent as possible with the intent of improving the educational experiences of the entire student body.*

Theme 7 (5, 6, 7, 8) Leadership matters! Although it is not clear exactly in what ways leadership matters, transformational, instructional, and distributed leadership all demonstrate influence on student outcomes, albeit through various pathways. *Principals and teacher leaders should carry in their minds the research finding that improving student achievement was never associated with weak leadership.*

Theme 8 (4, 7) In order to educate *all* students at a high level of quality, educational leaders must foster a culture of teacher learning that improves instruction. To increase the depth and quality of teacher learning, principals must ensure that robust webs of teacher collaboration are nurtured within the school. IL requires a *deep commitment* to working directly with teachers to understand and improve teaching and learning. *Grade-level leaders, department chairs, APs, and principals can collaborate to lead instruction by sharing expertise and learning together.*

Theme 9 (8) Growing awareness of the expanding complexity and intensification of principal work brought on by accountability demands has provoked much interest in shared leadership in schools. DL involves making difficult choices, reconciling disparate theories of instruction, and transforming schools into learning organizations aimed at improving classroom instruction. *Principals can use distributed leadership as a means to energize teachers in the overall effort to improve instruction. They should be mindful of what they are distributing, to whom they are distributing, and the responsibilities and expected outcomes they envision for those to whom leadership has been distributed.*

Theme 10 (the whole book) Leaders play multiple roles and in doing so are apt to step into multiple personae. More colloquially, they wear a variety of "hats." Each has a distinct focus, yet all are organically linked. At any given moment, the leader may be wearing a single hat *or* subset of hats. Furthermore, there are times when hats must be changed quickly. Effective leaders know which hat(s) to don, which hats to take off, and when. *Much is demanded of the contemporary principal. Recognizing that different constituencies have different expectations means that principals should be mindful of their audience for communication and action, all the while staying true to basic principles.*

We hope that these themes are easily recognized by this point. They can serve as touchstones as you encounter leadership challenges in the future. All of us need this kind of guidance as we deal with the mundane and unexpected in the daily life of schools. Possibly you will add your own themes to this list. We invite you to do so as your learning from this book, your class, and your experience continues.

ONE LAST PUZZLE: WHAT WILL YOU DO?

We could think of no better way to end this book than with a puzzle that asks you to piece together a vision of your future leadership. We recognize that most readers will be at the beginning of their administrative credential program—they are the readers whom we envision as our primary audience. But if you are already a practicing leader, we hope that this will be a moment for you to take stock of your leadership experience and determine how you might like to improve it moving forward. In any case, we recognize that there is much more to learn—in class, from experience, and from both—so we hope you will preserve your responses to this last puzzle and refer back to them often. If you are a credential candidate, we hope you will see how management tools will help you elaborate on your leadership thinking as you engage in more content-specific classes.

*Imagine that the principal of **the school where you currently work** has suddenly left the position. After a rapid search, the superintendent has determined that you are one of three top candidates for the permanent principal position, not wanting to have the school spin its wheels with an interim. You are elated to have made it this far in the process, yet nervous because you are eager for the position. The superintendent has asked you to come to a meeting that will include him and two board members. He has given you the questions below to prepare for the meeting. You will be asked* *for your answers to each of these questions. This is your last chance to make an impression before the superintendent and board decide whom to hire.*

1. *What is your overall vision for your school? Who will help you refine your vision and why would you involve them? What will your school look like in one, three, and five years?*
2. *If you could change one thing about your school, what would it be? Why? What consequences would ensue if you made this change?*
3. *What is some structural "maintenance" that must be taken care of in your school to help it function better? In other words, which of Herzberg's hygiene factors would you address right away?*
4. *What are the most critical faculty needs at this moment? How will you address these to maintain and boost faculty morale and motivation?*
5. *What are the top three learning challenges students encounter in your school? How do you know?*
6. *How will you manage competing demands from students, teachers, parents, and others while staying focused on district and school goals?*
7. *Do you envision a role for yourself in leading instruction? What will that look like?*
8. *How will you organize teachers and others to address the most important teaching and learning challenges?*
9. *Will you be a principal who distributes leadership? Why, or why not? In what ways is your school ready for distributed leadership and what further preparation might it need?*
10. *How will you sustain and enhance your own learning as you gain experience as a principal?*

REFERENCES

Drucker, P. (1997). *My life as a knowledge worker: A dialogue between Peter Drucker and Isao Nakauchi, Inc.* www.inc.com/magazine/19970201/1169.html.

Hall, C., & Lindzey, G. (1957). *Theories of personality.* New York: Wiley.

Johnson, Jr., B.L. (forthcoming). Organizations, organizing, and schools: Accessing theoretical tools and models in organization theory. In M. Conley (Ed.), *The SAGE handbook of school organization.* Thousand Oaks, CA: Sage Publications.

Schon, D. (1987). *Educating the reflective practitioner: Toward a new design for teaching and learning the professions.* San Francisco: Jossey-Bass.

Shulman, L. (2004). *The wisdom of practice: Essays on teaching learning and learning to teach.* San Francisco: Jossey-Bass.

Weick, K.E. (1982). Management of organizational change among loosely-coupled elements. In P. Goodman (Ed.), *Change in organizations.* San Francisco: Jossey-Bass.

Weick, K.E. (1976). Educational organizations as loosely-coupled systems. *Administrative Science Quarterly, 21*(1), 1–19.

Weick, K.E., & Quinn, R. (1999). Organization change and development. *Annual Review of Psychology, 50*(86), 361–363.

Index

Burnes, Bernard 164–167, 177
Bush, T. 8, 15, 152–153, 159–160, 210, 213, 219, 225, 235

calculus teachers 5, 7, 14, 20, 28, 194, 202
candidates for leadership 120, 125, 127–131, 142–143; credentials of 248; favorite 129; potential 127; strong 120
Carlyle, Thomas 124–125
case managers 106, 114
caseloads 29–30
CATS 163–165, 166–167, 178; *see also* "change as three steps"
CCSS 47, 190, 209
challenges xi–xii, 7, 57–58, 67, 71, 73, 84, 95, 98, 130–131, 147, 210, 237, 246; common 29; contextual 206; student outcome 53
change 15–16, 49–50, 60, 94–95, 108–110, 112–113, 136–141, 149–153, 159–161, 163–175, 177–180, 182–184, 215–217, 247, 249; educational xvii, 178, 207; efforts 168–170; environmental 59, 70; instructional 162, 200; management 150, 153, 177–178; managing 150–151, 165, 247; political 55; process 164–167; resistance to 167; social 131, 164; special education teachers 199; systemic 113; top-down 213
change agents 141, 167–168
"change as three steps" 163–165, 167
children 1, 10, 19–21, 45, 50, 72, 75, 96, 150, 184, 235; education of 43, 97; feeding of hungry 20; language minority 192; taught in unruly one-room school houses 10; unpredictable xiv
classes 37, 43, 46, 48, 53, 79, 81, 101, 106, 109, 111, 115, 186, 191, 248; advanced 133; college-preparatory laboratory science 194; content-specific 248; high school biology 188; managerial 16; online xvii; specialized 48
classical theories 35, 37, 51, 53, 59
classrooms 34–35, 39, 45–46, 48–49, 53, 72–74, 104–107, 179, 182, 184–185, 187–194, 197–199, 216, 218–219, 222; American 207; creating innovative 23; individual 218; management 44–45, 216; physical science 109
closed systems 12, 17, 35–36, 51–53, 59; categories of 51; models 34; theories 53; viewing of 52
collaboration 23, 44, 129, 195, 218, 221,

230, 232, 235; effective 199; long-term 197; spontaneous 222
collaborative teams xii, 1, 39, 184, 195–201, 203–204, 207, 218, 227, 233–234, 238–239
collective leadership 228
Collin, K. 211, 216, 226–227, 229
common core state standards 47, 190, 209
community 17, 24, 46, 49, 94, 96, 106, 109, 153, 156, 171–172, 174, 180, 182, 191; agencies 42; building 97, 117; inclusive 96, 110; involvement 214; members 36, 75
computer-mediated work practices 221
Conley, S. xvi, 213
content knowledge 184, 186, 189, 193–194, 202; enhancing pedagogical 199; pedagogical 72, 190, 193–194, 204; and term leadership 202
contingency theories 51–53, 63–64, 122, 131–134, 142, 234
core assumptions 51; of classical theories in terms of rationality 51; of structural contingency theory 52
Cuban, L. xi–xii, 10–11, 13–14, 23, 38, 45, 48–49, 52, 73, 182, 187, 218
curriculum xv, 13, 109, 111, 119–120, 129, 143, 160, 186, 190–193, 197–200, 202, 208, 228; audits 13; courses 192; coverage 46; district-mandated 120; documents 200; planning 190–191; school 13; well-constructed 193

decision makers 10, 15, 35, 68, 72, 76, 82–83, 196
decision-making process 59, 69, 72, 76–80, 84–85, 87, 92, 108, 196, 199, 234, 238
decisions 15–16, 59–61, 63, 68–69, 71–73, 75–88, 90–92, 110–111, 140–141, 196–197, 204, 213–216, 220–221, 233–235, 238–239; consequential 78, 214, 218, 226; effective 82; evidence-based 168; guiding educational 79; high-stakes 78, 87; important 211, 216, 221, 234; informed 52; of leaders 69, 214, 233; organizational 88; of principals 69–70, 73, 75, 79; rational 35; routine 173; school-based 16, 228; by school leaders 79–80; strategic 71–72; unilateral 101
design 5–6, 12, 17, 31, 35, 54, 64, 110, 179, 207, 235, 237, 246; components 197; factors 196; new 249; organizational 39, 51, 195, 197, 232–233, 237; perspectives 195, 207, 238
design work practices 237